THE
COVENANT:
GOD'S VOLUNTARY
CONDESCENSION

The Covenant:
God's Voluntary Condescension

Edited by

Joseph A. Pipa, Jr.
and
C. N. Willborn

Presbyterian Press
Taylors, SC

© 2005
Presbyterian Press
Greenville Presbyterian Theological Seminary
P.O. Box 770
Taylors, SC 29687
www.gpts.edu
bookstore@gpts.edu

Printed in the United States of America

The Covenant: God's Voluntary Condescension /
edited by Joseph A. Pipa, Jr. and C. N. Willborn
p.   cm.
Includes bibliographical references.
ISBN: 1-931639-06-X
1. Covenant Theology
BT155.P57   2005

Table of Contents

Preface   vii

1. The Unity of the Covenant
   Andrew McGowan   1

2. Federal Theology and the Westminster Standards
   Morton H. Smith   15

3. Jeremiah 31 and the New Covenant
   Richard Phillips   47

4. Scottish Covenant Theology
   Andrew McGowan   61

5. The Covenant and Our Children
   Joseph A. Pipa, Jr.   73

6. Covenant Confusion
   Richard Phillips   95

7. Justification by Faith Alone
    John Carrick   127

8. Defense of Paedocommunion
    Robert Rayburn   147

9. Pauline Communion vs. Paedocommunion
    Kenneth Gentry   163

Epilogue   213

List of Contributors   217

Preface

Since the Presbyterian Seminary in Greenville began its Spring Theology Conference in 1999, significant ecclesiastical issues have been the subject of investigation and explication. Topics have included Creation, Scripture, Sanctification, and Worship. When the topic has been one controverted within contemporary Reformed thought, the conferences often included leading spokesmen for the differing positions. All the while, the Conference primarily has been a forum for presenting classic Westminsterian Calvinism in a winsome, experimental manner.

We believe you will find the content of the present volume on Covenant Theology, from our 2004 Spring Theology Conference, to be no exception to our purpose. Covenant theology has been vital to the Church's life from her earliest days. It is, after all, within the covenant of grace that God "freely offereth unto sinners life and salvation by Jesus Christ," (WCF 7.3). Certainly ever since the Lord Jesus in instituting the Lord's Supper took the cup of wine and said, "this is My blood of the covenant," the Church has been acutely conscious of the centrality of the covenant theme in Scripture. This is certainly true of early fathers like Irenaeus, but the consciousness and emphasis seems to have escalated exponentially as the Church came through the Reformation and post-Reformation era. Peter Lillback (*The Binding of God*) has illustrated Calvin's covenantal consciousness, while Lyle D. Bierma (*German Calvinism in the Confessional Age: The Covenant Theology of Caspar Olevianus*), Charles McCoy and Wayne Baker (*Fountainhead of Federalism: Heinrich Bullinger and the Covenantal Tradition*), and others, have illustrated the same consciousness in a number of Reformation leaders. Likewise, a glance through Richard Muller's magisterial *Post Reformation Reformed Dogmatics* reveals the importance of covenant thought to the Scripture writers as well as those who studied the Scriptures throughout the period after Luther and Wittenburg.

It should surprise no one then for a school of the Church to devote an annual conference to this topic of eternal importance—the covenanted relationship of God to His people. Sadly, however, interest in the topic has not always persisted. Indeed, men like Thomas Boston believed it to be a neglected and often distorted doctrinal theme when he responded to Arminian denials of the covenant of works with his classic exposition of that essential covenant. The nineteenth century American theologian, John Girardeau, saw that interest and emphasis on covenant was waning and delivered a most useful paper on the topic under the title of "The Federal Theology: Its Import and Its Regulative Influence," which was subsequently published and remains in print. In the introduction to his brief, yet pregnant paper, Girardeau explained the practical or pastoral importance of maintaining the covenantal construct and theme of Scripture when he mourned the "growing tendency towards a departure from this type of theology." "Especially would it be for a lamentation," he continued, "should it disappear from the pulpit....And as surely as the pulpit drifts away from it, will it more and more cast its instruction in the mould of a wretched legalism; or losing the influence of this pervading genius of theological truth...it will more and more neglect its heavenly call to be an instructor of Christ's people, and sink its high didactic office into that of a vapid and sensational haranguer." From these two examples, Boston and Girardeau, we see the necessity of the Church to articulate afresh the covenant of works and the covenant of grace.

In the course of history, which is the progressive unfolding in time of God's eternal decree, we too often have seen the proverbial "pendulum swing" and this accounts for another reason our 2004 Theology Conference was important. From the low ebb detected in the latter quarter of the 19th century, we saw the Reformed church pass through a number of mood shifts—from a neglect of the topic to a radical hyper version of covenant theology. The latter has resulted in several distortions and sometimes radical movements away from classic confessional orthodoxy. In the present volume, we offer both a critique of some of the current tendencies troubling reformed and evangelical churches and a fresh exposition of classic Calvinism on the covenant theme. While the topics addressed are limited (by time, of course), we believe they may serve the Church to steer her way through some of the rough waters of controversy and to find the quieter waters of a theology derived from Scripture alone.

For the public appearance of this little book, we wish to thank a number of people who made it presentable. Of course, we thank the authors of each chapter for their love for Christ's Church and desire to expound the topics assigned them. Furthermore, we thank Mr. Andrew Wortman for his efforts to make the formatting of this volume pleasing to the eye; Mrs. Caroline Q. Brown for her editorial assistance; Ms.

Nancy Lambert-Brown for her fine cover design; and, Mr. Doug Robson for transcription of two sermons for the present publication.

So it is with thanksgiving to the Covenant Faithful One—Father, Son, and Holy Spirit—that we offer this contribution to the Church, with the prayer that the bride of Christ will be purer and richer from our efforts, as she seeks to present herself "spotless and blameless" to the Beloved. SDG!

Joseph A. Pipa, Jr.
C. N. Willborn

Chapter 1

The Unity of the Covenant

Andrew T. B. McGowan

INTRODUCTION

My dissertation at the Union Theological Seminary in New York, as part of my Master of Sacred Theology degree, was on the New England Puritans, treating the question of whether or not they were consistent covenant theologians. Then my doctoral dissertation at the University of Aberdeen was on the 'Federal Theology of Thomas Boston.' I also teach a course on "Scottish Covenant Theology" for Westminster Theological Seminary in their extension course in London.

The other reason for my being pleased to come and speak on this subject is that I am from Scotland, where covenant theology took an early hold. Not only so, but Scotland is a place where the whole notion of covenant took on a political expression. In 1638, while Charles I was seeking to re-impose Catholicism on the country, the protestant nobles called upon people to sign the 'National Covenant.' This was a plea for the preservation of the Reformed religion and contained a list of all the Acts of Parliament that supported and protected Protestantism. Those who signed or supported this document were called "The Covenanters." Later, when civil war broke out in England and Charles I was battling against our Parliament, the Scots entered into an alliance with the English Parliament against Charles, and they signed a document called 'The

Solemn League and Covenant.' The Covenanters were hunted down ruthlessly and many hundreds of them—men, women, and children—were killed for their beliefs, especially from 1680 until 1688, which was called the "Killing Time." Covenant, then, is not simply a theological theme but a concept of significant national importance.

Before going into the subject in detail, there is one further point I must make by way of introduction, and that is to emphasize that the current theological situation in Europe is very different from yours here in North America, not least in respect of the debates surrounding covenant theology. Whereas you have been debating the 'Federal Vision,' Norman Shepherd's doctrine and other North American controversies, our concerns have been different. We have been seeking to return the mainline denominations to their Calvinistic and confessional roots and have been battling against liberal, existentialist and post-liberal theologies. My own personal theological battles have largely been with neo-orthodoxy, particularly as represented by J. B. and T.F. Torrance, and re-fighting the Calvin versus Calvinism debate. If this means that I do not directly engage with matters relating to some of your internal North American debates, I trust that nevertheless the main argument of my two papers will be helpful to you.

In this chapter we will address the unity of the historical covenants, which manifest the covenant of grace. I take this title to mean that the covenant into which God entered with Abraham, thereby creating a covenant people, is essentially the same covenant which God maintains with his people today. In order to deal with this subject, I propose to break my paper into three parts: 1) The Old Testament: the Covenant Established; 2) The New Testament: the Covenant Consummated; and 3) The Continuity of the Covenant.

THE OLD TESTAMENT: THE COVENANT ESTABLISHED

The background for understanding the covenant is to be found in Genesis 3 where we read the story of the fall of mankind. After this had taken place, God made a promise, the first promise of the gospel, in Genesis 3:15: 'I will put enmity between you and the woman, and between your offspring and her offspring; he shall bruise your head, and you shall bruise his heel.' This promise was fulfilled when Christ came, but we might say that until then, God took some temporary measures. Genesis 15 is a useful place to begin in our understanding of these 'temporary measures,' pending the coming of the Lord.

Genesis 15 is one of the most significant passages in the whole of the Old Testament because it helps us to understand how a sinner can be in a right relationship with God. It does so by dealing with the key themes of faith and covenant. These two themes of faith and covenant are intertwined in Scripture and it is useful to deal with them together, but since there is to be a paper at this conference on justification by faith, I will focus my attention primarily on the theme of covenant. In order to do so, I want us to consider the chapter as a whole.

To understand Genesis 15, of course, we first have to understand Genesis 12, which gives the account of when God came to Abram and called him to leave his home and his father's house, and to set out on a journey. God said that he would be with Abram and guide him and also made two promises: first, that he was going to make of Abram a great nation with many descendants; and second, that he would give that great nation a land in which to live. That call to Abram in Genesis 12 to set out on this journey is the beginning of the story of the nation of Israel, the chosen people of God. In chapter 15, God confirms the promises which he made in chapter 12, and does so by entering into a covenant with Abram.

Here we consider Genesis 15:1-6: 'After these things the word of the Lord came to Abram in a vision: "Fear not, Abram, I am your shield; your reward shall be very great." But Abram said, "O Lord GOD, what will you give me, for I continue childless, and the heir of my house is Eliezer of Damascus?" And Abram said, "Behold, you have given me no offspring, and a member of my household will be my heir." And behold, the word of the Lord came to him: "This man shall not be your heir; your very own son shall be your heir." And he brought him outside and said, "Look toward heaven, and number the stars, if you are able to number them." Then he said to him, "So shall your offspring be." And he believed the Lord, and he counted it to him as righteousness.'[1]

Do you see what is happening here? God comes to Abram in a dream and declares himself to be Abram's shield and reward, but Abram is full of doubt and responds by asking God what good this is, when he has no heir to succeed him. In other words, Abram is asking how God can possibly fulfil the promise given to him in chapter 12, that he would be the father of a great nation, if he has no children. God then takes Abram outside, points up to the sky, and tells him that his descendants will be as numerous as the stars. Abram then moves from a position of

---

[1] All references are from the *English Standard Version*.

doubt to a position of faith and we have the important conclusion in verse 6: 'And he believed the Lord, and he counted it to him as righteousness.'

Having confirmed the first of his promises, God then goes on to confirm the second one, in verses 7 and 8: 'And he said to him, "I am the Lord who brought you out from Ur of the Chaldeans to give you this land to possess." But he said, "O Lord GOD, how am I to know that I shall possess it?"' Once again, Abram is doubtful and asks how he can be sure that he and his descendants will possess the land. At this point, God enters into a covenant with Abram. Notice verses 9-21:

> [9] He said to him, "Bring me a heifer three years old, a female goat three years old, a ram three years old, a turtledove, and a young pigeon." [10] And he brought him all these, cut them in half, and laid each half over against the other. But he did not cut the birds in half. [11] And when birds of prey came down on the carcasses, Abram drove them away.

> [12] As the sun was going down, a deep sleep fell on Abram. And behold, dreadful and great darkness fell upon him. [13] Then the Lord said to Abram, "Know for certain that your offspring will be sojourners in a land that is not theirs and will be servants there, and they will be afflicted for four hundred years. [14] But I will bring judgment on the nation that they serve, and afterward they shall come out with great possessions. [15] As for yourself, you shall go to your fathers in peace; you shall be buried in a good old age. [16] And they shall come back here in the fourth generation, for the iniquity of the Amorites is not yet complete."

> [17] When the sun had gone down and it was dark, behold, a smoking fire pot and a flaming torch passed between these pieces. [18] On that day the Lord made a covenant with Abram, saying, "To your offspring I give this land, from the river of Egypt to the great river, the river Euphrates, [19] the land of the Kenites, the Kenizzites, the Kadmonites, [20] the Hittites, the Perizzites, the Rephaim, [21] the Amorites, the Canaanites, the Girgashites and the Jebusites."

The covenant has been made! Abraham now stands in a particular relation to God. We should notice in passing that in these verses God also tells Abraham about the exile in Egypt and the suffering that this would bring to his chosen people (vv. 13-16). To read the Book of Exodus is to find the details of what is prophesied in these verses.

When we turn to Genesis 17, we find the covenant ratified and confirmed. It is clear from that chapter that the covenant consisted of three promises: 1) Abraham would be the Father of many nations. As a sign of this promise, his name was changed from Abram to Abraham; 2) He was going to have a son who would be his heir. As a sign of this promise, his wife's name was changed from Sarai to Sarah; 3) God promised to be his God and the God of his descendants. As a sign of this promise, the covenant of circumcision was given.

It is important to point out, however, that faith was the key to the covenant. By the time of Jesus, many of the Jews had forgotten that faith was the key and were trusting in the outward sign. As long as someone was circumcised, they said, he is a true Jew and is in a right relationship with God.

But that was not true, as Paul pointed out in Romans 2:25-29: 'For circumcision indeed is of value if you obey the law, but if you break the law, your circumcision becomes uncircumcision. So, if a man who is uncircumcised keeps the precepts of the law, will not his uncircumcision be regarded as circumcision? Then he who is physically uncircumcised but keeps the law will condemn you who have the written code and circumcision but break the law. For no one is a Jew who is merely one outwardly, nor is circumcision outward and physical. But a Jew is one inwardly, and circumcision is a matter of the heart, by the Spirit, not by the letter. His praise is not from man but from God.'

He makes the same point later in Romans 4:9-12: 'Is this blessing then only for the circumcised, or also for the uncircumcised? We say that faith was counted to Abraham as righteousness. How then was it counted to him? Was it before or after he had been circumcised? It was not after, but before he was circumcised. He received the sign of circumcision as a seal of the righteousness that he had by faith while he was still uncircumcised. The purpose was to make him the father of all who believe without being circumcised, so that righteousness would be counted to them as well, and to make him the father of the circumcised who are not merely circumcised but who also walk in the footsteps of the faith that our father Abraham had before he was circumcised.'

This covenant, which God made with Abraham and his descendants in Genesis chapters 15 and 17, is the third covenant that we find in these early chapters of Genesis. Earlier, in chapter 6, God made a covenant with Noah and his family. Then in chapter 9, God made a covenant with all the living. This covenant in Genesis 15 and 17, however, is somewhat different from those that have gone before. This is a covenant between God and his chosen people, which involves what Professor John Murray has called 'a sovereign administration' of grace.[2] By this covenant, God entered into a relationship with his chosen people such that he would be their God and they would be his people. Every descendant of Abraham was included in the covenant people of God. From this time on, every Jew would be related to God by covenant.

Nevertheless, we must constantly remind ourselves of Genesis 15:6, which makes it clear that Abraham's relationship to God was not based on the covenant alone; it was based on faith. It was an individual relationship, not simply a corporate relationship. We might put it like this: there were two levels on which it can be said that a descendant of Abraham could have a relationship with God. There is first of all the covenant relationship. In that sense, every Jew was outwardly related to God in and through the covenant. There was, however, another, deeper level at which they could have a relationship with God, and that was a personal relationship with God through faith. This means that it was possible to be included within the covenant people but to be a stranger to God's grace and mercy.

Having considered the covenant made with Abraham and his descendants, one important question which has to be answered concerns the relationship between this covenant and the Mosaic covenant, established at Sinai. This is a subject to which I intend to return in more detail in a later chapter,[3] and so for the moment I will simply give an indication of my position.

Two main views have been taken by Reformed scholars. On the one hand, there are those who see a fundamental continuity between the covenant with Abraham and the Mosaic covenant. They argue that what happened at Sinai was a spelling out of the obligations of the Abrahamic covenant, essentially detailing for the covenant people of God how they are to live. John Murray is among those who take this position. On the other hand, there are those who see the Mosaic covenant as a republication of what they perceive to be a Covenant of Works made with Adam in Genesis 2. On this basis they argue that there is a radical discontinuity with the Abrahamic covenant. John Owen is among those who take this position. I will explain why in more detail later, but for the moment let

---

[2] John Murray *The Covenant of Grace* (London: Tyndale Press, 1954), 14.

[3] See a later chapter entitled, " Scottish Covenant Theology: Thomas Boston and John Murray."

me say that I am in accord with Murray and continuity, and that I came to this position on the basis of Galatians 3, especially 3:17, 18: 'This is what I mean: the law, which came 430 years afterward, does not annul a covenant previously ratified by God, so as to make the promise void. For if the inheritance comes by the law, it no longer comes by promise; but God gave it to Abraham by a promise.'

The law given through Moses does not cancel the covenant made with Abraham; rather it was a continuation of it, a spelling out of the relationship between God and his people and of the obligations that came with this relationship.

THE NEW TESTAMENT: THE COVENANT CONSUMMATED

In the fullness of time, the promise of Genesis 3:15 was fulfilled and the seed of the woman was born. Now the covenant moves to a new dimension. Some of the very earliest statements concerning Christ in the gospels draw the connection between his coming and the covenant made with Abraham. Notice particularly the words of Zechariah in Luke 1:67-75: 'And his father Zechariah was filled with the Holy Spirit and prophesied, saying, "Blessed be the Lord God of Israel, for he has visited and redeemed his people and has raised up a horn of salvation for us in the house of his servant David, as he spoke by the mouth of his holy prophets from of old, that we should be saved from our enemies and from the hand of all who hate us; to show the mercy promised to our fathers and to remember his holy covenant, the oath that he swore to our father Abraham, to grant us that we, being delivered from the hand of our enemies, might serve him without fear, in holiness and righteousness before him all our days."

This was also part of the preaching of the early Church. Notice what Peter says in Acts 3:25-26: "You are the sons of the prophets and of the covenant that God made with your fathers, saying to Abraham, 'And in your offspring shall all the families of the earth be blessed.' God, having raised up his servant, sent him to you first, to bless you by turning every one of you from your wickedness."

One key passage for demonstrating the fundamental unity between God's sovereign administration of grace in the covenants of the Old Testament and his sovereign administration of grace in the new covenant is Romans 4. That passage makes it absolutely clear that Abraham was saved in precisely the same way as believers in Jesus Christ, namely, by grace through faith.

In the early chapters of Romans, Paul has been setting forth the gospel method of salvation, namely justification by faith. He now begins to prove his point with reference to the Old Testament. If you imagine a Jew approaching Paul and trying to disprove his teaching, then the scene will be set in your mind for what follows. Paul anticipates an objection about Abraham. The question at issue is how justification is to be obtained. The objector believes that Paul's argument will fall to the ground when measured against the case of Abraham; Paul, on the other hand, knows that if he can prove justification by faith in the case of Abraham, then his argument will be established. Paul is happy to take up the case of Abraham because no better example could be found.

Paul begins by agreeing with our supposed objector that if Abraham was justified by works then he had grounds for boasting. However, Paul goes on in verse 3 to quote Genesis 15:6 which, as we saw earlier, explicitly says that Abraham 'believed the Lord, and he counted it to him as righteousness.' As Professor Charles Hodge says, 'If the greatest and best men of the old dispensation had to renounce entirely dependence upon their works, and to accept of the favour of God as a gratuity, justification by works must for all men, be impossible.'[4] There is and has always been only one way of salvation, by faith.

There are many other passages to which we could turn to confirm this same point, not least Galatians 3. Faced with a church which was abandoning grace in favour of legalism, Paul insists on the continuity between Abraham's situation and that of the New Testament believers. Look at Galatians 3:1-9:

> O foolish Galatians! Who has bewitched you? It was before your eyes that Jesus Christ was publicly portrayed as crucified. Let me ask you only this: Did you receive the Spirit by works of the law or by hearing with faith? Are you so foolish? Having begun by the Spirit, are you now being perfected by the flesh? Did you suffer so many things in vain—if indeed it was in vain? Does he who supplies the Spirit to you and works miracles among you do so by works of the law, or by hearing with faith—just as Abraham "believed God, and it was counted to him as righteousness"?
>
> Know then that it is those of faith who are the sons of Abraham. And the Scripture, foreseeing that God would justify the Gentiles by faith,

---

[4] Charles Hodge, *A Commentary on Romans* (reprint, Edinburgh: The Banner of Truth Trust, 1972), 124.

preached the gospel beforehand to Abraham, saying, "In you shall all the nations be blessed." So then, those who are of faith are blessed along with Abraham, the man of faith.

This whole chapter of Scripture bears serious study and helps to demonstrate the unity of God's covenantal dealings with human beings. The covenant God made with Abraham, then, was a sovereign administration of grace whereby salvation by grace through faith was mediated. This helps us to see that this covenant which God made with Abraham was fulfilled and completed in Jesus Christ, so that we who are Christians are now God's covenant people. We have the promise, given by faith in Jesus Christ. This has important consequences for us. Just as the Jews were the covenant people of God in the Old Testament, so we are the covenant people of God today. As part of the family of the Christian Church, we are related to God as his covenant people. I noted earlier in relation to the Jews, that it was possible to be part of God's covenant people and yet not to be in a saving relationship with him. This is also true today. Perhaps this matter can be explained by giving the example of a child born to a covenant family. That child is part of God's covenant people from the moment of birth, but that child will still one day have to enter into a personal relationship with God by faith. (We should notice in passing that we do not baptise our children to bring them into the covenant: we baptise them because they are already in the covenant.)

Do you understand this? Let me put it in a more personal and direct way: is your relationship to God only on the corporate level or is it at the personal level? Are you related to God as part of the church, the covenant people of God, the visible and outward family of the faith? Or are you related to God individually and personally as a child of God who has come to him in faith and repentance because of the work of the Holy Spirit in your life? The first level, the level of the covenant people, is very important, because it marks us out from the world. But the second level, the level of individual faith in God, is the level which is of eternal significance.

We noted earlier that many of the Jews in Jesus' day made the mistake of assuming that if someone was circumcised, then that person, as part of the covenant people, was, by definition, in a right relationship with God. There are many today who make a similar mistake with baptism. As long as someone is baptised, they say, he is a true Christian and is in a right relationship with God. We must respond by saying that baptism fulfils for God's covenant people today the same function which circumcision fulfilled for the covenant people of God in the Old Testament, namely, as a sign and a seal of God's grace, and that faith is, and always has been, central to God's sovereign administration of grace through the covenants.

THE CONTINUITY OF THE COVENANT

That fine Scottish theologian, John Murray, about whom I will be saying more tomorrow, once gave an important lecture on this matter of the unity of the covenant at the British Tyndale Conference in Cambridge entitled *The Covenant of Grace.* That lecture was published fifty years ago, in January 1954. The arithmetic involved in working out that it was fifty years ago was not difficult for me, since that was also the month in which I was born! I can say with complete sincerity (and not a little national pride) that this is the best thing I have ever read on our subject today and I encourage you to read it. Murray looks at all of the covenants mentioned in the Scriptures and teaches us a number of important lessons.

His primary concern is to demonstrate that those who view the covenants principally in terms of a compact or agreement between parties have misunderstood the Scriptures. He recognises that in some of the covenants between human beings there is a 'mutual compact' but notes that, 'even should it be true that in these covenants the idea of mutual compact is central, it does not follow that the idea of compact is central in or essential to the covenant relation which God constitutes with man.'[5] Those who are familiar with Scottish theology will know that James B. Torrance has consistently over many years argued that covenant theology is misguided whenever it changes a covenant into a contract.[6] By responding to covenant theologians who have taken this unbiblical position, then, Murray is also able to defend covenant theology against the neo-orthodox.

Murray then considers the various covenants in the Old Testament, demonstrating their fundamental continuity. As he gradually builds up the picture he is able to define the key elements of covenant as 'a dispensation of grace to men, wholly divine in its origin, fulfilment, and con-

---

[5] Murray, *The Covenant of Grace,* 9.

[6] J.B. Torrance, "Covenant or Contract?" *Scottish Journal of Theology* (hereafter *SJT*) 23 (1970):51-76; "The Covenant Concept in Scottish Theology and Politics and its Legacy" *SJT*, 34 (1981): 225-243; J.B. Torrance, "Strengths and Weaknesses of the Westminster Theology," in, *The Westminster Confession in the Church Today,* ed., A.I. Heron (Edinburgh: St. Andrew Press, 1982), 40-54.

firmation.'[7]   When he comes to the Abrahamic covenant he maintains this definition and expands upon it:

> We are led to the conclusion that in the Abrahamic covenant there is no deviation from the idea of covenant as a sovereign dispensation of grace. We have found that grace is intensified and expanded rather than diminished and the greater the grace the more accentuated becomes the sovereignty of its administration. The necessity of keeping the covenant on the part of men does not interfere with the divine monergism of dispensation. The necessity of keeping is but the expression of the magnitude of the grace bestowed and the spirituality of the relation constituted. Even in this case the notion of compact or agreement is alien to the nature of the covenant constitution.[8]

We might suppose that when Murray comes to the Mosaic covenant, he will have much more difficulty in avoiding the notion of compact or mutual agreement—but not so. He is quite clear that in its fundamental character the Mosaic covenant has the same general character as the Abrahamic covenant. He does recognise that obedience is required, but he notes that this is true of all the covenants. The issue is rather whether this obedience is meritorious or necessary for the covenant to be established. He thinks not: 'Undoubtedly there is a conditional feature to the words, "If ye will obey my voice indeed, and keep my covenant." But what is conditioned upon obedience and keeping of the covenant is the enjoyment of the blessing which the covenant contemplates.'[9]   Murray then concludes in these words 'we find that the Mosaic covenant also is a sovereign administration of grace, divinely initiated, established, confirmed, and fulfilled.'[10]

In order to underline this point, he says,

> It is too frequently assumed that the conditions prescribed in connection with the Mosaic covenant place the Mosaic dispensation in a totally different category as respects grace, on the one hand, and demand or obligation, on the other. In reality there is nothing that is principally different in the necessity of keeping the covenant and of obedience to God's voice, which proceeds from the Mosaic covenant, from that which is involved in the keeping required in the Abrahamic. In both cases the keynotes are obeying God's voice and keeping the covenant

---

[7] Murray, *Covenant of Grace*, 15.
[8] Ibid., 18.
[9] Ibid., 21.
[10] Ibid., 22.

(cf. Gn. xviii. 17-19; Exod. xix. 5, 6).[11]

When he turns to the new covenant he is able to conclude that all the covenants which have gone before have a fundamental unity. He notes, 'The new covenant in respect of its being a covenant does not differ from the Abrahamic as a sovereign administration of grace, divine in its inception, establishment, confirmation, and fulfilment.'[12]

Indeed, he sees the new covenant as being not only in unity with the covenants of the Old Testament, but as representing the peak and consummation of God's covenant relationship with his people: 'To whatever extent the old covenant was the means of establishing the peculiar relation of the Lord to Israel as their God and their relation to Him as His people, the new covenant places this older intimacy of relation in the shadow. For it is the new covenant *par excellence* which brings to realization the promise 'I will be to them a God, and they shall be to me a people' (Heb. Viii. 10). In other words, the spiritual relationship which lay at the centre of the covenant grace disclosed in both the Abrahamic and Mosaic covenants reaches its ripest fruition in the new covenant.'[13]

And again, 'In all of this we have the covenant as a sovereign administration of grace and promise, constituting the relation of communion with God, coming to its richest and fullest expression. In a word, the new covenant is covenant as we have found it to be all along the line of redemptive revelation and accomplishment. But it is covenant in all these respects on the highest level of achievement. If the mark of covenant is divinity in initiation, administration, confirmation, and fulfilment, here we have divinity at the apex of its disclosure and activity.'[14]

Thus, Murray is able to draw together the threads of his argument respecting the unity of the covenants in this way: 'This brings to a close our review of the evidence bearing upon the nature of God's covenant with men. From the beginning of God's disclosures to men in terms of covenant we find a unity of conception which is to the effect that a divine covenant is a sovereign administration of grace and of promise. It is not compact or contract or agreement that provides the constitutive or governing idea but that of dispensation in the sense of disposition.'[15]

Finally, Murray concludes:

---

[11] Ibid.
[12] ibid, 27.
[13] Ibid., 28.
[14] Ibid., 29.
[15] Ibid., 30.

Hence, when we come to the climax and apex of covenant administration in the New Testament epoch, we have sovereign grace and promise dispensed on the highest level because it is grace bestowed and promise given in regard to the attainment of the highest end conceivable for men. It is no wonder then that the new covenant is called the everlasting covenant. As covenant revelation has progressed throughout the ages it has reached its consummation in the new covenant, and the new covenant is not wholly diverse in principle and character from the covenants which have preceded it and prepared for it, but it is itself the complete realization and embodiment of that sovereign grace which was the constitutive principle of all the covenants.[16]

CONCLUSION

It seems to me that Murray is fundamentally correct in his exegesis of the relevant Scriptures and fundamentally correct in his assertions regarding the unity of God's covenantal dealings with his people. We can say with real confidence that from the *protoevangelion* of Genesis 3:15 until the *eschaton* itself, God has sovereignly administered his grace and saved his people by that same grace, through faith.

---

[16] Ibid., 31.

Chapter 2

Federal Theology and the Westminster Standards

Morton H. Smith

INTRODUCTION

The Westminster Standards are the Confession and Catechisms produced by the Westminster Assembly of divines, meeting from 1643-1648, over a hundred years after the Reformation began. B. B. Warfield described the Westminster Confession as "the richest and most precise and best guarded instrument ever penned of all that enters into evangelical religion, and of all that must be safeguarded if evangelical religion is to persist in the world."[1] One of the particular distinctives of the Westminster documents is the inclusion of federal theology.

When we speak of Federal Theology, we are speaking of what is more commonly called Covenant Theology today. The word "federal" is derived from the Latin *foedus,* meaning league, treaty, or compact. In non-theological usage the term has come to describe a government, in which individuals or groups band together, relinquishing some of their

---

[1] Benjamin B. Warfield, "The Significance of the Westminster Standards a Creed" in *Selected Shorter Writings of Benjamin B Warfield,* ed. John E. Meeter (Nutley, NJ· Presbyterian and Reformed Publishing Company, 1973), 2:660.

own sovereignty for the sake of unity. In the United States it is used to describe the government of the whole nation, as distinguished from that of the individual states or local governments. During the War for Southern Independence, federal was used to describe the United States as distinguished from the Confederate States of America.

In theological usage it is virtually interchangeable with the term covenant, with special reference to the federal head of the covenant. It is this to which we shall be referring in this lecture. We shall use federal and covenant interchangeably.

DEFINITION OF FEDERAL OR COVENANT THEOLOGY

Before going further, let me give a couple of definitions of covenant theology. Donald Macleod defines covenant theology thus: "the use of the covenant concept as an architectonic principle for the systematizing of Christian truth."[2] Professor John Murray says: "From the beginning and throughout the development of covenant theology, a covenant has been defined as a contract or compact, or agreement between parties."[3] He sees it as "an organizing principle in terms of which the relations of God to men were construed."[4] Federal or covenant theology holds that God deals with man through covenants, which are stated in contractual form. Federal theology, in particular, sees the whole theological system held together by covenant. It is "characterized by a prelapsarian and a postlapsarian covenant schema centered around the first Adam and the second Adam, who is Jesus Christ."[5] Thus Adam was placed under the covenant of works, and upon his becoming a covenant breaker by his sin, God entered into a covenant of grace to provide a way of salvation for man.

J. I. Packer adds to the definition of covenant theology, the significance of this structure as a means of interpreting Scripture. He defines covenant theology as follows:

---

[2] Donald Macleod, "Covenant Theology," *Dictionary of Scottish Church History and Theology*, eds. David F. Wright, David C. Lachman, Donald Meek (Edinburgh: T. & T. Clark and Downers Grove, IL: Intervarsity Press, 1993), 214.

[3] John Murray, "Covenant Theology," *Collected Writings of John Murray* (Edinburgh and Carlisle, PA: The Banner of Truth Trust, 1982), 2:216.

[4] Ibid.

[5] Mark W. Karlberg, "Covenant Theology and the Westminster Tradition," *Westminster Theological Journal* 54 (Spring 1992): 137.

What is covenant theology? The straightforward, if provocative answer to that question is that it is what is nowadays called a hermeneutic—that is, a way of reading the whole Bible that is itself part of the overall interpretation of the Bible that it undergirds. . . . . Covenant theology is a case in point. . . . Once Christians have got this far, the covenant theology of the Scriptures is something that they can hardly miss.[6]

J. Ligon Duncan describes covenant theology thus:

Covenant theology is the Bible's way of explaining and deepening our understanding of (1) the atonement [the meaning of the death of Christ]; (2) assurance [the basis of our confidence of communion with God and enjoyment of his promises]; (3) the sacraments [signs and seals of God's covenant promises—what they are and how they work]; and (4) the continuity of redemptive history [the unified plan of God's salvation]. Covenant theology is also an hermeneutic, and approach to understanding the Scripture—an approach that attempts to biblically explain the unity of biblical revelation.[7]

WESTMINSTER: THE FIRST CONFESSIONAL STATEMENT OF FEDERAL THEOLOGY

The Irish Articles of 1615 was the first confessional standard to include the idea of the covenant of works as one of its articles. Article 21 reads:

Man being at the beginning created according to the image of God (which consisted especially in the wisdom of his mind and the true holiness of his free will), had the covenant of the law ingrafted in his heart, whereby God did promise unto him everlasting life upon condition that he performed entire and perfect obedience unto his Commandments, according to that measure of strength wherewith he was endued in his creation, and threatened death unto him if he did not perform the same.[8]

Though the phrase covenant of works is not used in the Irish Articles, the doctrine of this article is the doctrine Westminster designates under

---

[6] J. I. Packer, "Introduction, On Covenant Theology," in Herman Witsius, *The Economy of the Covenants Between God and Man* (Escondito, CA: The den Dulk Foundation, 1990), pages unnumbered.

[7] J. Ligon Duncan III, "Covenant Idea in Irenaeus," *Confessing Our Hope. Essays in Honor of Morton Howison Smith on His Eightieth Birthday*, ed. Joseph A. Pipa and C N. Willborn (Taylors, SC: Greenville Presbyterian Seminary Press, 2004), 32.

[8] Philip Schaff, *The Creeds of Christendom with a History and Critical Notes* (Grand Rapids: Baker Book House, 1966), 3:530.

that title.

The Westminster Standards are the first confessional standards that include the designations of the covenant of works and of the covenant of grace to describe their theology.

> The distance between God and the creature is so great, that although reasonable creatures do owe obedience unto Him as their Creator, yet they could never have any fruition of Him as their blessedness and reward, but by some voluntary condescension on God's part, which He hath been pleased to express by way of covenant (WCF Chapter VII, I).

> The first covenant made with man was a covenant of works, wherein life was promised to Adam; and in him to his posterity, upon condition of perfect and personal obedience (WCF VII, II).

> Man, by his fall, having made himself incapable of life by that covenant, the Lord was pleased to make a second, commonly called the covenant of grace; wherein He freely offereth unto sinners life and salvation by Jesus Christ; requiring of them faith in Him, that they may be saved, and promising to give unto all those that are ordained unto eternal life His Holy Spirit, to make them willing, and able to believe (WCF VII, III).

W. T. Hall of Columbia Theological Seminary at the beginning of the 20th century says federal theology is "the mould in which the Westminster Creed is cast. The plan of salvation is treated as a Covenant. Sin and Grace are alike taught in the light of the Covenants. One might almost venture to say that the doctrine of the Covenants constitutes the distinctive feature of the Westminster Creed."[9] Geerhardus Vos says, "The Westminster Confession is the first Reformed confession in which the doctrine of the covenant is not merely brought from the side, but is place in the foreground and has been able to permeate at almost every point."[10] Covenant theology combines both biblical theology and systematic theology. On the one hand the divines treated each of the *loci* of theology separately, and on the other hand, they interwove

---

[9] W. T, Hall, "The Federal Principle in the Westminster Standards," in *The Presbyterian Quarterly* XII, no. 6 (July 1898): 378.

[10] Geerhardus Vos, "The Doctrine of the Covenant in Reformed Theology," in *Redemptive History and Biblical Interpretation, The Shorter Writings of Geerhardus Vos*, ed. Richard B. Gaffin, Jr. (Phillipsburg, NJ: Presbyterian and Reformed Publishing Co., 1980), 239.

the whole with the historical doctrinal development of the covenants. Covenant theology gives the structure for the explanation of the
fall of man and the gospel of Christ.

Though he was critical of federal theology, Thomas F. Torrance of
Scotland describes the system of federal theology in these words:

> It gave Reformed theology a universal perspective, inasmuch as theol-
> ogy takes into account the whole economy of the Covenant before the
> Incarnation and the whole economy of the Covenant after the Incarna-
> tion. There can be no doubt that the Federal Theology achieved a mag-
> nificent and comprehensive unification of Biblical teaching. But it also
> gave theology its great historical perspective, as that which is concerned
> with the history of the people of God in Covenant relation and conver-
> sation with Him throughout all ages from the very beginning of the
> world to the present day, reaching out to the Parousia.[11]

In 1882, John L. Girardeau delivered a lecture at the semi-centennial
celebration of Columbia Theological Seminary entitled "The Federal
Theology: Its Import and Its Regulative Influence."[12] It was his
contention that covenant or federal theology is the Biblical and
thus the proper structure of Christian theology as set forth in the
Confession. Furthermore, he averred that the covenant theology
was vitally related to practical theology or preaching.

The Westminster divines saw the covenantal principle as the all-
encompassing theological theme of their system of theology. Adam in
his state of innocence was placed under the covenant of works on condition of perfect obedience. Sin is defined in terms of the law of God. By
sinning against God, he became a covenant breaker. God immediately
provided the covenant of grace, with the promised victory of the Seed of
the woman over the serpent. Immediately following the chapter on
God's Covenant with man in the Confession is the chapter on "Christ the
Mediator." The sin of Adam is seen as imputed to those represented by
Adam in the covenant of works. The justification of sinners under the

---

[11] Thomas F. Torrance, *The School of Faith* (London: James Clarke and Company,
Limited, 1959), lxv.

[12] John L. Girardeau, "The Federal Theology: Its Import and Its Regulative Influence," in *Memorial Volume of the Semi-Centennial of the Theological Seminary at Columbia, South Carolina* (Columbia, SC: The Presbyterian Publishing House, 1884), 96-
128. This essay has been republished in book form as John L. Girardeau, *The Federal
Theology: Its Import and Its Regulative Influence* (Greenville, SC: Reformed Academic
Press, 1994).

covenant of grace is by means of the imputed righteousness of Christ. The law as a rule of life for man, though first codified at Sinai, is seen as written on the heart of Adam as created. The curse on the human race as a result of Adam's disobedience is reversed by the obedience of Christ, the second Adam. The moral law continues as the rule of life for believers now. Christ the head of the New Covenant is the Head of the Church. The membership of the church visible included the children as well as the adult believers. The sacraments are explicitly defined as signs and seals of the covenant of grace. Thus we see that covenant theology underlies the Confession's teaching regarding the sacraments. This brief overview of the theology of the Westminster Standards shows how interrelated the idea of the covenants is with their statement of the gospel.

THE ATTACK ON FEDERAL THEOLOGY

Having sketched the significance of federal theology in the Westminster Standards, we need be aware that this theology is not held in the same high esteem by many today. There have been a number of attacks leveled against this theology in recent years from within Presbyterian circles. It is my intention, at this point, to examine some of these attacks, with some comment on them as we go along, and then afterward, time permitting, to go back to the Westminster Standards themselves, and to make some observations on the system they espouse. It is not possible in single lecture to set forth or to answer all of these positions, but we shall try to consider some of the most relevant.

NEW MODERNISM
(THE SO CALLED NEO-ORTHODOXY)

The new modernism of the existential theologians, which did not accept the orthodox Biblical Christianity of the Westminster Standards sought to discredit these Standards. They did this by attempting to draw a sharp division between the theology of the Westminster Standards and the theology of the Reformers. The Westminster Standards, which were produced a century after the Reformation, are alleged to be the product of protestant scholasticism. In Scotland this was the thrust of Thomas F. Torrance's critique of the Westminster Standards. For example, he says,

> The Reformation catechisms are less rationalistic than those of Westminster. That is to say, they expound Christian doctrine in the light of

its own inherent patterns, following the direction of the Apostle's Creed, whereas the Westminster divines abandoned that for a schematism of their own which they imposed upon the instruction they had received from their fathers. They schematised it to the scholastic pattern of the Federal Theology and thus expounded Christian doctrine from the point of view of a particular school of thought.[13]

I had the privilege of hearing Professor Torrance lecture on this subject at the Free University in Amsterdam. I asked Professor Berkouwer if he agreed with Torrance's thesis that the Westminster Standards were the result of protestant scholasticism. He said that he did not think this was valid. As a result of that question I was assigned Torrance's book *The School of Faith* for my final assignment to qualify me for the *doctorandus* degree, which essentially cleared me to write my dissertation.

It was maintained that Calvin and the other Reformers spoke only of a covenant of grace. They did not teach a covenant of works. It is true that Calvin and the Reformers did not use the language "covenant of works." They did, however, contrast law and gospel, or law and grace.

It was alleged that the Puritans developed the idea of the covenant of works, as a result of the popularity of Peter Ramus'[14] philosophical methodology, which favored the dichotomous pairing of ideas, such as nature and grace, reprobate and elect, mercy and justice, and so forth. Thus it is alleged that the federalists invented the covenant of works to contrast with the covenant of grace, without regard to Scripture. It may be true that the Puritans were influenced by Ramus and his simpler methodology. They were, however, so committed to the Bible, that anything they adopted from secular thought was only adopted because they believed it was Biblical.

It must be acknowledged that there was a distinct change in the testimony of the Reformed Confessions from the First Helvetic Confession (1536) to the Westminster Standards (1646) regarding covenant theology. The emphasis of the First Helvetic Confession was on the grace of God, where it is alleged that the Westminster Standards lay emphasis on

---

[13] Torrance, *The School of Faith*, xviii. For a fine recent treatment of Protestant scholasticism see Carl R. Trueman and R. S. Scott, eds., *Protestant Scholasticism: Essays in Reassessment* (Carlisle, UK: Paternoster Press, 1999).

[14] Peter Ramus was a French philosopher, who rejected the then popular Aristotelian logic for a much simpler method. He was a Protestant, and was killed in the St Bartholomew Day's massacre in Paris

law and duty, as a result of the covenant of works. The obligation of obedience is binding on all of Adam's descendants. The First Helvetic Confession was concerned with the fallen world and the grace needed to correct this world. The Westminster standards are more cosmic, beginning with man prior to his fall, and then dealing with fallen man.

Holmes Rolston, III, of the Southern Presbyterian ministry, in his book entitled *John Calvin versus the Westminster Confession*, asserts that the federalism of the Westminster Confession is a "theological anachronism."[15] He calls the federalism of the Westminster Standards a "myth," which he says was founded upon "the primacy of law."[16] Though he admitted that the Westminster Confession teaches, "a limited kind of grace is required even for a covenant of works,"[17] he felt that the federalism of the Confession really negates any meaningful understanding of grace in the covenant of works. He says of the covenant of works, that it "remains as the necessary precondition and framework of the second. Chronologically and logically for covenant theology, grace came and comes only after sin,"[18] which he held was the wrong order. He insisted on grace first and then the law.

To understand Rolston one must understand his Barthian presuppositions and skewed emphasis on grace, and therefore his erection of a "straw man." Contrary to Rolston, we hold that chronologically law does come before grace. The fact is sin comes before grace, and law comes before sin. It should be observed, however, that the very giving of the covenant of works was as the Westminster Standards says an act of condescension on the part of God to his creatures.

Both Rolston and J. B. Torrance object to the "contractual" understanding of Confession in describing covenants.

J. B. Torrance of Scotland asserts that the contractual understanding of covenants was a result of the social developments of the age. "With the break up of feudalism and the struggle for liberty," argues Torrance, "men made 'bands' and 'pacts' and 'contracts' and 'covenants' to defend their freedom and to preserve the rights of a people vis-à-vis their sovereign, and the rights of a sovereign vis-à-vis his subjects. The

[15] Holmes Rolston, III, *John Calvin Versus the Westminster Confession* (Richmond: John Knox Press, 1972), 11.

[16] Ibid., 14.

[17] Ibid., 35.

[18] Ibid , 22

Westminster Assembly met at a time when the whole nation was caught up in a struggle for freedom."[19]

Again, Torrance says, "The background of much theological controversy was the emerging socio-political philosophy of 'social contract', 'contract of government', 'the rights of man', 'natural law' —illuminated by the 'light of reason' and given divine sanction by 'revelation'.[20] Torrance's is objection is substantially weakened, however, when it is recognized that the Hebrew berith or covenant in the Old Testament often does describe a contractual relationship.

Both Torrance and Rolston maintain that the idea of social covenanting was so pervasive in the thought patterns of the day that it provided a conceptual federal theology framework within which Reformed theology was to be recast.[21] They see this as the ground for the "legalism" of the Westminster Standards. According to Torrance federalism has erred in placing the imperatives before the indicatives. It has replaced the love relationship (covenant) with a law relationship (contract).[22] To view the covenant of grace in contractual terms is to make grace conditional. "The whole focus of attention," Torrance would have us believe, "moves away from what Christ has done for us and for all men, to what we have to do IF we would be (or know that we are) in covenant with God."[23] Torrance and Rolston argue that the Westminster view of the covenants of works and of grace is based upon the priority of law over grace.[24] Their view, however, wants to insist on the priority of grace over law. In response it should be observed that the Bible teaches both law and grace, without necessarily setting one above the other. Donald Macleod observes, "the whole gospel story is about God's provision of just mercy."[25]

---

[19] James B. Torrance, "Covenant or Contract?," *Scottish Journal of Theology* 23, no. 1 (Feb 1970): 52.

[20] Ibid., 53.

[21] Torrance, "Covenant or Contract?," 53.

[22] Ibid , 56. See the discussion of David McWilliams, "The Covenant Theology of the Westminster Confession of Faith and Recent Criticism," *Westminster Theological Journal* 53 (Spring 1991): 111.

[23] Torrance, "Covenant or Contract?," 69.

[24] For a good response to the "law over grace" charge, see Donald MacLeod, "Federal Theology—An Oppressive Legalism?," *The Banner of Truth* 125 (February 1974): 21-28.

[25] MacLeod, "Covenant Theology," 217

Torrance argues that federal theology reverses the relation between forgiveness and atonement, insisting that forgiveness comes before atonement. Donald Macleod answers: "Yet this argument rests on a confusion between love and graciousness on the one hand and forgiveness on the other. All federal theologians . . . were adamant that God's love preceded atonement, and indeed provided it. But they did not confuse love with forgiveness."[26]

David McWilliams has an insightful analysis of the Rolston and Torrance position:

> It must be understood that Rolston and Torrance have predicated their positions upon the presuppositions of existential theology, presuppositions with far-reaching implications for the issue at hand. The Adam narrative, consequently, is not *Historie* but myth or saga. Modern concepts of the origin of man have radically altered the idea of a divine covenant with all men in Adam. But surely it should be obvious from the start that a denial of Adam's historicity is not without consequences. An *a priori* denial of the historicity of Adam (which is an explicit teaching of the WCF) necessitates a radical reappraisal of the biblical presentation of sin. Paul's presentation of sin and the gospel (Romans 5) stands or falls upon the historicity of the first Adam: "through one man sin entered into the world, and death through sin, and so death spread to all men, because all have sinned" (Rom 5:12). A rejection of the historicity of Adam must inevitably result in the rejection of federalism. Torrance, Rolston, and other existentialist theologians homogenize the pre-fall and post-fall situations, collapsing them into a sort of Ever Present. The "before" and "after" of the creation and fall are transmuted into a timeless "above" and "below" of the creation and the fall.[27]

CONTEMPORARY ATTACKS ON FEDERAL THEOLOGY

Wilson Benton, whom I judge to be essentially orthodox, and whom I hold in high personal regard, critiques federal theology as being found wanting because the starting point of the historical system is the cove-

---

[26] Ibid , 218.

[27] McWilliams, "The Covenant Theology of the Westminster Confession of Faith and Recent Criticism," 214. For an example of McWilliams' statement, "Modern concepts of the origin of man have radically altered the idea of a divine covenant with all men in Adam," see Rolston, *John Calvin versus the Westminster Confession*, 14.

nant of works, which he judges is "without biblical foundation."[28] He also feels that there is a subtle shift from theology to anthropology in this system.[29] These are charges, which it is proper for us to examine.

Is the covenant of works without biblical foundation? There have been respected men such as Professor John Murray who argued that there is no covenant of works, and this from a biblical theological perspective. However, we simply refer to the Scottish pastor-theologian Thomas Boston, who argued that where the various parts of a covenant are found, there a covenant exists.[30] This he found in connection with the command and threat regarding the tree of the knowledge of good and evil.

The second charge against federal theology of the Standards is that it moves the center of the system from theology to anthropology. One can see how this might be the understanding of the system, if one begins his consideration of the system with the covenant of works. Then it does seem to be a system centered upon man, and not upon God. Vos makes the following statement regarding the apparent anthropocentric character of federal theology: "When it first emerged, the doctrine of the covenant still betrayed the tendency to proceed from man and to survey his surroundings. By the outworking of the doctrine of the counsel of peace this danger was averted and the center placed in God."[31]

If anthropocentrism can be charged against federalism in general, is it true of the federal theology of the Westminster Standards? The Standards are certainly theocentric in their overall structure. Both of the Catechisms begin with the question about the chief end of man, and though this may appear to be anthropocentric the answer is theocentric. The chief end of man and of all of creation is to glorify God and to enjoy Him forever. The Standards view man as created in the image of God. As creature he is naturally obliged to obey his Maker. The God-centered

---

[28] Wilson Benton, "Federal Theology: A Review for Revision," *Through Christ's Words. A Festschrift for Dr Philip E. Hughes,* eds. W. Robert Godfrey and Jesse L. Boyd, III (Phillipsburg, NJ: Presbyterian and Reformed Publishing Co.), 1985.

[29] R. L. Dabney indicates that Principal Hill, on whom Dr. Benton wrote his doctoral dissertation, constructed his theology around the remedy for man's sin, thus taking an anthropocentric approach to theology. Dr. Benton may well have drawn his conclusions regarding the federal theology being anthropocentric from his studies of Hill.

[30] Thomas Boston, *The Beauties of Thomas Boston,* ed. Samuel Miller (Inverness: Christian Focus Publications, 1997), 365 f.

[31] Vos, "The Doctrine of the Covenant in Reformed Theology," 247.

emphasis underlies the whole of the covenant theology as set forth by the Westminster Standards.

Man's sin was ultimately a transgression of the law of God. Thus, even sin is God centered. The provisions of the covenant of grace are all God initiated, and God produced. It was God who sent his Son to accomplish the work of redemption. It was God the Son, who came and accomplished that work. It was the Holy Spirit who applies the redemption accomplished by Christ to the elect. The doctrine of effectual calling recognizes that without God man would not come to Him.

> As God hath appointed the elect unto glory, so hath He, by the eternal and most free purpose of His will, foreordained all the means thereunto. Wherefore, they who are elected, being fallen in Adam, are redeemed by Christ, are effectually called unto faith in Christ by His Spirit working in due season, are justified, adopted, sanctified, and kept by His power, through faith, unto salvation. Neither are any other redeemed by Christ, effectually called, justified, adopted, sanctified, and saved, but the elect only (WCF III VI).[32]

> Shorter Catechism Question 31:   What is effectual calling?

> Answer: Effectual calling is the work of God's Spirit, whereby, convincing us of our sin and misery, enlightening our minds in the knowledge of Christ, and renewing our wills, he doth persuade and enable us to embrace Jesus Christ, freely offered to us in the gospel.

As set forth in the Westminster Standards, federal theology is clearly theocentric.

This effort to separate the orthodoxy of the Westminster Standards from the Reformers is continued in more recent studies of the covenant,

---

[32] Additional Confessional statements on this subject: WCF X, I. All those whom God hath predestinated unto life, and those only, He is pleased, in His appointed and accepted time, effectually to call, by His Word and Spirit, out of that state of sin and death, in which they are by nature to grace and salvation, by Jesus Christ; enlightening their minds spiritually and savingly to understand the things of God, taking away their heart of stone, and giving unto them an heart of flesh; renewing their wills, and, by His almighty power, determining them to that which is good, and effectually drawing them to Jesus Christ: yet so, as they come most freely, being made willing by His grace. II. This effectual call is of God's free and special grace alone, not from anything at all foreseen in man, who is altogether passive.

such as David Weir's *The Origins of Federal Theology in Sixteenth-Century Reformation Thought.*[33] Mark Karlberg says, "One of the aims of David Weir's study of sixteenth-century covenant theology is to provide a rationale for the transformation of early covenant theology into the scholastic form called "federal" theology that obtained confessional status in the Westminster Confession of Faith and Catechisms written approximately one hundred years after the beginnings of the Reformation."[34]

Karlberg reviewed Weir's sources and other authors of the sixteenth-century and draws the following conclusion:

> Much of Weir's analysis of federal theology is marred by a misreading of the Reformation literature. At times Weir exaggerates differences between "federal" theology of the scholastic period and early "covenant" theology. A sharp demarcation between covenant theology and federal theology, in my judgment, is highly artificial and misleading. Weir's discussion, furthermore, contains a number of imprecise restatements and summaries of Reformed theology. Most serious is the virtual neglect of the medieval background for the covenant formulations, especially the influence of late medieval nominalism."[35]

The contemporary movement calling itself Federal Vision attacks the Westminster Standards and their view of federal theology. This may be seen in the essay of Richard Lusk entitled "A Response to 'The Biblical Plan of Salvation."[36] in which he rejects the whole covenantal understanding of the Westminster Standards, and seeks to restructure it all with a new understanding of the meaning of covenant as well as other theological *loci.* Lusk relies upon a volume entitled *The Eternal Covenant, How the Trinity Reshapes Covenant Theology* by Ralph Smith in which Smith concludes: "The Westminster Confession is in need of revision."[37] He cites Meredith Kline, who defends the idea of the covenant

---

[33] David Weir, *The Origins of Federal Theology in Sixteenth-Century Reformation Thought* (Oxford: Clarendon Press, 1990).

[34] Mark Karlberg, "Covenant Theology and the Westminster Tradition," *Westminster Theological Journal* 54 (Spring 1992), 135.

[35] Ibid., 136.

[36] Rick Lusk, "A Response to 'The Biblical Plan of Salvation,'" in *The Auburn Avenue Theology, Pros and Cons. Debating the Federal Vision,* ed. E. Calvin Beisner (Fort Lauderdale, FL: Knox Theological Seminary, 2004), 118-48.

[37] Ralph Smith, *The Eternal Covenant, How the Trinity Reshapes Covenant Theology,* (Moscow, ID: Canon Press, 2003), 101.

of works, but who believes "that the Confession is wrong when it speaks of God condescending to give Adam a covenant."[38]

Ralph Smith argues that the Trinity exists in a loving covenant, and that this should become the paradigm for Reformed covenant theology, instead of the covenant of works. He holds that "the covenant of works as traditionally conceived is clearly antiquated because of its notion of merit."[39]   He cites the Westminster Confession Chapter 7, paragraph 1 and 2, as expressing an "outmoded medieval conception of merit." Second, he affirms that "the traditional doctrine of the covenant of works is unbiblical."[40]   He cites Kline again as opposing the position of the Westminster Confession that the covenant was added after creation. Lee Irons, defending Kline's position says, "The covenant of works will of necessity now be viewed not as an additional structure superimposed on the created order, a created order that could very well have existed apart from a covenant relationship with the Creator, but as an essential part of God's creation of man after his own image."[41] Smith describes his view of the creation covenant thus: "The covenant in the garden, therefore, should be seen as an extension of the covenant fellowship of the persons of the Trinity, a covenant of love rather than a covenant of works."[42]

He states thirdly that the covenant of works is theologically inadequate. By this he is saying that the traditional concept of a covenant being contractual is an inadequate paradigm for the development of covenant theology. It is his view that there must be a covenant of love, not of works, that serves as the paradigm. In order to provide for this he posits that there is an eternal covenant of love within the Trinity. It is this eternal love covenant, which is reflected in the creation covenant of God's love for man as made in His image.

This concept of the Trinity existing in a loving covenant, without any contractual agreements between the persons is a speculation that is not backed by any clear teaching of Scripture. That there was a counsel

---

[38] Ibid.

[39] Ibid., 62.

[40] Ibid , 65.

[41] Lee Irons, "Redefining Merit: An Examination of Medieval Presuppositions in Covenant Theology," *Creator, Redeemer, Consummator: A Festscrift for Meredith G. Kline*, ed. Howard Griffith and John R. Muether (Greenville, SC: Reformed Academic Press, 2000), 268, as cited by Ralph Smith, *The Eternal Covenant*, 66.

[42] Ibid., 69.

of peace or *pactum salutis* or covenant of redemption within the God-head is a clear teaching of the Scripture. It is based upon passages such as Isaiah 53:11-2 and John 17. In this counsel or covenant of redemption, as it is sometimes called, those chosen by the Father are given to the Son. He, in turn, accomplishes the work of redemption for those the Father gives Him. The Holy Spirit then applies the redemption accomplished by Christ to the elect. Vos makes it clear that this counsel should not be confused with the predestinating decree. "In predestination," explains Vos, "the divine persons act communally, while economically it is attributed to the Father. In the covenant of redemption they are related to one another judicially. In predestination they are one, undivided, divine will. In the counsel of peace this will appears as having its own mode of existence in each person."[43]

We shall see that there are differences of opinion as to whether there was a covenant of redemption or a counsel of peace. Vos held that the counsel of peace preserves the theocentric doctrine of the covenant. He says:

> In the dogma of the counsel of peace, then, the doctrine of the covenant has found its genuinely theological rest point. Only when it becomes plain how it is rooted, not in something that did not come into existence until creation, but in God's being itself, only then has this rest point reached and only then can the covenant idea be thought of theologically. . . . When it first emerged, the doctrine of the covenant still betrayed the tendency to proceed from man and to survey his surroundings. By the outworking of the doctrine of the counsel of peace this danger was averted and the center placed in God.[44]

SOME IMPLICATIONS OF THE FEDERAL THEOLOGY AND THE WESTMINSTER STANDARDS

Having given the above overview of how basic covenant theology is to the Westminster Standards, and how it is now under attack, let me now go back and develop some of the particular themes that are a part of this kind of theology. As we have already noted the federal theology is a part of the warp and woof of the doctrinal teaching of Standards, involv-

[43] Vos, "The Doctrine of the Covenant in Reformed Theology," 246.

[44] Ibid., 247.

ing all of the doctrines set forth in them. What follows are some of those points where there have been differing viewpoints among the Reformed theologians.

MAN UNDER PURE MORAL GOVERNMENT

James Thornwell, who used the Westminster Standards to frame his system of theology, posits the concept of the original condition of man as that of being under pure moral government. He divides theology into three parts, that of pure moral government, and then moral government as modified by the covenant of works, and finally moral government as modified by the covenant of grace. This, of course, is an outline based upon the federal theology of the Standards. We shall follow this outline in our further discussions.

W. T. Hall points to the lack of clarity of the Westminster Standards regarding the difference between the conditions of man prior to and after the inauguration of the covenant of works. The Confession speaks of man as existing prior to the giving of the covenant of works, while the catechisms do not clearly make this distinction.

The Confession, chapter VII, paragraph 1, speaks of man existing in a primitive state prior to his being placed under the covenant. Francis Beattie comments: "The Confession does not clearly distinguish between this and the covenant state, and curiously enough it treats of the fall and of sin before it sets forth the covenant relations, and when it does set them forth it presents both covenants side by side."[45] It is clear from this paragraph, however, that the Confession views the covenants of God to be the result of his merciful condescension to the creature. Thus even the covenant of works is to be viewed as being granted to Adam as a special act of benevolent providence in order to provide a means for man to enter into blessings and reward as provided in the covenant. This is not something to which man had any claim, but it was a voluntary act on God's part.

The Shorter Catechism seems to speak of the moral law being given to man without any reference to the covenant of works, which would fit with Thornwell's concept of there being a period of pure moral government prior to the giving of the covenant of works:

---

[45] Francis R. Beattie, *The Presbyterian Standards. An Exposition of the Westminster Confession of Faith and Catechisms* (Richmond: The Presbyterian Committee of Publications, 1896; reprint, Greenville, SC: Southern Presbyterian Press, 1997), 89.

Q. 39. What is the duty which God requireth of man?

The duty which God requireth of man is obedience to his revealed will.

Q. 40. What did God at first reveal to man for the rule of his obedience?

The rule which God at first revealed to man for his obedience was the moral law?

Q. 41. Wherein is the moral law summarily comprehended?

The moral law is summarily comprehended in the ten commandments.

The Confession associates the giving of the law with the covenant of works.

> God gave to Adam a law, as a covenant of works, by which He bound him and all his posterity, to personal, entire, exact, and perpetual obedience, promised life upon the fulfilling, and threatened death upon the breach of it, and endued him with power and ability to keep it (WCF XIX.I).

Whether the moral law was given man as a rational creature prior to the giving of the covenant, Adam was to be obedient to his Creator. The most that such obedience secures is the continued favor of God, as long as the law is obeyed. Under such a system man's destiny must always be precarious. Since man was created under law, the definition of sin itself must relate to the law of God.[46] A single sin at any point would move him from innocence to a state of condemnation. Under pure moral government there is no principle of representation or federal headship and thus each man must continue in perfect obedience for himself.

The concept of sin being the transgression of the law of God is one that the modern critics on the covenants seem to miss. They want to define obedience as "covenant faithfulness." They really do not deal with the breach of the covenant of works in terms of transgression of the law of God, because they do not believe it to be a covenant of works. This comes out in their discussion of the meaning of merit as seen in Ralph Smith: "Adam is not earning favor in order to be justified and included

---

[46] Shorter Catechism Question 14: "Sin is any want of conformity unto or transgression of the law of God."

in the covenant. Adam is already in covenant. What is required of
Adam is simply faithfulness to the relationship already granted, something very different from earning 'merit' in order to receive a blessing."[47] Again, Smith says, "He is in covenant with God and what is required of him is just perseverance, faithfulness in the covenant."[48]

Having asserted that Adam existed under pure moral government,
his being placed under the covenant of works was seen as a gracious
provision of God to provide to man the possibility of "fruition of Him as
their blessedness and reward," (WCF 7.1). Thornwell, as well as Robert
S. Candlish in Scotland, argue that a part of this blessedness was the
adoption of Adam as a son, and being made a joint heir with Christ.[49]
Adam as created was the servant of his Maker, but by keeping the covenant of works could be granted the privilege of becoming a son of God.
This is based, in part, on the fact that adoption into the family of God is
clearly one of the specific benefits of the covenant of grace. That is to
say, since adoption is a benefit of the covenant of grace, one may deduce
that adoption would have been a benefit of the covenant of works, upon
Adam's obedience.

Though Vos does not refer to sonship as one of the blessings Adam
could have attained, he verges on it as he describes the Reformed view
of the original state thus:

"The Reformed view of the original state of man leads to a totally
different result. It was a state of perfect uprightness in which he knew
the good and did it consciously. As long as he remained in that state, he
could also be sure of God's favor.[50]

The Larger Catechism in question 20 may be read on either side of

---

[47] Smith, *The Eternal Covenant*, 65.

[48] Ibid., 70.

[49] See volume one of James Henley Thornwell, *The Collected Writings of James
Henley Thornwell*, eds. John B. Adger and John L. Girardeau, 4 vols. (1875; reprint, Edinburgh: The Banner of Truth Trust, 1986); and Robert S. Candlish, *The Fatherhood of
God*, 5th ed. (Edinburgh: Adam and Charles Black, 1870). The latter includes Professor
Candlish's reply to Thomas Crawford's work of the same title. For a helpful and salient
monograph on the doctrine of adoption see the reprint of John Kennedy, *Man's Relation
to God* (Aberdeen, UK: James Begg Society). Also, see John L. Girardeau, "The Doctrine of Adoption," *Discussion of Theological Questions* (Richmond: The Presbyterian
Committee of Publications, 1905; reprint, Harrisonburg, VA: Sprinkle Publications,
1986), 428-521.

[50] Vos, "The Doctrine of the Covenant in Reformed Theology," 243.

the question of whether Adam existed for a period without a covenant relationship with God.

> Q. 20. What was the providence of God toward man in the estate in which he was created?

> The providence of God toward man in the estate in which he was created, was the placing him in paradise, appointing him to dress it, giving him liberty to eat of the fruit of the earth; putting the creatures under his dominion, and ordaining marriage for his help; affording him communion with himself; instituting the Sabbath; entering into a covenant of life with him, upon condition of personal, perfect, and perpetual obedience, of which the tree of life was a pledge; and forbidding to eat of the tree of the knowledge of good and evil, upon the pain of death.

This question of the Larger Catechism parallels the first two paragraphs of Chapter VII of the Confession, but it does not clearly separate a pre-covenantal period from the covenantal period. The Catechism gives a listing of what have been called the creation ordinances. These ordinances are the privilege of Adam in the Garden to eat of the fruit of the trees of the earth. He also was assigned the task or work of keeping and dressing the garden. As a creature made in the image of God, Adam was given dominion over creation. Man as a rational creature was given the responsibility to keep the garden, which means that labor was not a part of the curse, but an original creation ordinance for unfallen man. In addition to this, God ordained marriage for the help of man. Adam enjoyed fellowship with God in the Garden. For his spiritual health he was given the weekly Sabbath as a time of rest from his labors, and a time of special communion with God.

PURE MORAL GOVERNMENT AS MODIFIED BY THE COVENANT OF WORKS

In addition to these creation ordinances, God entered into a covenantal relation with Adam, placing him under probation marked by His command concerning the tree of the knowledge of good and evil. The test was whether man would obey God because he is God. That is, would he obey regarding the tree, just because God had spoken. The Bible warns of the curse if he disobeyed, and from this we may by good and necessary consequence deduce the promise attached to obedience, namely, life.[51] The Catechism describes this as a covenant of life, while the Confession in Chapter 19 speaks of the covenant of works.

As we consider the teaching of the Standards regarding the covenant of works, we must first determine in response to Wilson Benton's charge whether there is a Biblical basis for this covenant? In response to this question, it must be admitted that the term covenant is not used in the opening chapters of Genesis, and even such a respected theologian as John Murray declined to speak of the covenant of works. He spoke of the Adamic administration, where he includes all the points maintained by federal theology while denying a covenant relationship.

O. Palmer Robertson in his *The Christ of the Covenants* treats the Biblical concept of covenant, and presents grounds for understanding the "orderings of creation" in Genesis 1 to be described by the term covenant in Jeremiah 33:20, 21, 25, 26 cf. 31:35f. He argues that Hosea 6:7 is a reference to the covenant with Adam.[52] As he says, "A bond of life and death clearly is present between God and man newly created (Gen. 2:15-17). If Adam would refrain from eating the forbidden fruit, he would live. But if he would eat of the tree of the knowledge of good and evil, he would die. This relationship of God to man is administered sovereignly."[53]

Robertson in distinction from Thornwell and Vos considers Adam to be under covenant from his being created in the image of God. He considers the creation ordinances as covenantal in the broad or general aspect, and the probation as a focal aspect of the Creation Covenant. As a covenant creature, man was to be obedient to his Maker. This agrees with the teaching of the Westminster Standards, which hold that man as created was given the law of God, to which was added the specific command regarding the tree: "The first covenant made with man was a covenant of works, wherein life was promised to Adam; and in him to his posterity, upon condition of perfect and personal obedience" (WCF VII, II).

---

[51] See Westminster Larger Catechism Question 99.4—"That as, where a duty is commanded, the contrary sin is forbidden; and, where a sin is forbidden, the contrary duty is commanded...."

[52] For a fine exegetical treatment of Hosea 6:7, see Benjamin B. Warfield, *The Selected Shorter Writings of Benjamin B Warfield*, ed. John E. Meeter (Nutley, NJ: Presbyterian and Reformed Publishing Company, 1973), 1:116-29.

[53] O. Palmer Robertson, *The Christ of the Covenants* (Phillipsburg, NJ: Presbyterian and Reformed Publishing Co., 1980), 25.

The last paragraph of the Confession cited describes the covenant into which God entered with Adam. It was termed a covenant of works, because the condition required of man to receive the promise, namely, life. This is a good and necessary inference from the Biblical statement made to man, that the day in which he ate the forbidden fruit he would die. In other words, by the act of disobedience he would forfeit the life he was then enjoying. On the other hand, if he met the terms of the probation and obeyed God, the implication is that he would continue to live. Further, Adam was representative of all his posterity, and thus his keeping or breaking of the probation was not only for himself personally, but also for all his posterity. Implied in this is the concept of federal or covenant head as well as natural generation. The federal headship is explicitly taught in the Larger Catechism in question 22, where it deals with the results of Adam's fall: "Did all mankind fall in that first transgression? The covenant being made with Adam as a publick person, not for himself only, but for his posterity, all mankind descending from him by ordinary generation, sinned in him, and fell with him in that first transgression."

The Shorter Catechism Question 12 speaks of the covenant as a covenant of life, giving only the threat of death if Adam disobeyed the command of God regarding the tree of the knowledge of good and evil.[54] Both of the catechisms speak of the fact that the covenant was on the "condition of perfect obedience." The Larger Catechism speaks of it as on the condition of "personal, perfect and perpetual obedience."

The language of the Standards does not state that the probation was one of a limited time, though most theologians hold that to be the case. Thornwell felt that with Adam being made the federal head of the race, the decision of whether he would keep or break the covenant needed to be made prior to the birth of any seed.

This covenant provided a specific command as a means of testing the obedience of man. It included the representative principle. Adam is not only the natural head of the human race but now also serves as the federal head of the race. This principle of representation necessarily in-

---

[54] Shorter Catechism Question 12: What special act of providence did God exercise toward man in the estate wherein he was created? When God had created man, he entered into a covenant of life with him, upon condition of perfect obedience; forbidding him to eat of the tree of the knowledge of good and evil, upon the pain of death.

troduces the principle of imputation, since the actions of the federal head are considered the actions of those he represents. The question of the allegiance of this federal head to his Maker needed to be determined prior to the birth of the first of his progeny. This has to do with the standing of man before God, or his justification.

As we have seen, the Confession affirms that God graciously gave the covenant of works so that man could rise to a higher state. Specific to our interest, the Confession reads: "The distance between God and the creature is so great, that although reasonable creatures do owe obedience unto Him as their Creator, yet they could never have any fruition of Him as their blessedness and reward, but *by some voluntary condescension on God's part*, which He hath been pleased to express by way of covenant" (WCF Chapter VII, I; emphasis added). Francis Beattie in his commentary on the Presbyterian Standards says of this paragraph:

> The covenant relation, even in its first form, was gracious in its nature. While its condition was legal and required obedience, still the constitution itself and the result which it aimed to secure was gracious. The Confession emphasizes this by pointing to the fact that there is a vital distance between God the Creator and man the creature. This distance is so great, and the demands of God's moral government are so exact, that although as reasonable creatures men did render perfect and constant personal obedience, they could never have any fruition of God. This simply means that men under pure moral government could never acquire any merit beyond that involved in meeting the strict demands of the perfect moral law of God; and men all the while under pure moral government would be servants, rendering a legal obedience, and not sons established in the favor of God, and enjoying the blessedness which was to be secured through the covenant relation. To secure for man such benefits, a voluntary condescension on God's part was necessary, which would transpose the status of pure moral servitude into that of covenant merit and reward.[55]

In describing Adam as a "publick person" the Larger Catechism is affirming that he was the covenant or federal head of the race, who are his posterity. Thus we see that the acts of Adam affected his posterity both by natural descent, "all mankind descending from him by ordinary generation" and also by virtue of his being the representative or federal

---

[55] Beattie, *The Presbyterian Standards: An Exposition of the Westminster Confession of Faith and Catechisms*, 93-94.

head. George P. Hutchinson in his book *The Problem of Original Sin in American Presbyterian Theology* says, "[W]ith the rise of the *Federal* theology, the notion of a covenant between God and Adam was to become the distinctive mark of the classical Reformed doctrine of original sin."[56] Hutchinson goes on to point out that the relation of the covenant of works to the doctrine of original sin is not clearly set forth in the Confession of Faith (VII, i, ii, XIX, i). He says, "The Confession simply traces original sin back to the specific sin of our first parents, with no mention of the covenant of works: 'They being the root of all mankind, the guilt of this sin was imputed; and the same death in sin, and corrupted nature, conveyed to all their posterity descending from them by ordinary generation' (VI, iii)."[57]

It is Hutchinson's view that "the primary motive behind the Federalist approach was the desire to ground the doctrine of original sin upon a wider basis than that of a mere natural union with Adam."[58] He indicates that it was thus that the covenant theologians spoke of the representative union as a judicial union. He cites J. H. Heidegger as teaching this judicial relation to the representative. "To represent is with a certain force of law to exhibit the presence of that which is not present."[59]

Jonathan Dickinson said: "We are guilty, not merely as Descendents from Adam, but as being naturally, as well as legally, in him when he violated the first Covenant."[60] Hutchinson's essay examines the various schools of thought regarding the relation of these two grounds for our guilt. Warfield indicates that there were in American Presbyterians four different interpretations of the imputation of Adam's sin.[61]

---

[56] George P. Hutchinson, *The Problem of Original Sin in American Presbyterian Theology* (Nutley, NJ: Presbyterian and Reformed Publishing Co., 1972), 8.

[57] Ibid., 8-9, notes 14 and 15.

[58] Ibid., 8.

[59] Hutchinson, *The Problem of Original Sin in American Presbyterian Theology,* 9; as cited from Heidegger X, 33 in Heinrich Heppe. *Reformed Dogmatics Set Out and Illustrated from the Sources,* ed. Ernst Bizer, trans. G. T. Thompson (London: George Allen & Unwin LTD, 1950), 313.

[60] Quoted from *The True Scripture-Doctrine Concerning Important Points of Christian Faith* (Boston, 1741) by Hutchison, *The Problem of Original Sin in American Presbyterian Theology,* 14.

[61] Benjamin B. Warfield, *Studies in Theology* (New York, London: Oxford University Press, 1932), 308

Hutchinson examines each of these schools of thought, and adds an additional view, which he designates as the Westminster Seminary view, which centers upon John Murray's viewpoint, which emphasizes the legal character of the relation of Adam to his posterity, but declines to speak of the Adam's prelapsarian relation to God as a covenant relationship.

PURE MORAL GOVERNMENT AS MODIFIED BY THE COVENANT OF GRACE

Upon Adam's fall man lost communion with God. Man as sinner now stands in need of God's grace because of his guilt. He is in need of the grace of mercy and of reconciliation. God now displays his grace as redemptive grace. By his fall man rendered himself "incapable of life" under the terms of the covenant of works. The Lord graciously made a second covenant, commonly called the covenant of grace. In this covenant God provided the fulfillment of the covenant of works through his Son. He accomplished this through his active obedience to the law of God, and in paying the debt of his elect. Salvation is freely offered to sinners on the basis of his accomplished work of redemption. The only requirement is faith in Jesus Christ as Savior. The Holy Spirit is promised to all those that are ordained unto eternal life in order to make them willing, and able to believe.[62]

These are (1) the "Federalistic" characterized by its adherence to the doctrine of "immediate imputation," represented, for example by Dr. Charles Hodge; (2) the "New School," characterized by its adherence to the doctrine of "mediate imputation," represented, for example, by Dr. Henry B. Smith; (3) the "Realistic," which teaches that all mankind were present in Adam as generic humanity, and sinned in him, and are therefore guilty of his and their common sin, represented, for example, by Dr. W. G. T. Shedd; and (4) one which may be called the "Agnostic," characterized by an attempt to accept the fact of the transmission of both guilt and depravity from Adam without framing a theory of the mode of their transmission of their relations one to the other , represented, for example by Dr. R. W. Landis.

[62] WCF VIII III. Man, by his fall, having made himself incapable of life by that covenant, the Lord was pleased to make a second, commonly called the covenant of grace; wherein He freely offereth unto sinners life and salvation by Jesus Christ; requiring of them faith in Him, that they may be saved, and promising to give unto all those that are ordained unto eternal life His Holy Spirit, to make them willing, and able to believe.

The first covenant was addressed to man as the creature of God. It promised life upon condition of perfect and personal obedience. The covenant of grace is addressed to man as a sinner. It promised life on the basis of the perfect obedience of Christ (8.5) to the elect who are redeemed by Christ. The Confession states: "The Lord Jesus, by His perfect obedience, and sacrifice of Himself, which He through the eternal Spirit, once offered up unto God, has fully satisfied the justice of His Father; and purchased, not only reconciliation, but an everlasting inheritance in the kingdom of heaven, for all those whom the Father has given unto Him" (WCF VIII.V). This paragraph sets forth the gospel as a response to the sin of Adam in breaking the law of God. God had announced death, separation from God, as the consequence of sin. Christ is seen as meeting this demand of God, satisfying divine justice. His work is seen as a "purchase" of the everlasting inheritance of the kingdom of heaven. This is certainly the language of his meriting this reward,[63] in contrast to the Federal Vision view, which denies merit.

The Westminster Standards teach that the redemptive work of Christ and the effectual call of the Spirit were designed particularly for the elect. W. T. Hall indicates there are "apparent inconsistencies in the statement of the doctrine of the Covenants" in the Standards.[64] One of these is the question of whether there are two covenants or only one relating to the salvation of fallen man. In other words, is there a covenant of redemption within the Trinity as well as a covenant of grace? Chapter VII only mentions one covenant of grace. On the other hand, two different answers are given by the Standards regarding the parties of this covenant. Chapter VII, paragraph 3 seems to speak of the parties as God and the elect—"Man, by his fall, having made himself incapable of life by that covenant, the Lord was pleased to make a second, commonly called the covenant of grace; wherein He freely offereth unto sinners life and salvation by Jesus Christ; requiring of them faith in Him, that they may be saved, and promising to give unto all those that are ordained unto eternal life His Holy Spirit, to make them willing, and able to believe."

---

[63] WCF III VI. As God hath appointed the elect unto glory, so hath He, by the eternal and most free purpose of His will, foreordained all the means thereunto. Wherefore, they who are elected, being fallen in Adam, are redeemed by Christ, are effectually called unto faith in Christ by His Spirit working in due season, are justified, adopted, sanctified, and kept by His power, through faith, unto salvation. Neither are any other redeemed by Christ, effectually called, justified, adopted, sanctified, and saved, but the elect only.

[64] Hall, "The Federal Principle in the Westminster Standards," 381.

The Larger Catechism Question 31 indicates that the parties are God and Christ and in him the elect, or his seed: "With whom was the covenant of grace made? The covenant of grace was made with Christ as the second Adam, and in him with all the elect as his seed."

In Chapter VIII, paragraphs 2 and 5, the Confession speaks of Christ as the Mediator between God and man. This paragraph seems to imply the gift of the people to Christ prior to his work of redemption. This arrangement has often been designated the covenant of redemption made between the Persons of the Godhead. It has also been designated the Council of Peace.[65]

Another place where some confusion has arisen is the references to the old and new covenants. The Standards include two paragraphs describing the differences of administration of the covenant of grace, between the time of the law and the time of the gospel. The first it calls the old Testament, and the latter the new Testament. The word "old" then is not referring to the covenant of works, which is still in force as to its effects, but to the Mosaic economy, which has passed away. Jesus' reference to the new covenant in his blood is in contrast to the old, Mosaic covenant, not to the covenant of works, which had no sacrificial system.[66]

---

[65] Theologians as eminent as the Scottish Divines Thomas Boston, John Brown of Haddington, and John Dick held to the combining of the two covenants in one. In this the Scottish theologians were followed by the American theologian John L. Girardeau, a student of Thornwell. B. G. McCrie in his Chalmer's Lectures *The Confessions of the Church of Scotland, Their Evolution in History* affirms that the development of the Covenant of Redemption concept was beyond the authors of the Confession. "There is the Covenant of Redemption, made between God the Father and Christ the Son in the councils of eternity; and there is the Covenant of Grace entered into by God and sinner in time." He goes on to affirm that as set forth in *The Sum of Saving Knowledge or a Brief Sum of Christian Doctrine, Together with the Practical Use Thereof*, often published with the Confession and Catechisms, though never endorsed formally by the Church of Scotland, it took an objectionable form.

"Detailed descriptions of redemption as a bargain between the First and Second Persons of the Trinity, in which conditions were laid down, promises held out, and pledges given; the reducing of salvation to a mercantile arrangement between God and the sinner, . . . have obviously a tendency to reduce the gospel of the grace of God to the level of a legal compact . . . "

[66] WCF VII, V. This covenant was differently administered in the time of the law, and in the time of the gospel: under the law it was administered by promises, prophecies, sacrifices, circumcision, the paschal lamb, and other types and ordinances delivered to the people of the Jews, all foresignifying Christ to come; which were, for that time, sufficient and efficacious, through the operation of the Spirit, to instruct and build up the elect

One of the covenantal doctrines that is particularly treasured by the Westminster Standards is the inclusion of the children of believers in the church visible. The Confession says, "The visible Church, which is also catholic or universal under the Gospel (not confined to one nation, as before under the law), consists of all those throughout the world that profess the true religion; and of their children: and is the kingdom of the Lord Jesus Christ, the house and family of God, out of which there is no ordinary possibility of salvation" (WCF XXV, II). The Larger Catechism Question 62 speaks in a similar way: "What is the visible church? The visible church is a society made up of all such as in all ages and places of the world do profess the true religion, and of their children."

In this connection, the Standards affirm that baptism is to be applied to children of believers or covenant children: "Not only those that do actually profess faith in and obedience unto Christ, but also the infants of one, or both, believing parents, are to be baptized" (WCF XXVIII, iv).[67]

Though some have argued on the basis of the fact that the whole family was gathered on the night of the Passover that children should be included at the Lord's Supper, the Westminster divines recognized that since both the Passover and the Lord's Supper are memorial feasts, those participating must be able to understand and remember the events being celebrated. They are to be able to examine themselves before coming to the Supper.

The Catechisms are explicit in teaching that those coming to the table must be able to examine themselves.

---

in faith in the promised Messiah, by whom they had full remission of sins, and eternal salvation; and is called the old Testament.

WCF VII, VI. Under the gospel, when Christ, the substance, was exhibited, the ordinances in which this covenant is dispensed are the preaching of the Word, and the administration of the sacraments of Baptism and the Lord's Supper: which, though fewer in number, and administered with more simplicity, and less outward glory, yet, in them, it is held forth in more fullness, evidence, and spiritual efficacy, to all nations, both Jews and Gentiles; and is called the new Testament. There are not therefore two covenants of grace, differing in substance, but one and the same, under various dispensations. See also LC Q. 33, 34, 35.

[67] Larger Catechism Question 166: "Unto whom is Baptism to be administered? Baptism is not to be administered to any that are out of the visible church, and so strangers from the covenant of promise, till they profess their faith in Christ, and obedience to him, but infants descending from parents, either both, or but one of them, professing faith in Christ, and obedience to him, are in that respect within the covenant, and to be baptized." See also Shorter Catechism Question 95.

> LC Q. 171. How are they that receive the sacrament of the Lord's supper to prepare themselves before they come unto it?
>
> A. They that receive the sacrament of the Lord's supper are, before they come, to prepare themselves thereunto, by examining themselves of their being in Christ, of their sins and wants; of the truth and measure of their knowledge, faith, repentance; love to God and the brethren, charity to all men, forgiving those that have done them wrong; of their desires after Christ, and of their new obedience; and by renewing the exercise of these graces, by serious meditation, and fervent prayer.[68]

This fits with the requirement of the Old Testament that the children in attendance be able to ask and understand the answer to the question, "What mean ye by this service" (Exod. 12:26b).

The Standards look to the last day as the final outworking of the covenant of works. The Larger Catechism says:

> LC Q. 84. Shall all men die?
>
> A. Death being threatened as the wages of sin, it is appointed unto all men once to die; for that all have sinned.
>
> LC Q. 85. Death, being the wages of sin, why are not the righteous delivered from death, seeing all their sins are forgiven in Christ?
>
> A. The righteous shall be delivered from death itself at the last day, and even in death are delivered from the sting and curse of it; so that, although they die, yet it is out of God's love, to free them perfectly from sin and misery, and to make them capable of further communion with Christ in glory, which they then enter upon.

Though the covenant of works is not mentioned here, it is obvious that the coming of death was because of the sin of our first parents, and that we are all under the judgment of God for sin, except for those whom Christ has redeemed in his death.

---

[68] Shorter Catechism Question 97: What is required for the worthy receiving of the Lord's supper?

A. It is required of them that would worthily partake of the Lord's supper, that they examine themselves of their knowledge to discern the Lord's body, of their faith to feed upon him, of their repentance, love, and new obedience; lest, coming unworthily, they eat and drink judgment to themselves.

CONCLUSION

Briefly we shall review what we have considered in this lecture. First, federal theology is recognized as the organizing principle by which the Westminster Standards present the original condition of man, his probation and his fall, and the gracious plan of salvation provided by God for fallen man. As we have observed it is a God centered presentation of the gospel. It faithfully preserves the doctrines of grace. It presents the Christ as both God and man in two distinct natures and one person forever. The three offices of Christ the Mediator of the covenant of grace are clearly proclaimed. It is the historic understanding of all those churches across the world, which have adopted the Westminster Standards. When one considers the history of Presbyterianism, it is significant to realize that it is the gospel of federal theology that has been an important part of the mission enterprise of Presbyterians throughout the world.

We have sought to lay out something of the attacks being made on the gospel of our Standards, and also to indicate the direction of answers to these attacks. It seems to me that before those who question the teaching of our Standards begin to teach and promote views that have not met the test of the Church, they should present their case to the proper Church courts for examination. If it should be found that the new interpretation is to be preferred over the historic understanding, then the Standards should be corrected by the proper means for amendment. As it is, the propagation of unapproved views in the Church causes division in the Church, which the Scripture clearly condemns.

Let me conclude this with the challenge that David McWilliams gives in his useful essay on Covenant Theology and the Westminster Standards. He makes the following important observation regarding the importance of federal theology:

> The conclusions of this paper suggest that federalism alone can adequately meet the challenge of modern theological thought, which is motivated to a large degree by historical relativism. Federal theology can only exist within an atmosphere of commitment to the historicity of the biblical text—of Adam, for instance. It is at this point that federalism and modern existential theology collide. Undoubtedly, federalism's commitment to the trustworthiness of biblical revelation is one reason that it is so distasteful to a theology of historical relativism. This being

so, federal thinking takes on an added dimension of monumental significance in the modern world. Or, to say it another way, the historical
relativism of existentialism can adequately be met, not simply by conservative theology, but only by Reformed federalism with its grounding
in the unity of redemptive history. This means that exegesis must be determinative of Reformed theology, whereas the same cannot be true of
the existential perspective. The result is, federalism is not to be seen as
an antiquated theological viewpoint, but one which sparkles with relevance. The Reformed, covenantal, perspective alone can best meet the
challenge of modern, relativistic theology.[69]

In the nineteenth century Hugh Martin of the Free Church of Scotland published *The Atonement*. In this fine work, Martin says, "May the
doctrine of the covenant of grace—the federal oneness of Christ and His
people—long remain in the hearts of Scottish piety!"[70] We would amend
Martin by saying, May it remain in the hearts of all Christian piety.

ADDENDUM REGARDING THE QUESTION OF WHETHER A BIBLICAL COVENANT INVOLVES A CONTRACT

As we have seen in the above presentation, one of the lines of attack on
the historic understanding of federal theology has been leveled against
the idea that a covenant involves a contract. New Modernists such as the
Torrance's in Scotland, and Holmes Rolston III in America make this a
particular part of their attack on the Westminster doctrine of federal theology. This same line of argument is adopted by the more contemporary
attacks of Weir, Ralph Smith and Richard Lusk. Even John Murray in
his unpublished notes on Biblical theology argues against the contractual
view as well. He indicates, for example, that the Noahic covenant is the
clearest example of a covenant that is not contractual in its form. He argues that there are six features of this covenant that point to the true essence of a covenant. They are:

---

[69] McWilliams, "The Covenant Theology of the *Westminster Confession of Faith*
and Recent Criticism," 123.

[70] Hugh Martin, *The Atonement* (New York: Smith, English & Co., 1871), 49.

1. The divinity of the covenant. "The covenant is conceived, devised, determined established and rendered secure by God."[71]

2. The universality of the covenant. "It is with Noah, his seed after him, and every living creature."[72]

3. The perpetuity of the covenant.

4. The confirmation of the covenant. "The stress is laid upon the Godward reference. 'I will see it (rainbow)."[73]

5. The unconditionalness of the covenant. "No commandment is appended that could be construed in any effect as being man's part in its fulfillment."[74] There is no concept of a contract in this covenant.

6. The divine monergism. "The very sign is produced by conditions over which God alone has controls. It is not an act performed by man at the Divine behest. In this respect it differs from other covenants."[75]

Murray states his conclusion, "When you appreciate these six features of this covenant's administration, you discover *the true essence of the* ברית (berith) is, this making it more clear than any other covenant given in the Old Testament."[76] He goes on to give his definition of a covenant in its bare essence, "A sovereign, divine disposition in administration, and is such in its conception, determination, disclosure, sanction and fulfillment. Of course it is a divine assurance for man's benefit, but that is secondary."[77]

Professor Murray indicates that in many cases "certain circumstances and conditions may be attached to a *berith*, but such do not belong to a *berith ipso facto*."[78] By his careful examination of the Biblical

---

[71] "Old Testament Biblical Theology," unpublished mimeographed Mss., 22.

[72] Ibid.

[73] Ibid., 23.

[74] Ibid.

[75] Ibid

[76] Ibid.

[77] Ibid.

[78] Ibid

usage of the term covenant Professor Murray has brought out the fact
that the Biblical concept of covenants is not of mutual contract, but of a
divinely imposed administration. This corrects a misimpression that
could arise from defining a covenant as a contract. It is clear that Biblical covenants between God and his people are not bi-lateral covenants in
which each party bargains with the other. Rather they are sovereignly
imposed divine administrations, which may include conditions. These
conditions are like a contract in that God binds himself to reward upon
the compliance by man to the stipulated condition. Thus to think of
covenants as contractual is not entirely wrong, so long as the sovereign
imposition of the terms is by God, without any bargaining on man's part.
They are voluntary contracts on God's part. As such they are all gracious in character, since God is not under obligation to his creatures to
provide such a covenantal relation.

Chapter 3

Jeremiah 31 and the New Covenant[1]

Richard D. Phillips

Behold, the days are coming, declares the LORD, when I will make a new covenant with the house of Israel and the house of Judah, *Jeremiah 31:31*

One of the notable innovations of recent times is the no-fault divorce. A couple meets, starts dating, gets married and moves in together (usually in that order). As man has found since time immemorial, it is then that real life sets in, a real relationship has to be worked out; it is then that faults are recognized and magnified and getting along becomes less than easy. In so many cases today, marital failure leads to frustration and misery. That is why we have devised the no-fault divorce. The point is not really that no one is to blame, but that everyone is to blame. Instead of trying to untie the convoluted knot, thus prolonging the agony, the knot is simply cut. There is no blame, no fault, no hassle. That is just the way it goes, an apparent inevitability in a world where breaking promises is much easier than breaking habits. There are few tragedies, I think, that so sadly testify to the despair that grips our time as the no-

---

[1] This is a sermon preached during the 2004 Spring Theology Conference of Greenville Presbyterian Theological Seminary.

fault divorce.

Divorce is something that is found in the Bible, too. God's word recognizes grounds for divorce, namely infidelity and abandonment. But divorce is never "no-fault," nor is it ever "no big deal." It is always a big deal and the result is always lamentable. "I hate divorce," God said in Malachi 2:16,[2] just as He always hates the breaking of faith.

It is especially a tragedy when someone is forced into an unwanted divorce. Usually this happens because a spouse has been unfaithful and rejects his or her partner. It may surprise you to learn that this very thing has happened to God. This is why the old covenant was shattered, because of Israel's infidelity: her worship of other gods and rejection of the Lord. The old covenant was a marriage agreement between God and his people, just like that between a man and a woman today. Jeremiah 3:8 explains what happened: "For all the adulteries of that faithless one, Israel, I had sent her away with a decree of divorce." God knows what it is like to be a rejected lover, to be forced into an unwanted divorce.

A marriage begins with the exchange of vows: "I take thee to be my wedded wife or husband, for richer or poorer, in joy and in sorrow, in sickness and health, so long as we both shall live." Yet, when someone is faced with the infidelity of a partner, he or she is not able to keep his own wedding vows. That is one of many tragedies in divorce. When faced with rejection, when unable to change our spouse's heart or erase the devastation of what has been done, all we can do is walk away from our own promise, with a broken marriage, a broken heart, a broken vow.

But there is a difference here between God and us, and the difference is that He is able to remake what has been broken. He is able to keep the promise He has made. "I will be your God and you will be my people," He vowed to His bride Israel (Ex. 6:7). And though God's people broke that marriage covenant, God had prepared a new covenant in which His promise would be fulfilled. That is what this great passage is about this evening, God's promise of a new covenant that secures God's wedding vow to his people, the new covenant that has better promises and actually secures a people for God forever.

A NEW COVENANT

It would be hard to imagine a more dramatic scene than the one in which

---

[2] Unless otherwise noted, all Scripture quotations are from the English Standard Version.

this promise is given. Jeremiah's ministry took place at an epochal turning point in redemptive history. We think of the great moments in covenant history, such occasions as God's great promise to Abraham and the covenant He made by walking alone between the two halves of the severed carcasses. We think of the giving of the Law amidst all the fire and storm of Mt. Sinai. We think of the coming of the ark of the covenant into Jerusalem and God's promise to David of a temple-building son. The scene played out during Jeremiah's life fits into that company. Here we witness the end of the Old Covenant in punishment, destruction, and wrath.

Jeremiah is not called the weeping prophet for nothing. "How desolate lies the city," he opened up the Book of Lamentations, "once so filled with people." But Jeremiah gazed with weeping eyes upon not merely a broken city and a broken people, but the tragedy of a broken covenant with the living God.

It is significant, therefore, that Jeremiah is one of the great gospel preachers of the Old Testament. Jeremiah 31 is in a portion of the book that is heavily reinforced by promises of grace. Chapter 29 contains the letter to the exiles in Babylon, telling them to "seek the welfare of the city where I have sent you into exile," because, "I know the plans I have for you, declares the Lord, plans for wholeness and not for evil, to give you a future and a hope" (Jer. 29:7, 11). Chapter 30 speaks of restoration for Israel and Judah: "I will restore the fortunes of my people, Israel and Judah, says the Lord... for I am with you to save you" (Jer. 30:3, 11). Jeremiah 31 starts off on this same theme: "The people who survived the sword found grace in the wilderness" (v. 2).

We hear from some today that we are saved through our faithfulness to the covenant; Jeremiah had no such delusions. He lived in a time when the faithlessness of his people rose up like a stench before him from the ruins of Jerusalem, one that is biblically compared to the smoke wafting up before Abraham from Sodom and Gomorrah. The only salvation Jeremiah saw or hoped for was one based on the faithfulness of the Lord, the saving God who offered grace to the faithless and hope to the covenant-breakers. According to Jeremiah, Israel's salvation rested not on her covenant-keeping but on God's electing love. The Lord explained, "I have loved you with an everlasting love; therefore I have continued my faithfulness to you" (Jer. 31:3). Here we see that covenant salvation rests on election, rather than election resting on the covenant.

Israel had broken her covenant like a faithless wife, giving herself to her lovers and despising her husband-God. For that reason, the curses associated with that covenant from the start fell on her in full force. If God's people would not obey his voice and fulfill all that he commanded, then "The Lord will send on you curses, confusion, and frustration in all that you undertake to do, until you are destroyed and perish quickly on account of the evil of your deeds, because you have forsaken me" (Deut. 28:20).

The question, then, is how could God still speak of restoration and grace? God had entered into covenant with his people. The covenant made promises, but had conditions and curses in the case of failure. The outcome of that covenant had now been seen and the settlement of affairs was taking place. So far as the Old Covenant is concerned, there is nothing more to happen except the final extermination of Judah. Nonetheless the just and holy God promises amidst His judgment a future restoration. How could that be? How could He say that He had a plan for the good of the covenant-breakers? How could the people who had passed through the sword into the wilderness find grace there from God?

The answer is found in Jeremiah 31, beginning in verse 31: God would provide a new covenant for the salvation and establishment of his people. He promised not that the old covenant would be patched up and restored, for it was broken, but that its aims would be accomplished through a new and different covenant. "I will be your God and you will be my people," was always the purpose of God's covenant. Jeremiah 31 promises that a new covenant would come to bring that to pass.

UNDERSTANDING THE OLD COVENANT

But first we need to understand what was wrong with the Old Covenant. This was not a no-fault divorce, and the blame is clearly assigned all through Jeremiah. Sometimes you will hear that the problem with the old covenant was that it was not a covenant of grace, but a covenant of works. But verse 32 demonstrates that the Mosaic covenant was indeed an administration of the covenant of grace. The old covenant was given amidst the greatest manifestation of grace in the entire Old Testament, namely the Exodus, "When I took them by the hand to bring them out of the land of Egypt." God saved Israel by grace, He led them out of Egypt and betrothed them, and only then brought them to Mt. Sinai to receive his Law. The problem with the Old Covenant was not an absence of grace.

What, then, was the problem? Verse 32 tells us plainly: "my covenant that they broke." The problem with the Old Covenant was the infidelity of the people. Read the Old Testament and you will find a continuous history of idolatry and faithlessness. Jeremiah 3:2 delivers the formal charge: "Lift up your eyes to the bare heights, and see! Where have you not been ravished? By the waysides you have sat awaiting lovers... You have polluted the land with your vile whoredom."

Hebrews 8:9, a great New Testament reflection on this passage, shows the chilling cause-and-effect relationship so well displayed in the Old Testament: "They did not remain faithful to my covenant, and I turned away from them" (NIV). That is what happens when people reject God – He turns away from them. The result for Old Testament Israel was military defeat, vast destruction, and national bondage. If salvation meant deliverance from slavery in Egypt, rejection of God meant a return to bondage in the form of the Babylonian captivity.

The same principle applies today. People think that rejecting God opens the door to freedom. They can do with impunity what they want without fetters or restriction. But that is not the case, because they are not free from the consequences of their sin. As Romans 6:23 declares, "The wages of sin is death." Although our nation is not in covenant with God, it is a large-scale illustration of this principle: having rejected God we now are left to deal with godlessness and its consequences on a vast scale. "They did not continue in my covenant, and so I showed no concern for them, declares the Lord." That is the worst thing that could ever happen to any people, entailing both the withdrawal of God's special care and the infliction of sin's terrible wages.

All of this goes to show that while the Old Covenant was an administration of the covenant of grace, it contained within it a republication of the covenant of works. I am always astonished by claims that there is no legal aspect to the Mosaic Covenant; the Mosaic covenant is not called the Law for nothing! In Exodus 24, the great passage depicting the confirmation of that covenant in the valley beneath Mt. Sinai, the people took their vow: "All the words that the LORD has spoken we will do" (Ex. 24:3). It is often explained that the legal provisions of the Old Covenant dealt with the status and blessing of the nation as the typological kingdom, and that certainly is true. Israel's peace and prosperity depended on her keeping of the Law. But I think we are mistaken if we stop there. For the Law as the republished covenant of works extended into the body politic to the people themselves. "Do this and live" (Lev. 18:5), was spoken to the people. This why Paul said, in Romans 10:5,

"For Moses writes about the righteousness that is based on the law, that the person who does the commandments shall live by them."

The works principle in the Old Covenant was calculated to lead the people to Christ, as he was so vividly represented in the ceremonial law, so that the Old Covenant presents both law and gospel as they work together in the covenant of grace. The relationship between the two is demonstrated in the great covenant ceremony on Mounts Gerizim and Ebal in the Promised Land. Half the tribes stood on Mt. Gerizim proclaiming blessings on obedience. The other half cried out curses for disobedience from Mt. Ebal. Together, they presented the way of law and works. But included there was an altar—significantly, it was placed on Mt. Ebal, where God's curse on the failure and sin of his people was declared—an altar of uncut stones on which sacrifices could be offered. This portrayed Christ and his gospel, the provision of grace in the context of the demands for works. The emblem of the gospel was placed not among those proclaiming blessings, but among those proclaiming the curses, thus demonstrating the way for the atonement of their sin.

The point is that covenant-keepers do not need the gospel; for them the law is sufficient, if only they can keep it. I have recently read claims that the law was given for sinners to keep in order to be saved, but that is a fatal mistake. The altar that represented the gospel was placed on Mt. Ebal among those who represented the covenant-breaking sinners precisely because the law brings only condemnation and death for them. No altar was placed on Mt. Gerizim, because there, as Paul said in Romans 2:13, "The doers of the law . . . will be justified."

THE FIRST PROMISE: THE SPIRIT'S TRANSFORMING WORK

The Old Covenant, therefore, was an administration of the covenant of grace. It republished the covenant of works in the form of the Law, not as a way of salvation to those who cannot keep it because of their sinful nature, but to lead them to the atoning altar that represented Christ. We ask again, therefore, what was the problem with the Old Covenant? Why did it fail? It did not fail because there was no grace offered. Nor did it fail because it was a legal covenant. It is true that the Law could not succeed because it "was weakened by sinful flesh" (Rom. 8:3). The Old Covenant, however, contained within itself the remedy for the failure of the Law; namely, the atoning sacrifices of the ceremonial law that pointed to Christ. It would seem to be a nice, tidy covenant, with every prospect of success. And yet it was not.

According to Hebrews 8:7 the problem was in the Old Covenant itself. It was inadequate to achieve its aims. The writer of Hebrews explains, "For if that first covenant had been faultless, there would have been no occasion to look for a second." A better covenant was needed, with a better mediator than Moses and better promises than those from Mt. Sinai (Heb. 8:6).

The main problem of the Old Covenant was not that it lacked grace, but that it was an external administration of salvation. The problem was in the kind of grace it offered; namely, an outward and ritual grace rather than the transforming grace needed to achieve its aims. This is what Paul meant in 2 Corinthians 3:6, when he wrote of the "new covenant, not of the letter but of the Spirit. For the letter kills, but the Spirit gives life." What sinful mankind needs is a transformed life, and the Old Covenant did not and could not give it. The Israelites' hardened hearts, Paul explained, were like a veil that kept them from seeing Christ in the Old Covenant (2 Cor. 3:14-15), leaving them to the ineluctable justice of the law. Therefore, in the weakness of their flesh they fell under the axe of the Law before the weeping eyes of Jeremiah.

But the new covenant of which the prophet spoke is better precisely in this respect. It is no surprise that the first promise he associates with the New Covenant to come is an inner transforming work of God's grace. Verse 33 says, "I will put my law within them, and write it on their hearts." In the Old Covenant, God gave the people his law without giving them the ability to receive it, to love it, to keep its demands. In Romans 8:3 Paul says the Old Covenant law was compromised by the weakness of human nature; that is why the relationship between God and his people broke down. Therefore, in the New Covenant, God makes provision for human weakness, promising not only to give the law, but also actually to place it within us. This, of course, points to the work of the Holy Spirit as Jesus sends him to his own.

I mentioned 2 Corinthians chapter 3 as an eminent New Testament reflection on this passage. There, Paul contrasts the external work of the old covenant to the internal work of the new, repeating the metaphor of tablets of stone in contrast to tablets of the heart. The chapter concludes with an explanation of how this takes place, namely that believers in Christ "are being transformed into his likeness with ever-increasing glory, which comes from the Lord, who is the Spirit" (2 Cor. 3:18, NIV).

Every true Christian has personal acquaintance with this. If you

possess eternal life through faith in Christ, you have experienced at least
something of this. You start wanting to do things you never did before,
while old pleasures seem disturbing. You find yourself eagerly attend-
ing church, praying, reading the Bible, serving others, while shunning
sin more and more as Christ leads you, because God has written His law
upon your heart.

This is the first of three promises that makes this a better covenant.
God promises that he will work faithfulness into us. What the Old
Covenant could not do, actually give us a heart to obey and glorify God,
the New Covenant can do. This means that if you have faith in Christ, if
you are saved under the New Covenant, God is sanctifying you. "For it
is God who works in you," Paul says, "both to will and to work for his
good pleasure" (Phil. 2:13). Genuine, saving belief in Christ proceeds
from a change in our will and our affections; otherwise it is not the faith
that saves us by means of this New Covenant.

One of our most troubling controversies today comes from an attempt by some to recast covenant theology. I mentioned earlier that they
argue that our faithfulness to the covenant is the condition of our receiving its blessings. But this is not how Jeremiah saw it. In the promise of
a new covenant, which speaks of the ministry of Jesus Christ, faithfulness is not what we do to receive salvation; rather, it is a component of
the salvation God gives us. Faithfulness is not a condition upon which
our receipt of the new covenant salvation depends. It is not what God
looks for in us in order to give us salvation, but it is what God works into
and through us as the blessing of his covenant grace.

Does that mean that those who come to God through the new covenant must be faithful? The answer is yes, not as a condition either of entering into the covenant blessings or of maintaining them, but as a consequence. We need to emphasize this against the antinomianism and
easy-believism rampant today. It is true, as Paul says in Romans 8:3,
that "the law was weakened by sinful flesh." In our sinful state of nature, we are, as Augustine phrased it, *non posse non peccare*, that is, *not
able not to sin*. We cannot stop sinning and thus keep the Law. Regeneration, however, changes that. We need to emphasize that because of
the transforming work of the Holy Spirit, those who are born again are
now *posse non peccare, able not to sin*. This was Paul's point in the full
statement of Romans 8:3-4:

> For God has done what the law, weakened by the flesh, could not do.

By sending his own Son in the likeness of sinful flesh and for sin, he condemned sin in the flesh, in order that the righteous requirement of the law might be fulfilled in us, who walk not according to the flesh but according to the Spirit.

We are not saved *by* law-keeping, but we are saved *to* law-keeping (Eph. 2:10). This is not yet perfectly realized in our experience, though we are to be moving forward in this respect. It is the *telos*, the goal and end point of our salvation, not the beginning, and will be perfectly realized only in glory, when we will perfectly say what our Lord Jesus said during his earthly sojourn: "My meat and drink is to do the will of the heavenly Father" (John 4:34).

Under the New Covenant, God's people will be characterized by faithfulness. Far from being a source of worry, this should be a great encouragement to you, since it is presented in Romans 8 not as a command, but as a promise. In this matter, as all others, our assurance rests on God's promise, not our performance. You may come before God and say, "Lord, I believe on Jesus, but I am not faithful. I am not trustworthy." But he says here that if you trust in him, if you walk with him by the blood of Jesus, he will make you faithful. He will work faithfulness into you; he will engrave his law on your heart. You lament, "Lord, I love things that are wicked and find precious little attraction in holy and good things." What a great promise we have here in the new covenant in Christ! He will reveal his law to your mind, he will give you understanding and sanctify your affections and give you the will to embrace it. He will change you so that you will increasingly reflect his character.

This passage promises that God *will* do this, and I think it also contains insight into *how* it happens. In Hebrews 8:10, Jeremiah 31's promise is set forth with a clear progression: "I will put my laws into their minds and write them on their hearts." Note how this begins with the mind and moves to the heart. The point is that God will give us an understanding of his Word, and that light will shine through the mind to warm the heart. Head religion and heart religion are not in opposition but in cooperation. Therefore, the apostle Paul says, in Romans 12:2, "Do not be conformed to this world, but be transformed by the renewal of your mind, that by testing you may discern what is the will of God, what is good and acceptable and perfect" (Rom. 12:2). God changes us by his Word, applying it to us, illuminating our hearts, and regenerating our will by the work of the Holy Spirit. It is through God's Word that he saves us and changes us.

Therefore, trusting in this great promise, we are to be people of God's Word. You say, "I cannot change my heart," and that is true. But you can give your mind to the Word of God, you can seek the light that shines forth from Scripture – and as your mind is transformed by the word and the work of the Spirit, God will shine that light into your heart, warming it to himself.

THE SECOND PROMISE: FORGIVENESS OF SINS

The second great promise comes third in the passage, although logically it comes next. It is found in verse 34: "I will forgive their iniquity, and I will remember their sin no more." This promise comes last because it is the preeminent and foundational promise that is the basis for the superiority of the New Covenant. As John Owen writes, "This is the great fundamental promise and grace of the new covenant... The first thing that is necessary is the free pardon of sin."[3]

There are two parts to this promise and both of them are wonderful good news. The first is that God will forgive our iniquity. There is a connection that is elucidated especially in the New Testament rendition of this verse. "I will be merciful towards their iniquities," God says. The Greek word merciful, *hileos*, is the same word that is used in the description of the mercy seat that sat atop the ark of the covenant, the *hilesterion*. That was the place where the blood of the sacrifice was brought by the high priest on the Day of Atonement. The high priest came into the Holy of Holies, the inner sanctum, where the golden cherubim rested atop the Ark of the Covenant. That was God's throne, and he looked down upon the Ten Commandments, which were kept in the ark. Before him came the high priest, representing all the sinful and wicked people. According to God's Law he must be struck down immediately, except that he brought before him the blood of the sacrifice, shed for the sins of the people. The blood was poured upon the mercy seat, so that God looked down and no longer saw the Law that was transgressed, but the blood that paid the debt of sin. We might well read the promise, "I will be mercy-seated towards your iniquities"

That is how God forgives our sin, by means of the blood of a spotless sacrifice. Jeremiah looked forward to the coming of the Messiah, Jesus Christ, who was identified by John the Baptist with these words: "Behold the Lamb of God, who takes away the sin of the world" (Jn.

---

[3] John Owen, *Hebrews* (Wheaton, Ill.: Crossway, 1988), 189.

1:29).

God is merciful towards our wickedness when we acknowledge our sin and put our faith in Christ's blood that was shed for us. That was the point signified in the Last Supper. Jesus took the cup of wine, gave thanks, and used it as a symbol for his sacrificial, vicarious death. He told the disciples: "This cup is the new covenant in my blood, which is poured out for you" (Lk. 22:20). The cup Jesus offered his disciples is one of blessing and gladness; he can offer to us a cup without a tinge of sin's curse because of the cup he went out into the Garden of Gethsemane to receive, the cup of God's wrath without a tinge of mercy and grace.

Jeremiah received the promise of a New Covenant during the era in which the curse of the Old Covenant fell in full force upon the people. What most especially makes the New Covenant better is the Savior who takes the curse of God in our place, so that the covenant in his blood is offered without threat of cursing to those who trust in him. It is because of Jesus' atoning death for his people that God promises, "I will forgive their iniquity."

The second part of this promise is that God will remember our sins no more. How, we might ask, is it possible for God to forget? How can God know all things and be perfect in knowledge, and yet forget the wicked things we have done? The answer is found in the prior statement. God's forgetting is based on his forgiving.

This was symbolized in the other ritual that took place on the Day of Atonement. Two goats were involved, only one of which was sacrificed. The other was the scapegoat. When the high priest came out from making atonement in the Holy of Holies, he then laid his hands on the scapegoat to signify that the sins of the people were placed there. The goat was then sent away into the wilderness, the sins never to be seen again (Lev. 16:20-22).

Is this not how it usually works among us? You owe a debt to someone and you haven't paid it. The one thing you can count on is that he will not forget. The man you owe will remind you, probably every time you see him, which of course makes you want to avoid him. But if someone else comes along and pays the debt for you, the man will no longer bother you about what was owed. He has forgotten your debt because he has received full payment. That is similar to what has happened with God in his perfect justice towards the debt of our sin. It has been fully satisfied, fully paid, and God remembers our sin no more.

The scapegoat of our sin has vanished forever. You can see what a difference this makes to our relationship with God. Instead of wanting to avoid him, this draws us near to his love.

Many, many marriages are embittered by the remembrance of sin, despite claims of or efforts toward forgiveness. Sometimes the sin happened years and years ago. Nevertheless, the husband or wife still brings it up, still holds it before the other. "I have never forgotten what you said at such and such a time!" "I want you to know that I remember what you did back then!" "Don't think I forget the time you let me down!" There it is, always, like poison in the well of the relationship, making everything bitter and dead.

Now here is the point: a believer in Christ will never hear that from God. He has put away your sin. He has forgotten all the dreadful things you have done and failed to do. Psalm 103:12 celebrates: "As far as the east is from the west, so far does he remove our transgressions from us." How far is the east from the west? Infinitely far! That is the great promise of this New Covenant in Jesus Christ. God has forgiven you, and so your sin is no more!

That is the kind of grace that allows Christians to overcome sin and guilt in our own relationships, truly forgiving and putting aside another's sin because of the grace we have received through Jesus Christ. We forgive as God forgave us. Many Christian marriages have been saved and others should be saved, because of the power of forgiveness through the blood of Jesus Christ.

THE CULMINATING PROMISE: "I WILL BE THEIR GOD"

That leaves one more great promise, and it is the promise that flows from the two by which it is surrounded: "I will be their God, and they shall be my people. And no longer shall each one teach his neighbor and each his brother, saying, 'Know the LORD,' for they shall all know me, from the least of them to the greatest, declares the LORD" (Jer. 31:33-34). This promise also has two parts, the first of which is God's promise to be our God.

"Personal, direct fellowship with God: this is the crowning blessing of the new covenant, writes Andrew Murray."[4] Positively, this fellowship requires holiness, for God is holy – and God has promised to make

---

[4] Andrew Murray, *The Holiest of All· An Exposition of the Epistle to the Hebrews* (Grand Rapids, MI: Revell, 1993), 295.

us holy, writing his law on our hearts. Negatively, the obstacle to such fellowship is our sin – and he has promised to forgive and forget it completely through Jesus Christ. Therefore, God brings to fruition what he promised of old: "I will be their God, and they will be my people."

This is the sealing of a marriage – one that had been broken by God's covenant people but can be restored because it rests upon the unbreakable promise and electing love of God. He replaces the old covenant with a new one, a covenant that deals both with our internal problem – a sinful nature – and our external problem – the guilt of our sin – so that he can in justice keep his promise of old: "I will be your God" (Ex. 6:7). "Be of sin the double cure," we sing, "cleanse me from its guilt and power." That is what God promises. Instead of a no-fault divorce, or even a covenant broken by the guilt of an adulterous spouse, God has overwhelmed our sin with the power of his grace. Therefore, at the heart of this new covenant promise, our faithful God says not, "I'm sorry, but I have to let you go." Instead, in a triumph of his grace, he speaks anew his vow of love: "I will be your God."

With that, and as its consequence, comes our responding vow to God, which he also promises. "They will be my people... They shall all know me, from the least of them to the greatest." This is the affirmation from God's purchased and betrothed people, each of them and all of them, their acknowledgment that he is their Lord and God.

That is what God desires, an expression of fidelity, of marital commitment and intimacy, the loving declaration of the faithful bride: "I know him – he is my Lord." Here, then, is the glory of the new and better covenant. What God desires from us, what he requires of us, he bestows upon us and works within us by grace: "They will be my people." Not only will God fulfill his vow, but all of his will speak and faithfully fulfill their vows to him. Sadly, we know too little of this in our present experience, although God continues to work in us towards this end. But this is the scene with which the whole Bible comes to its culmination, the future day when all of this will fully come to pass, in the glory of the consummated new creation. Revelation 21:2-3 tells us:

> I saw the holy city, new Jerusalem, coming down out of heaven from God, prepared as a bride adorned for her husband. And I heard a loud voice from the throne saying, "Behold, the dwelling place of God is with man. He will dwell with them, and they will be his people, and God himself will be with them as their God."

SO LONG AS WE BOTH SHALL LIVE

One of my greatest joys as a gospel minister is to perform wedding ceremonies, establishing a covenant of marriage between a man and a woman. I always like to point out that the bride, in her resplendent joy, in all her shining beauty and white attire, is a wonderful picture of what it means to be a Christian. This is not just my idea, but the teaching of Isaiah 61:10, which says: "I will greatly rejoice in the LORD; my soul shall exult in my God, for he has clothed me with the garments of salvation; he has covered me with the robe of righteousness." Isaiah goes on to say that these garments are like those of a groom and a bride on their wedding day.

A bride purchases her gown and wears it just for that one day, by current custom. Afterward she will change into regular clothes and that white wedding gown will be put away. But here is the point: the way we see the bride on one day in all of her life is the way God sees you every day of your life in Jesus Christ. That is what this New Covenant is all about –an inviolable compact sealed by the blood of Jesus and the ministry of the Holy Spirit flowing from the eternal covenant love of God the Father. Because Jesus has woven your robe of righteousness and taken away your sin, what Isaiah said is true of you: "As the bridegroom rejoices over the bride, so shall your God rejoice over you" (Isa. 62:5).

He has given you a garment of salvation, a robe of righteousness, even the imputed righteousness of Jesus Christ. And he is working in you the love and affection suitable for a bride to such a husband. There will be no divorce, for this covenant is made effectual by God himself. He says, "So long as we both shall live, I will be your God." And by his work within us, all God's people will respond in love: "So long as we both shall live, we will be your people." We will know him and acknowledge him as Lord and God; we will follow him with minds renewed in truth, with hearts transformed in holiness, and we will be to him forever a bride in shining white. He has promised it. He has accomplished it in Christ. And what he has begun he will complete, so that we will live forever in the loving embrace of our God, to the praise of his glorious grace. Amen.

Chapter 4

Scottish Covenant Theology: Thomas Boston and John Murray

Andrew T. B. McGowan

INTRODUCTION

Two of the most significant Reformed theologians ever produced by Scotland were Thomas Boston and John Murray. I came to know and value the writings of Boston as a postgraduate student, having chosen to study him because he was a pastor-theologian, one who never left the parish and yet produced some writings of the highest academic quality of his day. At the time, my own aspiration was to be a pastor-theologian. Indeed, when I was writing my dissertation I was a Church of Scotland minister in a Highland parish, where I had six churches, five of which could only be reached by boat, including four Hebridean Islands. It was only after sixteen years as a parish minister that the Lord called me, with others, to begin a new Reformed theological seminary.

Until we began the Highland Theological College, my acquaintance with John Murray was entirely through his writings. Then I came to know his nephew, the Rev. Alex Murray, who became chairman of the Board of our College, and I learned a little more about the man and his life. Mr. Murray showed me the house where John Murray was born and the house where he died, both of which are still in the family. He also took me to see his grave. All of these historic sites are only about an hour's drive from our College. Because of our links with the Murray family and in honour of his great importance as a Scottish theologian, this coming October we are to establish an annual lectureship, to be called the John Murray Lecture, in his memory.

There are many similarities between Murray and Boston, and many points of common interest. To give one example: John Murray was famous for his distinction between 'definitive' and 'progressive' sanctification;[1] over two hundred years earlier, Boston had spoken of 'initial' sanctification and 'progressive' sanctification,[2] making essentially the same point. Today, however, we are looking at a subject on which they were not in complete agreement, namely, the interpretation of Genesis 2 and whether or not we may describe what took place there as the establishment of a covenant.

I have divided the essay into four sections. First, we will consider Thomas Boston's teaching on the 'Covenant of Works'; second, John Murray's teaching on the 'Adamic Administration'; third, two significant points of agreement and two significant points of disagreement; and fourth, I will offer an assessment of the issues at stake and propose some further developments.

THE COVENANT OF WORKS IN THOMAS BOSTON

Thomas Boston[3] (1676-1732) was a minister of the Church of Scotland and a gifted theologian. He served for many years in the parish of Ettrick in the Scottish borders and became well known through his preaching and his writing. His collected writings were published in twelve volumes in 1853.[4] The most famous of his writings is *The Fourfold State* which in its day was one of the most popular books among devout Christians in Scotland. It has been said that the library of many a crofter (tenant farmer) and shepherd of the Border hills consisted of a Bible, the

---

[1] John Murray, *Collected Writings of John Murray* (Edinburgh: The Banner of Truth Trust, 1977), 2: 277ff..

[2] Samuel McMillan, ed., *The Complete Works of The Late Rev. Thomas Boston* (London: William Tegg & Co., 1853), 1: 653ff.

[3] This summary of Boston's life and significance is taken from my article on Thomas Boston in T.A. Hart, ed., *The Dictionary of Historical Theology* (Carlisle: Paternoster, 2000).

[4] They have subsequently been republished three times: (Wheaton, IL: Richard Owen Roberts, 1980); (Lafayette, IN: Sovereign Grace Publishers, 2001); and (Stoke-on-Trent, UK: Tentmaker Publications, 2002).

Westminster Shorter Catechism, a copy of Bunyan's *Pilgrim's Progress,* and Boston's *Fourfold State.*

Boston also came to public notice because he was involved in certain controversies within the Church of Scotland. The first of these concerned Professor John Simson (1667-1740), who was Professor of Divinity in the University of Glasgow. Simson was accused of heresy on a number of occasions and was ultimately suspended (but not deposed) from the ministry. On one occasion at the General Assembly Boston was the only person prepared to protest against the leniency of the treatment accorded Simson. This was not an easy matter for him because he was not a natural controversialist, but his convictions were such that he felt under compulsion to take this action.

The more significant controversy in which Boston was engaged and the one with which his name is inextricably linked, was the Marrow controversy. This concerned a book, *The Marrow of Modern Divinity,* which was condemned by the General Assembly of the Church of Scotland in 1720, but which Boston and others regarded as containing a true account of the gospel. The book was published anonymously in 1645, but was probably written by Edward Fisher. It was a pastiche of quotations from the works of many reformed scholars including Calvin, Beza, Sibbes and Rutherford and was one of the books 'approved' by the Westminster Assembly of Divines. In the course of this controversy it became apparent that there were two parties within the church, both holding to the *Westminster Confession of Faith* but with radically opposing views. The one group, led by Principal Hadow of St Andrews rejected the free offer of the gospel on the grounds that such an offer could not be made in all conscience without also holding to a universal atonement. Boston and the other Marrowmen, as they were called, believed that the gospel should be preached to 'every creature without exception.' The dispute extended to the nature and place of repentance, the doctrine of assurance and various other matters. Ultimately, the Marrowmen were rebuked by the General Assembly of 1722 but permitted to continue to serve in their parishes.

The Marrowmen were accused of being antinomian, but a more accurate judgment would be that they were anti-neonomian. To be precise, they were protesting against a legalistic strain which had crept into Scottish theology at this time. Some of them, led by Ralph and Ebenezer Erskine, ultimately left the Church of Scotland to found the original Secession Church in 1733. Although Boston died in 1732, it is clear that he would not have seceded.[5] He remained a faithful member and minister of the Kirk to the end of his days.

Thomas Boston was undoubtedly a consistent Calvinist who faithfully held to the *Westminster Confession of Faith* and we are in his debt for clarifying and expounding the great doctrines of grace. With particular relation to our subject today, we can also say that he was one of the finest covenant theologians Scotland has ever produced, not least because of his two treatises, one called 'A View of the Covenant of Works'[6] and the other called 'A View of the Covenant of Grace.'[7] Interestingly, he turned his attention to these subjects as a direct result of the actions of the General Assembly in respect of the *Marrow*.[8]

Covenant theology (or Federal theology) can be defined as that system of theology in which the relationship between God and humanity is described in covenantal terms. It was developed in the sixteenth century, first as a one-covenant system (the Covenant of Grace) and then subsequently as a two-covenant system (the Covenant of Works and the Covenant of Grace). Some theologians, though not Thomas Boston, also included a Covenant of Redemption between God the Father and God the Son. In this paper I am concerned with Boston's view of the Covenant of Works, and to that we now turn.

Boston taught that God entered into a covenant with Adam in Genesis 2:16, 17. He describes this as 'the original transaction between God and our first father Adam in paradise, while yet in the state of primitive integrity.'[9] Adam had the law of God 'engraven on his heart in his creation'[10] but in the making of this Covenant of Works he was given an additional commandment, namely, that he should not eat from the tree of the knowledge of good and evil. The condition of the covenant was perfect obedience to the whole law of God, including this prohibition. .

Crucially, Boston taught that when God entered into that covenant with Adam described in Genesis 2, he was entering into covenant with Adam not as a 'private person' but as federal head of the human race yet unborn. When the President of the United States signs a treaty he does so as President and not as a private individual, so that if he ceased to be

---

[5] Andrew T. B. McGowan, Should We Leave Liberal Denominations?," *Reformation and Revival Journal* 13, no. 1 (Winter 2004):61-74.

[6] McMillan, ed., *The Complete Works of The Late Rev. Thomas Boston*, 11:178-339.

[7] Ibid., 8:379-604.

[8] Ibid., 11:176.

[9] Ibid., 11:178.

[10] Ibid., 11:179.

President the treaty would still be binding. He signs as the representative head of the nation, and the whole nation is thereby bound by the treaty. Similarly, argues Boston, Adam was our representative head and so when he broke the covenant (and Boston would subsequently argue that Hosea 6:7 refers to this breach) the consequences of the breach came not upon him alone, but upon all whom he represented in the covenant. That is why you and I are born with a sinful nature and are objects of God's wrath. We were in Adam and so share in the judgment upon all his posterity. In other words, Adam's sin was imputed to every human being except Christ (because he was born of a virgin).

Boston goes on to speak about the Covenant of Grace and how Christ is the federal head of the elect, whereby his righteousness is imputed to us. This is how he interprets Romans 5:12-21 and 1 Corinthians 15:21, 22; 44b-49. The conclusion is that all human beings are either in Adam, under the Covenant of Works, or in Christ, under the Covenant of Grace. If we are in Adam then we are subject to death, and if we are in Christ we shall be made alive.

As I mentioned earlier, some covenant theologians argued for a Covenant of Redemption between the Father and the Son as the basis for the Covenant of Grace, but Boston denied the need for a covenant of redemption. He argued that it was simply another way of looking at the covenant of grace.[11]

GENESIS 2 AND JOHN MURRAY'S ADAMIC ADMINISTRATION

John Murray, late Professor of Systematic Theology at Westminster Theological Seminary, was one of the finest theologians Scotland has produced in a very long time. He was a Reformed theologian, yet always willing to challenge the tradition if it did not conform to the Scriptures. There are some today who appear to regard the *Westminster Confession of Faith* as immutable and almost treat it as if it were Scripture, but Murray was not of this inclination. He recognised that theology did not end in 1647 and understood that through the Scriptures God would continue to shed light on our understanding. The interpretation of Genesis 2 was one of these areas where he challenged the traditional covenant theology, on the basis of Scripture.

---

[11] Ibid., 8:396,397,404,405.

In his article 'The Adamic Administration'[12] Murray notes that Adam was created 'in the image of God, a self-conscious, free, responsible, religious agent.'[13] He was created good and righteous, such that he was 'approved and accepted by God.'[14] In other words, he stood in a right relationship to God. This justified state would have continued indefinitely, so long as Adam had maintained his obedience to God and fulfilled his obligation 'to love and serve God with all the heart, soul, strength, and mind.'[15]

Nevertheless, as Murray points out, there were two respects in which Adam's relationship to God might be regarded as falling short of a 'higher' situation. First, Adam's position was 'a contingent situation, one of righteousness but mutably so, and likewise of justification and life. There is always the possibility of lapse on man's part and, with the lapse, loss of integrity, justification, [and] life.'[16] The second problem is that in Adam's natural condition, There is the absence of full-orbed communion with God in the assurance of permanent possession and increasing knowledge.[17]

Murray notes that the specific command not to eat of the tree of the knowledge of good and evil was intended to create a new and better situation for our first parents. Effectively, they were on probation; if they had obeyed God perfectly during that period of probation they would have been allowed to take of the tree of life and would have received the gift of eternal life, from which state it would no longer have been possible to fall into sin.[18]

Like Boston, Murray also makes the point that Adam 'acted in a public capacity.'[19] Drawing attention to Romans 5:12-19 and 1 Corinthians 15:22,45,46, Murray shows that, just as Adam's sin brought judgment and death upon the human race, so his obedience would have brought life to the human race. He states it like this,

> Analogy is drawn between Adam and Christ. They stand in unique relations to mankind. There is none before Adam – he is the first man.

---

[12] John Murray, *Collected Writings of John Murray* (Edinburgh: The Banner of Truth Trust, 1977), 2:47-59.

[13] Ibid., 47.

[14] Ibid.

[15] Ibid.

[16] Ibid.

[17] Ibid.

[18] Ibid., 48.

[19] Ibid., 49.

There is none between – Christ is the second man. There is none after Christ—he is the last Adam (1 Cor. 15:44-49). Here we have an embracive construction of human relationships. We know also that in Christ there is representative relationship and that obedience successfully completed has its issue in righteousness, justification, life for all he represents (1 Cor. 15:22). So a period of obedience successfully completed by Adam would have secured eternal life for all represented by him.

Murray calls the relationship established by God with Adam in Genesis 2, the 'Adamic Administration.' He speaks of this administration as the means by which God, 'by a special act of providence, established for man the provision whereby he might pass from the status of contingency to one of confirmed and indefectible holiness and blessedness.'[20] In other words, Adam would have been confirmed in a state in which it would have been impossible for him to sin.

Adam having disobeyed God, however, the consequences of that disobedience came upon us all. Only thus can we properly explain why it is that human beings are born with a sinful nature. As Murray says, 'We are sinners and come into the world as such. This situation demands explanation. It cannot stand as an empirical fact. It requires the question: Why or How? It is the Adamic administration with all its implications for racial solidarity that alone provides the answer. This is the biblical answer to the universality of sin and death.'[21]

John Murray, then, stands in essentially the same tradition as that of Thomas Boston, noting that all of humanity is either in Adam or in Christ and recognising Adam and Christ as representative heads of the human race. In some respects, however, their views were divergent. Let us now move on to consider certain important points of agreement and disagreement.

POINTS OF AGREEMENT AND DISAGREEMENT BETWEEN BOSTON AND MURRAY

There are many points of agreement between Boston's view of the Covenant of Works and John Murray's Adamic Administration. We will consider only two of these points of agreement, however, because it seems to me that they are fundamental.

---

[20] Ibid., 49.
[21] Ibid., 58.

POINTS OF AGREEMENT

The first significant point of agreement is their shared conviction that what God's words related in Genesis 2 (whether we call it a covenant or an administration) constituted an act of grace. That is to say, the establishment of this covenant or administration involved God's unmerited favour, the gracious action of a gracious God. Now do not misunderstand what I am saying here. Boston, for example, was quite clear that the Covenant of Works was a legal covenant and that the successful completion of his probationary period would have obliged God to grant Adam the benefits implied in the covenant. He writes that God '(made) over to him a benefit by way of a conditional promise, which made the benefit a debt upon the performing of the condition.'[22] Yet Boston was also clear that the very decision of God to establish such a covenant was an act of grace. Notice, he is not saying that the covenant made with Adam was a covenant of grace, but he is declaring that God's decision to establish the covenant was itself an act of grace.

The other point of agreement concerned imputation. Boston and Murray are quite clear that our relationship to Adam and our relationship to Christ, as spelled out in the passages mentioned above from Romans 5 and 1 Corinthians 15, are vital if we are to maintain imputed sin and imputed righteousness. Interestingly, Murray believes that it is perfectly possible to conceive of the headship of Adam without a Covenant of Works as the basis for this imputation.

POINTS OF DISAGREEMENT

The first significant point of disagreement between Boston and Murray concerns whether or not it was correct to call what God stipulated in Genesis 2 a covenant. Boston, as we have seen, called it a Covenant of Works. Murray on the other hand, called it the 'Adamic Administration'. Boston makes his argument in these words:

> Now it is true, we have not here the word *covenant*; yet we must not infer, that there is no covenant in this passage, more than we may deny the doctrine of the Trinity and sacraments, because those words do not occur where these things are treated of in scripture, nay, are not to be found in the scripture at all. But as in those cases, so here we have the thing; for the making over of a benefit to one, upon a condition, with a penalty, gone into by the party it is proposed to, is a covenant, a proper

---

[22] McMillan, ed., *The Complete Works of The Late Rev. Thomas Boston,* 11:178.

covenant, call it as you will.[23]

Murray disagrees with this argument and states his position in this way:

> This administration has often been denoted 'The Covenant of Works'.
> There are two observations. (1) The term is not felicitous, for the rea-
> son that the elements of grace entering into the administration are not
> properly provided for by the term 'works'. (2) It is not designated a
> covenant in Scripture. Hosea 6:7 may be interpreted otherwise and
> does not provide the basis for such a construction of the Adamic econ-
> omy. Besides, Scripture always uses the term covenant, when applied
> to God's administration to men, in reference to a provision that is re-
> demptive or closely related to redemptive design. Covenant in Scrip-
> ture denotes the oath-bound confirmation of promise and involves a se-
> curity which the Adamic economy did not bestow.[24]

The second significant area of disagreement concerns the Mosaic
Law, given on Mount Sinai. One of the problems faced by covenant
theologians is to interpret what Paul means in Galatians 4:24 when he
says that there are two covenants, one of which is 'from Mount Sinai.'
Those who have structured their theology round a Covenant of Works
and a Covenant of Grace, have to explain the relationship between these
covenants and this covenant from Mount Sinai. Two main possibilities
present themselves, one represented by Boston and the other by Murray.

Boston, following John Owen on this matter, takes the view that Sinai was a republication of the Covenant of Works. Commenting on Galatians 4:24, he writes,

> This covenant from Mount Sinai was the covenant of works as being
> opposed to the covenant of grace, namely, the law of the ten com-
> mandments, with promise and sanction, as before expressed. At Sinai
> it was renewed indeed, but that was not its first appearance in the
> world.[25]

Murray, on the other hand, is not satisfied exegetically with this interpretation. He writes,

> The view that in the Mosaic covenant there was a repetition of the so-
> called covenant of works, current among covenant theologians, is a
> grave misconception and involves an erroneous construction of the
> Mosaic covenant, as well as fails to assess the uniqueness of the Ad-

[23] McMillan, ed., *The Complete Works of The Late Rev. Thomas Boston,* 11:180.
[24] Murray, *Collected Writings,* 2:49.
[25] McMillan, ed., *The Complete Works of The Late Rev. Thomas Boston,* 11:181.

amic administration. The Mosaic covenant was distinctly redemptive in character and was continuous with and extensive of the Abrahamic covenants. The Adamic had no redemptive provision, nor did its promissory element have any relevance within a context that made redemption necessary.[26]

In other words, the proper way to interpret Galatians 3 is to view the covenant at Sinai as a spelling out of the obligations of the covenant of grace, rather than as republication of the covenant of works.

ASSESSMENT AND NEW PROPOSALS

I have a tremendous appreciation for both Boston and Murray and trying to choose between them is rather like choosing between your father and your grandfather! Nevertheless, on the matters mentioned above where they disagree, I am convinced that Murray was right! I am also impressed by the way in which Murray constantly subjects our theological tradition to the bar of Scripture.

In the above chapter on the unity of the covenant of grace I spoke of John Murray's published lecture entitled *The Covenant of Grace*. In that lecture, Murray said this:

> It would not be, however, in the interests of theological conservation or theological progress for us to think that the covenant theology is in all respects definitive and that there is no further need for correction, modification, and expansion. Theology must always be undergoing reformation. The human understanding is imperfect. However architectonic may be the systematic constructions of any one generation or group of generations, there always remains the need for correction and reconstruction so that the structure may be brought into closer approximation to the Scripture and the reproduction be a more faithful transcript or reflection of the heavenly exemplar. It appears to me that the covenant theology, notwithstanding the finesse of analysis with which it was worked out and the grandeur of its articulated systematization, needs recasting. We would not presume to claim that we shall be so successful in this task that the reconstruction will displace and supersede the work of the classic covenant theologians. But with their help we may be able to contribute a little towards a more biblically articulated and formulated construction of the covenant concept and of

---

[26] Murray, *Collected Writings,* 2:50.

its application to our faith, love, and hope.[27]

In other words, we are not bound to the formulations of an earlier genera-tion if we can show that Scripture can usefully be understood in a differ-ent way. This subject of covenant theology might well be one of the ar-eas where reformulation takes place. After all, the expressions 'covenant of works', 'covenant of grace' and 'covenant of redemption' do not ap-pear in Scripture. Could it be that other terms might make the position clearer?

In my view, the theological explorations of John Murray in this area might usefully be regarded as 'unfinished business' and taken further. In a lecture given to the British Tyndale Fellowship earlier this year, I ex-plored that possibility:

> It seems to me that Murray greatly advanced the cause of Reformed theology by indicating that a relationship of solidarity between God and Adam could be established without the requirement of calling it a covenant. Further, he rightly noted that grace has priority over law in God's relationship with Adam. His assertion of continuity between the Abrahamic and Sinaitic covenants is also important, namely, that the Sinaitic covenant does not annul or cancel the earlier covenant but is rather a spelling out of the obligations of the covenant of grace....

> It is my contention, however, that John Murray's reconstruction of the notion of a covenant of works into what he called the 'Adamic Ad-ministration' went part of the way to dealing with an incipient problem within federal theology but that a further step has to be taken, namely, speaking about a 'Messianic Administration', thus turning aside from over-emphasis on the covenants and re-focussing attention upon Adam and Christ as the two 'heads' of administration. This then leaves us free to see the covenant of grace as an overarching theme, rather than as a counterpoint to a covenant of works. In this way, I intend to chart a way forward for federal theology which I shall rename 'Headship Theology'....

> When we step back and ask what it is about the covenant of works and covenant of grace which was so central to Reformed theology as it de-veloped in the late sixteenth century, we have to conclude that it is the parallel between Adam and Christ as recorded in Romans 5 and 1 Co-rinthians 15. The vital element of federal theology is that all human

---

[27] John Murray, *The Covenant of Grace* (1953; reprint, Phillipsburg, NJ: Presbyte-rian and Reformed Publishing, 1988), 4, 5.

beings are either 'in Adam' or 'in Christ' and that death or salvation come by means of our relationship with one or other of these 'representative heads'. It is, however, perfectly possible to maintain this relation of headship without positing covenants as the basis for the relationship. Murray partially accomplished this by speaking of the Adamic Administration instead of the covenant of works, thus freeing that gracious relationship between God and mankind from the strictures of being called 'a covenant'. Why, then, can we not go further and speak of a 'Messianic Administration' where the emphasis is on union with Christ rather than upon the covenant of grace? By this means we can place the emphasis of Romans 5 and I Corinthians 15 where it belongs, namely on headship solidarity. Either we are 'in Adam' as a result of that solidarity created by the establishment of the Adamic Administration in Genesis 2, or we are 'in Christ' as the result of a spiritual union with Christ.[28]

At this stage, I am merely exploring these ideas and it may be that they do not solve all of the problems inherent in various traditional forms of the covenant theology. I do believe, however, that they are worth pursuing and it is my intention to develop them in a more sustained form in the near future. I would greatly appreciate any comments or suggestions (or even damning criticism!), which would assist me in this study.

May God help us to maintain our Calvinistic theology but always to be re-evaluating the traditional forms in which it has come down to us, in the light of Scripture.

---

[28] To be published in the volume from the Tyndale Triennial Conference of 2003, edited by A.I. Wilson and J. Grant.

Chapter 5

The Covenant and Our Children[1]

Joseph A. Pipa, Jr.

Imagine three children playing; we will call them Bobby, Paul, and Rebecca. As we watch these children from the distance, their behavior does
not appear to differ significantly; they are playing quite well together.
However, we know them and their families. Bobby, though he is a well-
behaved, gentle boy, comes from a non-Christian home. Nevertheless, he
is a fine boy—one with whom you would not object to your children's
playing. Paul comes from a Christian family of an evangelical persua-
sion. His parents hope that one day Paul will become a Christian, but
they do not recognize God's covenant purposes in Paul's life. Rebecca,
however, is being reared in a covenant home. She has been baptized and
is recognized as a member of the church, and her parents are bringing her
up as a Christian, seeking God's grace in her life. We recognize these
distinctions and do not have a great deal of difficulty in distinguishing
the fundamental spiritual difference between Bobby on the one hand and
Paul and Rebecca on the other, but in terms of spiritual benefits and
privileges, can we assert that Rebecca has an advantage over either of the
others, and particularly whether she has advantages that Paul does not
enjoy? This is a question that many Presbyterian and Reformed people

---

[1] This a transcription of a sermon preached at the 2004 Spring Theology Conference
of Greenville Presbyterian Theological Seminary.

have difficulty answering, and yet our answer to this question influences how we will rear our children. Are there differences, and if so, what are they? How ought the differences to affect the rearing of our children?

I will seek to answer these questions from Romans 9:4, 5: "...who are Israelites, to whom belongs the adoption as sons and the glory and the covenants and the giving of the Law and the *temple* service and the promises, whose are the fathers, and from whom is the Christ according to the flesh, who is over all, God blessed forever. Amen."[2] To address these questions, I have chosen this passage because, despite Paul's awareness that those of whom he speaks as being in the covenant had not yet obtained the saving benefits of the covenant, Paul nevertheless asserts that they possess certain objective privileges and benefits. I suggest that if these things were true for them, they are equally true for all those who are under the administration of the covenant of grace.

In Romans 9 Paul returns to the question he first raised in chapter 3. Before he delivered his final indictment of the sinfulness of mankind (both Jews and Gentiles), he wrote, "Then what advantage has the Jew? Or what is the benefit of circumcision? Great in every respect. First of all, that they were entrusted with the oracles of God" (Romans 3:1, 2). He leaves the discussion of their advantage undeveloped as he launches into a discussion of depravity, justification, sanctification, glorification, and God's overarching eternal plan (chapters 3-8). Not until chapter 9 does he return to this question of advantage. What about the Jew? The question is important, because the great majority of the Jews had rejected Jesus of Nazareth as Messiah. What does their rejection say about God's covenant faithfulness? What does it say about God's righteousness if the people to whom God had promised the Messiah refused to believe in Him? Paul begins to answer this question by expressing his sorrow. He uses a grammatical form indicating that if it were possible (though it is not), he would give his soul for the salvation of theirs. To indicate the depth of their loss and his grief for them, he delineates the great privileges they possessed as a consequence of being part of God's covenant people. In this list of privileges we find the *non-saving* benefits that belong to the covenant people; here God also teaches that our children are members of the church and as such receive covenant benefits that are sealed to them by the sacrament of baptism.

We shall consider three things: First, our covenant children are

---

[2] Unless otherwise noted Scripture quotations are from the New American Standard Version.

members of the church; second, our covenant children are beneficiaries of covenantal good; and third, our covenant children are recipients of the covenant sign and are to be reared accordingly.

In the first place, our covenant children are members of the church. Paul teaches that even those Jews who were in the process of being cut off from the olive tree (Romans 11:17) had belonged to the covenant people. We notice that he speaks of them in verse 4 as those "who are Israelites," and in verse 5, "whose are the fathers." What does this reveal about these Old Covenant people? To be an Israelite was not simply a matter of a national or racial identity, as we shall see when we consider Deuteronomy 29 and Ezekiel 47 below. To be an Israelite meant that one belonged to the covenant people of God and was a member of the church; it meant that he was in covenant succession[3] from the fathers; it meant he was numbered among the seed that God had promised to Abraham, when he said, "I will be a God to you and to your seed" (Genesis 17). Because he was a part of that seed, born into a covenant household, he was registered in the citizenry of the covenant people, in the church of the Lord God (Psalm 87:6) and was counted among the people of God.

Through Moses, God taught (and teaches) that children born to covenant families were members of the Old Covenant people. When Moses began the second reading of the law, he addressed the people: "Then Moses summoned all Israel and said to them, 'Hear, O Israel, the statutes and ordinances which I am speaking today in your hearing that you may learn them and observe them carefully. The Lord our God made a covenant with us at Horeb. The Lord did not make this covenant with our fathers, but with us, with all those of us alive here today'" (Deuteronomy 5:1-3). When the Lord said through Moses that He did not make this covenant with their fathers, but with them, with all those alive there that day, He was reasserting that He also made the covenant at Mt. Sinai with the children, even those not yet born. The significance of this is the principle that when God makes covenant, He makes it with both believers and their children and their descendants. There is no other way to understand what God is saying here. He stated this principle more spe-

---

[3] By "covenant succession" we mean "The children of the covenant are the heirs apparent of the promises. God has graciously promised to show mercy unto thousands of them that love Him and keep His commandments; the decree of election runs largely in their loins, and through their faithfulness in rearing a godly seed, the Church is perpetuated, and new recruits are constantly added to the communion of saints. They are all incorporated into the church, because many of them hereafter are to be of the Church," (James H. Thornwell, *Collected Writings,* 4:340).

cifically in Deuteronomy 29. As his people were about to enter the promised land, He had assembled them to renew the covenant.

> You stand today, all of you, before the Lord your God, your chiefs, your tribes, your elders and your officers, even all the men of Israel, your little ones, your wives, the alien who is within your camps . . .that you may enter into the covenant with the Lord your God, and into his oath which the Lord your God is making with you today, in order that He may establish you today as His people and that HE may be your God, just as He spoke to you and as He swore to your fathers, to Abraham, Isaac, and Jacob. Now not with you alone am I making this covenant and this oath, but both with those who stand here with us today in the presence of the Lord our God and with those who are not with us here today." (Deuteronomy 29:10-15)

The emphasis is clear. He is renewing a covenant that reaches back to the one He made with Abraham, Isaac, and Jacob; through covenant succession, He established it with their fathers at Mount Sinai and with their children. As He renews it with them and their children, He also includes those not yet born ("those not with us here today").

That covenant children under the Old Covenant were members of the church He elucidates in the second commandment, saying He will be "visiting the iniquity of the fathers on the children, on the third and the fourth generations of those who hate Me, but showing lovingkindness to thousands, to those who love Me and keep my commandments (Exodus 20:5, 6). The promised threats and blessings affect future generations of covenant people. These passages clarify what Paul means by "who are Israelites and of whom are the fathers." Because the Jews descended from the fathers, they were members of the church. Although multitudes would soon be cut off because they rejected the covenant Savior, until that time they were members of the church, part of the covenant seed.

The New Testament explicitly teaches that this principle is in effect. Paul writes in Galatians 3:29 that Christians are the seed of Abraham, and at the conclusion of Galatians, he calls Christians "the Israel of God" (Galatians 6:16). Peter teaches the truth of covenant succession for those in Christ in Acts 2:39: "For the promise is for you and your children, and for all who are far off, as many the Lord our God shall call to Himself." His choice of wording includes the children of Gentile converts as well as of Jewish. Joel Beeke writes, "It is unthinkable that in the fullness of the gospel era, the children of the New Testament church would have less a place in the covenant than children of Old Testament Israel."[4] The basis of Peter's remarks is Ezekiel 47:21-23:

> So you shall divide this land among yourselves according to the tribes of Israel. And it will come about that you shall divide it by lot for an inheritance among yourselves and among the aliens who stay in your midst, who bring forth sons in your midst. And they shall be to you as the native-born among the sons of Israel; they shall be allotted an inheritance with you among the tribes of Israel. And it will come about that in the tribe with which the alien stays, there you shall give him his inheritance, declares the Lord God.

In this passage God established the principle that when an alien, that is, one not descended physically from Abraham and therefore not formerly under the covenant, was brought into the covenant community, he with his children was assigned a portion in Israel. This pattern was practiced in the Old Covenant Church, and God uses it in Ezekiel 47 as a New Covenant prophecy. I affirm that it has a New Covenant fulfillment because of its position in Ezekiel's prophecy. He gives these instructions about the alien and his children after describing the great, glorious temple with its river of water. These are figures depicting the work of Christ, on account of which Gentiles of all nations with their children are brought into the church.

We find further proof for this doctrine in the book of Ephesians. Paul addresses this letter to the church ("the saints at Ephesus," v.1). As he addresses various categories of church members, he speaks not only to wives and husbands, parents, slaves and masters, but to children as well (6:1), reminding them that they are responsible for obeying their parents. All those in each category are members of the church.

Therefore, what Paul says of Old Covenant people in Romans 9 is true of the New Covenant people as well. There is but one covenant of grace and one administrator of that covenant, the Lord Jesus Christ. Throughout the covenant of grace, God has always dealt with believers and their children. Every covenant throughout the Scriptures is with both the person with whom God covenants and His descendants. This is an inviolable, unbreakable principle of the God's dealing with His people as revealed in Scripture. Thus we understand that our children are mem-

---

[4] Joel Beeke, *Bringing the Gospel to Covenant Children* (Grand Rapids: Reformation Heritage Books, 2001), 6.

bers of the church, a part of the New Covenant people. This doctrine is stated clearly in the *Westminster Confession of Faith*: "The visible church...consists of all those throughout the world that profess the true religion, together with their children" (XXV.2).

In anticipation of what we shall consider later, let us note here that we baptize our children because they are members of the church. This is the same reason we baptize adult professors. The *Westminster Confession of Faith* does not distinguish between the baptisms of adults and children. Whether one comes by profession of faith or birth, he is solemnly inducted into the church by baptism (*Westminster Confession of Faith* XXVIII.1). Hence, it is incorrect to speak of children who make professions of faith as "joining the church." Rather they move from one status within the church (that of non-communicant member) to another (communicant member).

We must consider also a serious reality with respect to this membership: *there is no necessary, absolute correlation between election and covenant church membership.* Paul addresses this difficulty in Romans 9:6. Can members of the church refuse to embrace the Savior? Yes, "But it is not as though the word of God has failed. For they are not all Israel who are descended from Israel; neither are they all children because they are Abraham's descendants." This answer is sobering: "For they are not all Israel who are descended from Israel; neither are they all children because they are Abraham's descendants, but 'through Isaac your descendants will be named.'" In other words, God's election is not exactly co-extensive with membership in his covenant. Having introduced the doctrine of election in chapter 8, Paul provides greater detail in the context of covenant membership and covenant rejection, because he wants us to know that there is no absolute correlation between election and church membership. Election is God's sovereign, eternal purpose, and it is secret until it manifests itself in effectual calling and a professing Christian's subsequent life of faith and obedience.

God's election, however, works in part in and through the covenant community, through covenant succession. God teaches in Genesis 18 how election works through covenant succession. In Genesis 18:19, as He explained why He was taking Abraham into His confidence about His impending judgment of Sodom and Gomorrah, He said, "For I have known him (The New American Standard translation is, "I have chosen him"; Paul uses the word "know" that means "elect" here) that he may command his children and his household after him to keep the way of the

Lord by doing righteousness and justice in order that the Lord may bring upon Abraham what He has spoken about him." Again we see that God's covenant promise included Abraham's seed; He would be a God to him and his seed, who would be blessed and innumerable, and a blessing to the earth. In Genesis 18:19, God says that he will accomplish these covenant promises as Abraham rears his children in the nurture and admonition of the Lord. In other words, God brings those whom He saves from the world into the church. In the church, they and their children enjoy the means of grace; it is in the church that God's people come to the realization and the assurance that they are elect and His covenant is with them and their children. He promises to save their children and does so through the ministry of the church. So election ordinarily works through covenant succession.

God, however, never promises to save every one of our children. He does not even promise to save every one of our children if we are faithful. Rather, He has promised to save a seed, and from passages like Revelation 7, the numbers appear to be vast. We must never forget that He in His sovereign wisdom may pass by some of our children, as heartbreaking as that is to us. He alone is God, and like Job we must lay our hands over our mouths and consent to His holy will. We have great hope for our children and bring them up them in the hope of the gospel. He has placed them in a Christian home; He has put them in the church; He ordinarily works through covenant succession.

Moreover, He will not violate His purpose for the covenant family; He delights in working through the family, which is the primary means through which God gathers His elect, as the Bible makes quite clear. Of course, we desire to see multitudes brought from the world to Christ, and most of those who come from the world will come with families or will establish families. These families will belong to the Lord God; in and through them He shall gather His elect to Himself.

Hence the first thing that Paul teaches us is that our children are members of the church, the covenant community, and that God's election is ordinarily manifested through covenant succession. There is, we reiterate, no absolute guarantee that *every* covenant child is elect. We rear them by God's grace, recognizing that the Lord is sovereign; He saves whom He will save; He has mercy on whom He will have mercy. Nevertheless, His revelation is clear: the fullest manifestation of that mercy shall be in our homes and to our children.

Second, we learn that covenant children, who are members of the church, are beneficiaries of many great covenant blessings. Paul lists these benefits for us in verses 4 and 5. First, to them belongs adoption as sons. The Old Covenant doctrine of adoption was not as fully worked out as the Pauline doctrine of adoption, particularly regarding the individual who has the testimony of the Spirit. Nevertheless, God considered the Old Covenant people to be his children. He instructed Moses, "Then you shall say to Pharaoh, 'Thus says the Lord, "Israel is My son, My firstborn. Let My son go that he may serve Me. But you have refused to let him go. Behold, I will kill your son, your firstborn"'" (Exodus 4:22). The Old Testament ends with the same declaration—that the covenant people of God are the children of God. So testified Malachi: "A son honors his father and a servant his master. Then if I am your father, where is My honor?" "Do we not all have one father? Has not one God created us? Why do we deal treacherously each against his brother so as to profane the covenant of our fathers?" (Malachi 1:6; 2:10).[5]

Because the children were in the covenant, God was their Father. Although many of the Jews would prove themselves to be reprobate covenant breakers, Paul says they had the benefit of adoption; within the covenant they related to God as Father. How much more glorious is the revelation of the doctrine of adoption in the New Testament! In Romans 8:15-17, Paul lays out the doctrine: "For you have not received a spirit of slavery leading to fear again, but you have received a spirit of adoption as sons by which we cry out, 'Abba! Father!' The Spirit Himself bears witness with our spirit that we are children of God, and if children, heirs also, heirs of God and fellow heirs with Christ, if indeed we suffer with Him in order that we may also be glorified with Him." Paul clearly states in Ephesians 5 and 6 that our children are our Lord's children. In Ephesians 5:1 Paul bases his exhortation to wives, husbands, children, fathers, slaves, and masters on their being the children of God: "Therefore be imitators of God, as beloved children." Our children are to imitate God as His beloved children, just as all those in the covenant have the glorious privilege of relating to God as Father.

Consider some of the practical outworking of covenant adoption.[6]

---

[5] See also Ezekiel 16:20, 21 where God indicts the Jews for sacrificing their children, who were preeminently God's children.

[6] Here we refer our readers to Thomas Boston, *The Complete Works of the Late Rev. Thomas Boston,* ed. Samuel M'Millan (reprint, Wheaton, IL: Richard Owen Roberts, Publishers, 1980), 1:615 for the distinction of "covenant adoption" and "saving adoption."

We cannot assure little Bobby (in the absence of a credible profession of faith), who is from a non-Christian home, that God loves him, but we can tell Paul and Rebecca, "Jesus loves you, this I know, for the Bible tells me so." We can tell Paul and Rebecca that they belong to God, just as we pray with our own children and teach them to pray to God as their Father. What Christian would not long for his children to pray to God as Father? We include them in family worship and bring them into corporate worship, where the congregation addresses God as Father. Our children have the benefit of covenant adoption, being federally a part of the family of God.

The second benefit is "the glory." What does Paul mean by this phrase? When God led the children of Israel out the land of Egypt, He manifested Himself to them by the *Shekina* glory, a cloud by day and a pillar of fire by night. That glorious cloud was a theophony, a manifestation of the presence of God in the midst of the people. No matter where one was in the camp, he could look up and be assured that he was in the presence of God. At the dedication of the tabernacle at Mount Sinai, the cloud of God descended on the tabernacle (Exodus 40:34-38), and later when Solomon dedicated the temple (1 Kings 8: 10, 11), the presence of God manifest by this cloud filled the temple. The tabernacle and the temple contained the mercy seat, which was a manifestation of the throne of God; God was enthroned amongst His people in such a visible manner that they knew they lived in His presence. To them belonged the glory of God.

Moreover, they experienced God's glorious works in answers to prayer and mighty deliverances. You can imagine what a great privilege it was to live with those fearsome manifestations of God's glory.

We and our children enjoy an incomparably greater manifestation of God's glory, for the glory of God is made evident by the Spirit of God Himself, who does not dwell in one place (as in the Tabernacle, for instance), but in the hearts of all Christians and their congregations (1 Corinthians 3:16-18; 6:19). The Spirit of Christ indwells each individual believer and is in our midst when assembled. Every time Christ is proclaimed in family worship and particularly in the preaching of His Word and the Lord's Supper, we see His glory. As Paul contrasts the Old Covenant glory with that of the New Covenant, he says, "Now the Lord is the Spirit; and where the Spirit of the Lord is, there is liberty. But we all, with unveiled face beholding as in a mirror the glory of the Lord, are being transformed into the same image from glory to glory, just as from the Lord, the Spirit" (2 Corinthians 3:17). Jehovah the Spirit dwells in our midst. We do not need to look on any purported physical image of Christ. No, we have the glory of Christ set before us in the preaching of the gospel, the glory of Christ placarded before us in the sacrament, the glory of Christ experienced in every answer to prayer. Every time Christ is exalted we behold His glory, and are transformed by that glory.

In Paul's teaching we perceive how our children experience God's glory. They live in the home where God dwells. They participate in corporate worship, which takes place in God's presence. It is essential that children be in the corporate assembly, because God manifests Himself to us in glorious ways during corporate worship. Jesus says, "he who loves Me will be loved by My Father, and I will love him and manifest Myself to him,"(John 14:21, NKJV). Where does He do this more fully than in corporate worship, in our prayers and singing, and particularly in the Holy-Spirit-anointed preaching of His Word?

I trust that you have some acquaintance with such things, that you and your children are experiencing them —in answers to prayer, in God's great work on your behalf, in spiritual worship. You and your children live in the midst of the people among whom God dwells. What an incomparable privilege!

Third, Paul says that they possess "the covenants." "Covenants" refers to the covenant of grace by which God legally binds Himself to His people and them to Him. Paul speaks of the covenant in the plural because he is referring to the various administrations of the one covenant of grace. We saw in Deuteronomy chapter 29 that the covenant made with Abraham, Isaac, and Jacob was the covenant that was being renewed under Moses. By the time Paul wrote to the Romans, the Old Covenant people had lived with the reality and privileges of all the Old Covenant administrations: the post-fall Adamic covenant, the Noahic covenant, the Abrahamic covenant, the Mosaic covenant, and the Davidic covenant. These covenants with their promises (particularly the great declarative promise "I am your God and you are My people"), responsibilities, threats, signs, and types, were the possession of the Old Covenant people of God. Their children lived legally within the covenant. They legally possessed all of the covenanted privileges which God had granted in the covenants, and their concomitant responsibilities.

The covenant people were also recipients of the progressive unfolding of the revelation of Christ in those covenants. That is why Paul goes on to state that the Christ was from them: "whose are the fathers and from whom is the Christ according to the flesh who is over all, God blessed forever" (verse 5). The central truth of these Old Covenant administrations was that God was going to come in the flesh as covenant head, as mediator, as surety to deliver them from their sins. Moreover, the covenants revealed to them the mystery of the Godhead, although they only saw it darkly in the Old Covenant. You will notice that Paul clearly states the deity of the Lord Jesus Christ in this passage; he uses similar language in Titus 2:13. There is no other way to understand his language than as a reference to the deity of the Lord Jesus Christ. "From whom is the Christ according to the flesh, who [i.e., Christ] is over all, God blessed forever"—a clear statement that our wonderful Savior is God blessed forever. How were they to have known this truth? They had learned it in the covenant, particularly in the Davidic covenant through which God revealed the deity of the Christ (Psalm 45; Isaiah 7:14; Isaiah 9:6, 7; Psalm 110:1).

Because we and our children live under the New Covenant, which fulfills all the types and shadows and through Christ guarantees to us all that was promised in the Old Covenant (Jeremiah 31:31-35), we no longer live under the shadows, types, and prophecies. We do not wonder, "How can David's son be David's God?" No, we understand these things. We and our children can see clearly that our Savior, who established the New Covenant, is the God-man, God blessed forever. We live under the covenant headship of the Lord Jesus Christ. Our children are part of the people to whom God has covenanted to give this Savior given to redeem His church, of which our children are part. God has legally bound Himself to them and them to Him. They have God saying to them, "You children remember this: I am your God and you are My children." Our children may not understand now, but there is nothing in this entire world they could ever hear that is more glorious. The God who created all things by His Word in six days, the God who by that same Word governs all things, He that is absolutely holy, powerful, and infinite says, "I am your God, and you are My child." That is what it means to say that they possess the covenants.

Fourth, Paul says that they have the law. This benefit reverts to Paul's question and answer in Romans 3:1, 2: "Then what advantage has the Jew? Or what is the benefit of circumcision? Great in every respect. First of all, that they were entrusted with the oracles of God." Remember the difference between general revelation and special revelation: in works of creation and providence, God has revealed Himself generally to the entire world. This revelation manifests that God is and that all are accountable to Him. God, however, gave to the church His special revelation, which alone teaches us about salvation. Similarly, God gave His revelation in the Old Covenant to the church, His covenant people. Who was the guardian of that revelation in the Old Covenant? Was it not the church? Where were the Scriptures read and preached? In the church; Israel had the law of God, the oracles; they knew the mind of God, for He revealed His will to them. The Psalmist says, "The secret of the Lord is for those who fear Him, and He will make them know His covenant" (Psalm 25:14). God has revealed His will to those in covenant with Him.

In the New Covenant, we live in the full light of completed revelation. Our Bibles contain God's perfect and final revelation until Christ returns. Paul declares in 1 Timothy 3:14 and 15 that the New Covenant church is "the pillar and support of the truth." By "truth" he means the Word of God. God has given that Word to the church with the attendant responsibility to study that Word, to defend it, to teach it, and to preach that Word. Our children live in the midst of the people who possess God's Word. They are nurtured in families that have family worship. Faithful parents teach them the Bible; they memorize Scripture and catechism before they are able to read; they learn to read and study the Bible; they attend the worship of God's church and hear the Bible read and preached, which is the primary means God uses for conversion and strengthening of faith (Romans 10:14,15; Larger Catechism 155). Many live and die today without having heard one word of Scripture. Even in our own country, many do not own a Bible and have never read a Bible. Thankfully, covenant children possess the word of God.

Fifth, in connection with the word of God, is the worship of God—that is what "service" means in this context. "Service" is one of the Greek words that is used for the worship of God—and it is in the worship of God where the other benefits are most wonderfully manifested. The children in the Old Covenant were reared with the temple worship, and in all of their cities and villages they attended the synagogue. Only God's people knew how to worship God, how to approach Him acceptably. When Jesus spoke with the Samaritan woman, He contrasted Samaritan worship and Jewish worship: "You worship that which you do not know; we worship that which we know, for salvation is from the Jews" (John 4:22). He was asserting that the Samaritans worshiped God falsely; they did not know how to approach God; they and their worship were unacceptable to God. In contrast, the Jews had the revelation of God, which taught them how to worship Him acceptably.

How much more is this true of the New Covenant people? We worship in the fullness of the gospel, in spirit and in truth. We know what God requires us to do in worship and how we are to respond to Him. We know that He meets with us in worship. Our children have the privilege of being in the worship of God, where all these benefits come to bear--both in family worship and particularly in corporate worship. The privilege of acceptable worship belongs to them.

Sixth, Paul says they have the promises. We have already mentioned the great covenant promise; "I am your God, and you are My people." God unfolds that promise by promising the two things necessary to accomplish it, namely, the forgiveness of sins and the gift of the Holy Spirit. Those promises belonged to the Old Covenant people and were renewed to them in covenant succession. God often promised them the forgiveness of sin, as He did in Isaiah 1:18: "Though your sins are as scarlet, they will be as white as snow; though they are red like crimson, they will be like wool." We all are familiar with David's canticle on forgiveness in Psalm 32.

In Isaiah 59:21, God promised the gift of the Holy Spirit: "'And as for Me, this is My covenant with them,' says the Lord, 'My Spirit which is upon you and my words which I have put in your mouth shall not depart from your mouth nor from the mouth of your offspring nor from the mouth of your offspring's offspring,' says the Lord, 'from now and forever.'" Not just for three or four generations, but now and forever God's people possess His promises.

God fully accomplished these promises in the New Covenant. He had said, "'But this is the covenant which I will make with the house of Israel after those days.' declares the Lord, 'I will put My law within them, and on their heart I will write it; and I will be their God, and they shall be My people. And they shall not teach again, each man his neighbor and each man his brother, saying, "Know the Lord," for they shall all know Me, from the least of them to the greatest of them,' declares the Lord, 'for I will forgive their iniquity, and their sin I will remember no more'" (Jeremiah 31:33,34). Our children are heirs of these promises. They have a legal right covenantally to these promises. Peter declared on the day of Pentecost, "For the promise is for you and your children" (Acts 2:39).

Pierre Marcel expands on the concept of heir of the promise:

Scripture teaches us that children born in the covenant are *heirs*. But their heritage is *that of promise*, of which the Holy Spirit is the pledge. We can never insist too much on this point in opposition to those who obstinately maintain that according to us the heritage has to do with salvation. These children do not inherit salvation and eternal life. Salvation is not hereditary! They inherit only the promises. It behoves them thereafter to receive the *content* of the promise by faith and repentance, and thus by regeneration and conversion, and to live a life consecrated to the Lord. Then, and then only, will they be heirs of *the things promised*. The heritage is only communicated to the heir who receives the promise *with faith*.[7]

Having noted the covenantal benefits that belong to our children, let us consider an inference related to baptism. The children who are members of the church and have these benefits of covenant, have their membership and benefits sealed[8] to them with the covenantal sign. The Old Covenant members had these benefits confirmed to them by circumcision. Circumcision was a sign of spiritual blessings, as Paul points out with respect to Abraham, "And he received the sign of circumcision, a seal of the righteousness of the faith which he had while uncircumcised, that he might be the father of all who believe without being circumcised that righteousness might be reckoned to them" (Romans 4:11). While circumcision was a sign of membership in the Old Covenant church, it spoke as well of the necessity of regeneration and salvation (Deuteronomy 10:16; 30:6). It sealed the reality of these things to the one who possessed them. Baptism has the same significance. Thus since our children are members of the church and have all the benefits the Old Covenant people had, and since baptism has replaced circumcision (Colossians 2:11, 12), we baptize our children. The Westminster Standards state this doctrine while identifying the proper recipients of baptism: "Not only they that do actually profess faith in and obedience unto Christ, but also the infants of one, or both, believing parents, are to be baptized" (*West-*

---

[7] Pierre Marcel. *The Biblical Doctrine of Infant Baptism*, trans. Philip Edgcumbe Hughes: (London: James Clarke & Co. LTD., 1959), 107, 108.

[8] Francis Beattie, *The Presbyterian Standards* (1896; reprint, Greenville, SC: Southern Presbyterian Press, 1997), 300, gives a simple and clear definition of "seal" when he says, "The idea here is somewhat obscure by reason of the meaning of the word used....The sacraments, as seals of the covenant of grace, are the divine marks that God will make good the contents of the covenant to those who accept its term." See also A. A. Hodge, *The Confession of Faith* (1869; reprint, Edinburgh: The Banner of Truth Trust, 1983), 331.

minster Confession of Faith XXVIII.IV).

The purpose of this chapter is not to defend infant baptism; rather it is to show what the baptism of our children signifies and how we are to regard them. So we look, in the third place, at the practical outworking for us of our children's being in covenant with us. At this point, we clearly see the difference between Bobby, on the one hand, and Paul and Rebecca, on the other. Bobby is the recipient of none of these promises with their benefits, whereas Paul and Rebecca have this great inheritance.

We see, moreover, a difference between Paul and Rebecca. In Paul's case, if his parents seek to nurture him according to Scripture, they rear him in the fullness of these privileges and benefits whether they recognize them or not. They, however, deprive themselves of the comfort of the covenant, as well as an understanding of the great utility of this inheritance to bring Paul to conversion and assurance (if he had not been regenerated in infancy). Rebecca and her parents enjoy this inheritance and have the great comfort of knowing that God is her God and these promises are hers as she lives according to the covenant by repentance, faith, and obedience. Furthermore, Rebecca enjoys the additional benefit of her baptism. But what is the import of her baptism for Rebecca and her parents?

A wide range of divergent views exists with respect to the significance and efficacy of Baptism.[9] To some it means very little. Failing to understand God's inclusion of their children in the covenant, they treat their children as unconverted and outside the covenant. Too often even Reformed and Presbyterian parents regard their children as if baptism makes no difference at all to their spiritual well-being. Such parents, even if Presbyterians by profession and practice, are Baptists in their view of and rearing of their children. In like manner, some Presbyterian Churches do not teach or act consistently with their doctrine of baptism:

> Many ministers, rather than getting a handful of water, get so little as to perform a virtually 'dry baptism.' Some of us say hardly anything in sermons about the importance of baptism or about baptism as a real means of grace. We often teach, by practice, that baptism is nothing but a Baptist dedication of infants service with a few drops water. We so emphasize what the parents say to God that we diminish what is more important – what God says to the community in baptism. Often, influ-

---

[9] I am indebted in this section to an article written by William Smith, "Does Baptism Work?" *The Westminster Message*, (February 2004), a newsletter of Westminster Presbyterian Church, Huntsville, Alabama.

enced as we are by revivalism and pietism, we do not treat children as those who are to be brought up in the faith, but as those who must wait for 'something to happen' – regeneration, or conversion, or maybe a 'decision.'[10]

We also manifest our error by saying that our baptized children have "joined the church" when they make profession of faith.

If some place too low a premium on baptism, others attribute too much to it. They teach that baptism regenerates the children as it incorporates them into the body of Christ. Rich Lusk writes, "Scripture is clear: baptism is the means through which the Spirit unites us to Christ. No other means is said to have this function; it is the peculiar grace attached to baptism. . . . Since baptism is the instrumental means of union with Christ, it is sometimes said to be the instrument of forgiveness and regeneration (Acts 2:38; 22:16; Tit. 3:5)....In other words, baptism is simply the gospel in aqueous form."[11] This view is a serious error and clearly contradicts the Westminster Standards. The Confession clearly avoids tying the efficacy of baptism to its moment of application. The Confession does not teach that the grace is exhibited and conferred at the time of the administration of the sacrament; rather, it is conferred at God's appointed time. Baptism does not work automatically. "The grace...is not conferred by any power in (it) ...but...the efficacy of (it) depend(s) upon the work of the Spirit and the word of institution...." One may receive the grace promised before, at the time of, or after baptism: "The efficacy of Baptism is not tied to the moment of time wherein it is administered" (WCF 28.6). Hodge wrote, "But that this actual conveyance of the grace sealed is not tied to the moment in which the sacrament is administered, but is made according to the precise provisions as to time and circumstance predetermined in the eternal covenant of grace. So property may be sealed and conveyed in a deed to a minor, but the minor may not actually enter into the fruition of it until such time and upon such conditions as are predetermined in his father's will."[12]

---

[10] Smith, "The Westminster Message."

[11] Rich Lusk. "Some thoughts on the Means of Grace: A Few Proposals" *Theologia,* 2003, accessed at: http://www.Hornes.org/theologia/content/rich_lusk/some_thoughts_on_the_means_of_grace.httm.

[12] A.A. Hodge. *Commentary on the Confession of Faith* (Philadelphia: Presbyterian Board of Publication and Sabbath School Work, 1916), 477. See further critique in this volume—Richard Phillips, "Covenant Confusion."

The biblical position as stated in the Westminster Standards, avoids the two extremes (one ignoring the significance of baptism, and the other virtually attributing regenerative grace to it at the time of its administration). The temperate position of Scripture is seen when the Confession says, "By the right use of this ordinance, the promised grace is not only offered, but really exhibited and conferred by the Holy Ghost, to such (whether of age or infants) as that grace belongeth unto, according to the counsel of God's own will, in his appointed time," (*Westminster Confession of Faith*, XXVIII.VI).

In Rebecca's family, baptism reminds her parents and will testify to her as she begins to think on her baptism, that she was born in sins and trespasses and needed to be born again. At the time of her baptism God promised her parents that she was and is with them federally in covenant with Christ; she is a member of the church and a recipient of covenant benefits; and she is an heir to all the covenant promises. Moreover, through her baptism God has declared to her, I am your God and you are my child, so you must keep covenant with me by faith. As the Confession says, when she experiences the reality of God's grace in her life, her baptism will exhibit and confer grace on her.

Since we have already noted that this does not mean that Mary or any other covenant child invariably will be converted, how then are we to view our baptized children? Do we presume they are unregenerate? Do we presume they are regenerate? We must acknowledge that not everyone baptized as an infant continues in the covenant. Of course, the same holds true of those who are baptized upon later profession of faith, Biblical examples being Simon the Magician and Demas. We do not baptize our children because we presume they are regenerate, but because they are members of the covenant.

We do not, however, assume our covenant children to be unregenerate. The Westminster Directory for Worship teaches "That they are Christian, and federally holy before baptism, and therefore are they baptized."[13] Federally or covenantally they are viewed as Christians and are separated unto Christ. Although some of them may not be

converted until they are older, we do not demand or necessarily expect some decision or later-life extraordinary experience. They are heirs of the promise. We remind them of what God has promised and of their responsibility to be repenting and believing. We recognize that federally

---

[13] *The Directory for the Publick Worship of God.* (Glasgow: Free Presbyterian publications, 1985), 383.

or covenantally they are Christians. As they manifest grace in their lives, we encourage them. If they manifest patterns of persistently sinful behavior, we warn them of the necessity of being born again, and we continually set before them the necessity of faith in the Lord Jesus Christ.

Thus we rear our children with the hope and expectation that they are Christ's. Some, if not many of them will be regenerate from the womb, never remembering a day when they did not know Christ. Others will not come to saving faith until later. But when a two-year old says he loves Jesus, we ought not to assume that is impossible. Rather we accept his profession of faith and teach him what it means to believe in Jesus. Thus, although some of our children will be converted later, we do not treat them as objects of evangelism, as we would those living outside God's covenanted relationship, but rather we nurture them in covenant truth. What then, are our responsibilities, and what do we teach them?

Before answering this question, let us recall that baptism also places a solemn obligation on parents. We take vows: We "unreservedly dedicate" our children to God. We promise we will "set before (them) a godly example," that we "will pray with and for (them)," "teach (them) the doctrines of our holy religion," and "strive by all the means of God's appointment to bring (them) up in the nurture and admonition of the Lord," (*Presbyterian Church in America Book of Church Order*, "Directory for Worship," 56-4). Although I find no promise in Scripture that if parents are faithful and believe God's promises, each of their children will of necessity be converted, I am quite certain that *ordinarily* God does not operate savingly when parents are unfaithful, nor should we expect Him to do so (Exodus 20:5). He operates within the means he has appointed. Bill Smith says, "Still, there is a part parents play, and, when we consider the quality of spiritual life in some homes and the influences parents allow from outside, we must say that some "baptismal failures" are attributable in whole or part to parental vow breaking."[14] James H. Thornwell, likewise, emphasized the importance of the parents "faithfulness in rearing a holy seed."[15]

What then do we teach them? First, teach them about their baptism and what God signifies and seals in baptism. Show them the privilege it is to be in the covenant of grace and the wonderful promises God makes to them. Explain that they are members of the Church and the benefits that belong to them. Teach them as well, the obligations God places on

---

[14] Smith, *Westminster Message.*
[15] Thornwell, *Collected Writings,* 4:340.

them to receive Christ in the covenant and to obey God's law. Teach them about the great benefits of the covenant: regeneration, justification, adoption, sanctification, perseverance, assurance, and glorification. Remind them of God's sovereign election and that they may not presume on their covenantal membership for automatic salvation. In connection with the covenant, teach them their "baptismal identity"—because they have been baptized, God has marked them as His own; they have become "engaged" or solemnly bound to Him. We expect them to believe the Scriptural truths that we teach them. We encourage them to affirm the gospel and to walk worthy of their privileges. Moreover, we teach them to "improve" their baptism, as our forefathers in the Faith used to say. The Larger Catechism (Q. 167) teaches:

> The needful but much neglected duty of improving our Baptism, is to be performed by us all our life long, especially in time of temptation, and when we are present at the administration of it to others; by serious and thankful consideration of the nature of it, and of the ends for which Christ instituted it, the privileges and benefits conferred and sealed thereby, and our solemn vow made therein; by being humbled for our sinful defilement, our falling short of and walking contrary to, the grace of baptism, and our engagements; by growing up to assurance of pardon of sin, and of all the other blessings sealed to us in that sacrament; by drawing strength from the death and resurrection of Christ, into whom we are baptized for the mortifying of sin, and the quickening of grace; and by endeavoring to live by faith, to have our conversation in holiness and righteousness, as those that have therein given up their names to Christ; and to walk in brotherly love, as being baptized by the same Spirit into one body.

Second, teach them about God.[16] Show them His greatness and beauty as He reveals His character in His person, names, titles, attributes, and works. Explain to them that they are to love God and serve Him.

Third, teach them about their sinful natures. Explain original sin, total depravity, and the miseries resulting from sin in this life and the life to come. Teach them about the corruption of their hearts, and that outward conformity to the covenant is not sufficient.

Fourth, teach them the law of God as summarized in the Ten Commandments and applied in the Old and New Testaments. Show them they are to love God's law and express their gratitude to Him by obedience.

---

[16] I have adapted these precepts from Joel Beeke, *Bringing the Gospel to Covenant Children,* 13-21.

Show them their sin in breaking the law and the necessity of repentance when they disobey.

Fifth, teach the necessity of regeneration. They must be born again. Help them to understand that because mere outward conformity to God's law is not sufficient, they must love and obey from the heart, which they cannot do unless God has given them a new heart. Show the marks of a new heart: love for God, love for his work, love for his people, love for righteousness, and hatred of sin. If they develop sinful patterns of behavior, exhort them that they are not manifesting evidence of a new heart. Remember you are not looking for an adult's marks of grace, but marks commensurate with their age.

Sixth, teach them about the person and work of the Lord Jesus Christ as savior of his people. Explain his three-fold office and all He has done for them. Teach them their need of faith in Him. Constantly hold Christ before them, reminding them that they must be resting in Jesus Christ alone for their salvation. Remember you are not looking for a "decision." Many of our children will from their earliest days trust in Christ. Others, though they may have confessed Christ early on as savior, will realize at some point that they have not yet been converted. Exhort them to call on God to save them for Christ's sake, and pray with them to that same end.

Seventh, teach them about the nature and necessity of sanctification. They must daily be dying to sin and growing into conformity to the Lord Jesus Christ. Beeke lists some inducements to holiness to use with children:[17]

- God calls us to holiness for our good and His glory (1 Thess. 4:7).

- Holiness makes us resemble Christ and preserves integrity (Phil. 2:5-13)

- Holiness gives evidence of justification and election, and fosters assurance (1 Cor. 6:11; 2 Thess. 2:13; 1 John 2:3)

- Holiness is essential for effective service to God (2 Tim. 2:21)

- Holiness fits us for heaven (Heb. 12:14; Rev. 21:27)

---

[17] Ibid., 20,21.

Eighth, teach them about the beauty and joy of heaven. "Focus on the blessedness of being with God, the holy angels, and all the redeemed, and of the believer finally becoming what he has desired to be ever since his regeneration. . . Explain from Hebrews 12:1-2 how Jesus was motivated to endure His sufferings by anticipating the joy of His reward. Let your children see that you long for the day when Jesus Christ returns to establish a new heaven and a new earth (2 Pet. 3:13-14)."[18]

By this point, we have seen that Rebecca has great advantages over Paul. Not recognizing the benefits that belong to Paul in the covenant, his parents will treat him as if he is unconverted until he makes a decision. Because he is unbaptized, or is being brought up as if her were not baptized, he will have no awareness of God's great covenant mercy and benefits.

Therefore, recognizing God's promises and the great benefits our children have in the covenant, let us prayerfully use the means that God has appointed for their nurture. If we are faithful, I believe we will see the great majority of our children growing up and affirming their faith in Christ through lives of faithfulness to their merciful Savior.

---

[18] Ibid., 21.

Chapter 6

Covenant Confusion

Richard D. Phillips

Thus says the Lord, "Stand by the crossroads, and look, and ask for the ancient paths, where the good way is; and walk in it, and find rest for your souls. *Jeremiah 6:16*

There is a fine line between the use and the overuse of a word. The same is true with public figures. When someone is getting exposure, we are pleased for them. But when they are over-exposed we are embarrassed for them. In my view, the word *covenant* has crossed that line in Christian circles. As such, one often hears it applied in dubious ways. We have gone from covenant people and covenant children to covenant schools and covenant businesses. I recently was given a bag of covenant coffee beans, which, by the way, I received as an effectual means of grace. Today, if you want to express a zeal to be distinctively Christian, and especially if you are Reformed-leaning, you are very likely to apply the word *covenant* to your activity or group or product. In the process, the word has begun to lose definition and become little more than a vague nimbus.

I believe, however, that we are faced today with more than the over-exposure of the word and idea of covenant. Perhaps aided by its ill-defined usage, new definitions are being given to covenant, and with the new definitions comes a new theology. There is an increasing confusion over what covenants are and how covenants shape our relationship with God. I believe the result is the propagation of a new and different gospel from the one taught in the great Reformed confessions and in the Bible.

In this paper, I intend to present the main points that I believe are shaping this new covenant approach to salvation. The Bible says that we are to "stand at the crossroads" and select the good way, the way that leads to life. I believe that at certain key crossroads, many figures within the Reformed movement are taking wrong turns, and they are leading growing numbers of people down false paths and into a false assurance of salvation. The thing to do, then, is to retrace our steps, go back to the crossroads, biblically assess our choices, and take the good road that leads to life.

COVENANT RECAST BY TRINITY?

First, we need to consider a proposal that is relatively recent, but which rapidly has come to play a vital role in the reworking of covenant theology. Its main exponent is Ralph Smith, in two books published by Canon Press, *Paradox and Truth: Rethinking Van Til on the Trinity* (2002), and *Eternal Covenant: How the Trinity Reshapes Covenant Theology* (2003). In the first of these, Smith posits covenant as the basis of unity among the three eternal and divine Persons of the Godhead. He writes, "The persons of the Trinity are eternally united in a covenantal bond of love."[1] He cites James Jordan as describing the covenant as "a personal-structural bond which joins the three persons of God in a community of life, and in which man was created to participate."[2]

The purpose of the second book is to defend this assertion and work out some of its implications. Smith begins with a tour of Reformed Theology's view of what is generally called the covenant of redemption, that is, the eternal pact among the members of the Trinity to accomplish the work needed for the redemption of God's elect. Smith provides a fairly conventional history in support of this teaching, culminating with the observation that Reformed Theology has accepted the biblical evidence in support of this eternal covenant and, moreover, has consistently considered this covenant, as all covenants, as an agreement or pact.

---

[1] Ralph Smith, *Paradox and Truth* (Moscow, ID: Canon Press, 2002), 73.

[2] James B. Jordan, *The Law of the Covenant* (Tyler, TX: Institute for Christian Economics, 1984), 5.

Smith thus concludes, "Perhaps without exception they [Reformed theologians] have viewed the Trinitarian covenant as a mere agreement entered into in order to respond to the situation of sin."

The exception to this is Abraham Kuyper, who insinuates that the economic covenant relations of the Trinity for redemption must signal an ontological covenant relationship between the divine persons. Smith argues that this is indeed the case, that on an ontological level, the relationship within the Trinity is covenant. Thus covenant is viewed not as an agreement, as is by Smith's own reckoning the overwhelming consensus of the Reformed tradition, but as a "form of life," or "a community of life." According to Smith, Trinity must therefore serve as the paradigmatic covenant in the place of God's covenant with Adam, which classically has been understood as providing the paradigm for all other covenants.

Smith gives three arguments in support of this assertion, only one of which is at all to the point.[3] This is the rule provided by theologian Karl Rahner, that "the economic Trinity reveals the ontological Trinity."[4] Smith points out that from the time of Adam onward, God dealt with mankind exclusively in terms of covenant. Therefore, he argues, "If history reveals truth about who God is in Himself, then it reveals that the covenant is something essential to the eternal reality of God. It is precisely this conclusion that is required by the overwhelming predominance of covenant as the one and only manner of God relating to man and the creation."[5] He then states that this puts the burden of proof on his opponents. Unless we can offer some better explanation for the fact that God relates with his creatures via covenant, we must conclude that covenant is something ontologically inherent to the Trinity.

A couple of observations are worth making at this point. The first is that Smith intends a wholesale recasting of covenant theology, not on the basis of any clear teaching of Scripture, nor on the basis of good and necessary consequences from Scripture, but on the basis of an argument from silence involving abstract reflections on the doctrine of the Trinity. He thus concludes forty-seven pages of argument by doing nothing more than asserting his original premise, that covenant is the basis of the onto-

---

[3] His second two arguments consist of defending the traditional covenant of redemption and then asserting that this economic covenant demands an ontological covenant, which amounts to a repetition of the first argument.

[4] Ibid , 33.

[5] Ibid., 37.

logical union within the Trinity, then demanding that unless we can prove it wrong we must accept this assertion, for which even Smith has provided no demonstration.

Second, Smith's analogical reasoning is without control. If God does something in history, he says, history must reveal something about the essence of God. So far, so good. But in this case he argues that the structure of God's relations with his creation in history must be assumed as the basis for the ontological inner-Trinitarian relations, unless proved otherwise. The problem with this is that the two situations in view are not comparable. The differences between the inner-Trinitarian relations and the relation between God and the creation must be accounted for before Smith can simply demand that a direct analogy be assumed.

With this in mind, I would like to suggest that there are in fact better explanations for the preponderance of covenant in history than that the Trinity must involve an essential covenant relationship. The first is that the Creator-creature relationship necessarily involves lordship, and lordship expresses itself through covenant, a point Smith himself labors to make. But this situation does not pertain ontologically to the Trinity. Covenant is the out flowing of God's lordship as manifested in commands, sanctions, and promises of blessing. But as the Council of Nicea insisted so long ago, there is no ontological subordination within the Godhead, hence no lordship, and hence no covenant, which is, by Smith's own reckoning, a function of lordship.[6]

Furthermore, the covenants we see in the Bible do inform us about the ontological Trinity, as Rahner demands. What they reveal are the attributes of God that dictate how these covenants work. God is just, and so his covenants have conditions and sanctions. God is good, so he offers blessings through covenant with his creatures. God is true, as his faithfulness to his covenants demonstrates. Moreover, the biblical evidence regarding the fellowship between the persons of the Trinity shows forth qualities such as love, truth, and honor. That these same attributes find expression in God's historic covenants with man shows how the historic covenants reveal truth about the ontological character of the Triune God. But this revelation of attributes does not give us warrant to read back covenant into the Trinity itself.[7]

---

[6] See Smith's argument about creation, lordship, and covenant, in *Eternal Covenant*, 33-37.

[7] J.I. Packer's treatment of this is notable in that he makes much of the correspondence between the nature of inner-Trinitarian fellowship and God's covenant dealings

Here, then, are two explanations to satisfy Smith's demand that the history of covenants reveal truth about the being of God: the Creator-creation relationship which prompts covenant and that attributes of God which find their expression in the character of the covenants God has made. These adequately explain the preponderance of covenant in history, without recourse to covenantal union in that one community that does not involve ontological lordship, namely, the Trinity.

Apart from its intended recasting of covenant theology, Smith's teaching does grave damage to the doctrine of the Trinity. Smith, following James Jordan, argues that the form of unity within the Trinity is covenant. This is a serious departure from orthodox Trinitarian theology, falling into a tacit tri-theism. Instead of the classic view that the Trinity is three persons united in one being, this view argues that the Trinity is three divine persons united by a social bond. Smith presents his final conclusion in strikingly tri-theistic terms: "God is three persons united in covenantal love."[8]

As Smith proceeds from this thesis, he seems to be aware of the tri-theistic leanings of his argument. Thus he tries to temper it by advancing perichoresis, that is, mutual indwelling, as the basis of Trinitarian union – in which case there is no need for covenant as the basis of union. Later still, he tries to distinguish covenantal union from ontological union, noting vaguely that "in God covenant and ontology intersect or share common ground."[9] But the damage is done: if the three divine persons of the Trinity have an ontological union of essence – one based on a shared being and mutual indwelling – then it is hard to see how one being is joined together by covenant, unless we totally redefine the meaning of the word *covenant*, which is the whole point of Smith's exercise.

The only way for Smith to sustain any idea of an inner-Trinitarian covenant is simply to assume a different definition for covenant. Indeed,

---

with mankind, while explicitly insisting that we must not go beyond this observation in postulating the nature of the inner-Trinitarian relationship. See J.I. Packer, "Introduction: On Covenant Theology" in Herman Witsius, *The Economy of the Covenants Between God and Man* (Kingsburg, CA: den Dulk Christian Foundation, 1990).

[8] Ibid., 47.

[9] Ibid., 56. Smith perhaps forgets that his whole thesis rests upon the argument that the economic covenants of history reveal an ontological Trinitarian covenant via Rahner's rule. That argument requires covenant to operate at the level of ontology. The indication that Smith himself cannot stomach the implications of this formula is fatal to his whole thesis.

here is the function of Smith's argument, to redefine covenant so that it no longer is understood to mean a pact or agreement but simply as a form of relationship and life. Covenant is no longer the *way* God brings us into a saving relationship, but it is *that to which* God saves us, defined vaguely as a union in love.

In his classic study of covenant theology published in 1677, Herman Witsius wrote, "A covenant of God with man, is an agreement between God and man, about the way of obtaining consummate happiness."[10] This definition has stood through the centuries on the basis of the Bible's testimony. J. I. Packer emphasizes that covenants provide "a basis for a life with God of friendship, peace, and communicated love."[11] Covenant is the *means* by which two parties are bound in relationship; it is a *basis* for relationship and not the relationship itself. Covenants provide the terms of agreement that structure a relationship, setting forth the means of entry, the obligations, and the privileges that the relationship will entail, along with the penalties for breaking the stipulated conditions. But now, based on abstract speculation, we are expected to understand covenant to be simply God's gift of love in the form of relationship.[12]

Following this revisionist approach in which the biblical structures of covenant are removed, Smith proceeds throughout *Eternal Covenant* to apply covenant to practically everything with little definition. Covenant is relationship, and so it becomes hard to know what it is about a relationship that makes it a covenant, except that it becomes whatever Smith wants to make of it at any given time. As such, covenant serves as an ideal vehicle for Smith and his cohorts' purpose, which, it becomes clear, is to define salvation in such a way as to remove the forensic theory of justification as classically understood in Reformed thought.

This redefinition of covenant as relationship is especially important

---

[10] Herman Witsius, *The Economy of the Covenants between God and Man* (Kingsburg, CA: den Dulk Christian Foundation, 1990), I.1.9.

[11] J.I. Packer, "Introduction: On Covenant Theology" in Herman Witsius, *The Economy of the Covenants between God and Man.*

[12] Smith is not the first to argue against covenant as a pact or agreement. This is a standard of Barthian theology, as exemplified in James B. Torrance, "Covenant or Contract? A Study of the Theological Background for Worship in Seventeenth-Century Scotland," *Scottish Journal of Theology* 23 (1970): 51-76. Torrance wrote, "The God and Father of our Lord Jesus Christ is a Covenant-God and not a contract-God," (66).

to the Auburn Avenue theology.[13] Steve Schlissel asserts, "A covenant
is a relationship."[14] Douglas Wilson makes the same assertion, writing
in the title article of *Credenda/Agenda*, Vol. 15, Issue 1, "A covenant is
a relationship between two parties... a relation between persons." In the
place of what is evidenced in every single covenant depicted in the Bible, namely, a pact or agreement for the attainment of blessing, we are to
accept Smith's speculations on the Trinity in order to redefine covenant
as a simple gift of love.[15]

This amounts to a collapsing of the structure of covenants as long
identified in God's covenants with man, starting with Adam and pro-
ceeding throughout the biblical record. Instead of the classically identified elements of a covenant – the parties involved, the condition, the
promised blessing, and the threatened sanction – all that now is involved
is a mutual commitment to relationship. As a result, everything in salvation becomes synonymous with everything else. What is election?
Smith says it is "the gift of covenant." Similarly, God's commands are
the same as God's covenant. Smith says, "Keeping the commands is
keeping the covenant." Likewise, love equals obedience equals covenant
equals election. The same is true of law and of righteousness. They are
covenant, which is love, which is election, which is holiness.[16]

I do not want unfairly to overstate this position, for Smith and others
try to assert some sense of distinct meaning for these terms. But the in-
ter-relatedness is so overly stressed that the biblical structure provided
by covenant is demolished. In this new paradigm, God gives the covenant, and with covenant comes everything else. The problem is that with
no differentiation in the function of things like faith and works, the biblical structure of salvation is up for grabs. What this view of covenant
gives in its purported emphasis on grace (since covenant is a mere gift of
relationship), it takes away in its teaching that we retain those blessings
only by covenant-keeping works, as we shall see.

KEY FEATURES OF THE NEW APPROACH TO COVENANT

This new definition of covenant, grounded in unsound Trinitarian specu-

---

[13] See my critique of this, "Covenant and Salvation," in *The Auburn Avenue Theology, Pros and Cons. Debating the Federal Vision*, ed. E. Calvin Beisner (Ft. Lauderdale:
Knox Theological Seminary, 2004).
[14] Steve M. Schlissel, *What Does God Require?*, 1.
[15] Smith, *Eternal Covenant*, 49-53.
[16] Ibid., 50.

lation, serves to advance three features notable in the current debate. The first is the supplanting of traditional soteriology with a re-charged ecclesiology. Indeed, this seems to be one of the main motives for this new theology of covenant. The argument goes like this (here I am following Peter Leithart): none of us exists on our own, so being is being-in-relationship; I only am what I am with respect to the community in which I relate to others. For instance, I am named Phillips not because of something essential about me, but because of my relationship with other people named Phillips. Thus what makes me a Christian is being in the church. Leithart writes, "Entry into the church is always a soteriological fact for the person who enters... If the church is the 'house of God' (WCF 25.2), then membership in the church makes the person a member of that household."[17] Note the word *makes*. Membership in the church is not correlative with becoming a child of God; it *makes* a person a child of God.

This is what I mean by the supplanting of soteriology with ecclesiology. Instead of realizing that our relationship with God is primary, so that salvation is primarily a spiritual reality in which our relationship one with another in the church is derivative from our relationship with God, this revamped covenant theology puts it precisely backward. Under this view, our relationship with the church is primary, so that salvation is primarily a social and cultural reality, and our relationship with God is derivative from our relationship in the church.

A second and related feature of this approach is its emphasis on the external and the objective over the internal and subjective. This is touted as its main attraction. Douglas Wilson boasts of "recovering the objectivity of the covenant," the sub-title of his book *Reformed Is Not Enough*. This means I can know objectively I am right with God because I am in the church. He exults, "Covenants of God have a physical aspect, like an oak tree."[18] Presumably, the point is that we can physically climb into it.

This is supposed to deliver us from the so-called plague of "morbid introspection" – that is, from ascertaining the presence of a real and per-

---

[17] Peter J. Leithart, "Trinitarian Anthropology: Toward a Trinitarian Re-casting of Reformed Theology" in *The Auburn Avenue Theology, Pros and Cons: Debating the Federal Vision*, ed. E. Calvin Beisner (Ft. Lauderdale: Knox Theological Seminary, 2004), 69-70.

[18] Douglas Wilson, *Reformed Is Not Enough· Recovering the Objectivity of the Covenant* (Moscow, ID. Canon Press, 2003), 64.

sonal faith that brings me into relationship with God through Jesus Christ. I am freed from all this simply by noting that I am physically in the church and therefore in covenant with God. This emphasis would not be so dangerous if its proponents, such as the Auburn Avenue theologians, allowed for the distinction between the visible and the invisible church that is so essential to the system of doctrine taught in the Westminster Standards. But since they insist that there is no other church than the one that is visible and physical, their emphasis on ecclesiology over soteriology and the external over the internal is all the more alarming.

Both of these first two features come together in the great importance assigned to baptism, which in this system exerts a controlling influence over the assurance of salvation. Since they believe that we enter into a saving relationship with God through entry into the church (rather than vice versa), then since baptism is the rite of entry into the church it is also the route of entry into all of salvation's blessings. Instead of serving as a visible sign and seal of the covenant promise, baptism becomes the way the promise is made real to the recipient. As an example, Rich Lusk writes, "Baptism is the means through which the Spirit unites us to Christ. No other means is said to have this function; it is the peculiar grace attached to baptism... Since baptism is the instrumental means of union with Christ, it is sometimes said to be the instrument of forgiveness and regeneration (Acts 2:38, 22:16; Tit. 3:5)... In other words, baptism is simply the gospel in aqueous form."[19]

The problem with this is that salvation comes by grace alone through faith alone (Eph. 2:8-9) and, according to the Westminster Confession, baptismal grace does not create faith, but strengthens existing faith (see WCF XIV.1). That is true even for infants who come to faith sometime after their baptisms. "The grace of faith," says the Confession, "is ordinarily wrought by the ministry of the Word, by which also, and by the administration of the sacraments, and prayer, it is increased and strengthened." Therefore, we must distinguish between the respective ministries of the Word and of the sacraments: the former both creates and strengthens saving faith, whereas the latter does not create saving faith but does strengthen it. The point is that salvation's blessings come

---

[19] Rich Lusk, "Some Thoughts on the Means of Grace: A Few Proposals" *Theologia*, 2003, accessed at: http://www.Hornes.org/theologia/content/rich_lusk/some_thoughts-_on_the_means_of_grace.httm.

via faith, which faith is wrought by the Holy Spirit through the ministry of the Word. Baptism does not grant those blessings but confirms them, just as it does not create but strengthens faith.

What this means is that we should not look to the rite of baptism as the ground of our assurance, for the simple reasons that we may be baptized without believing, and that if we believe it is because of God's Word and not because of baptism. Here, too, we have a confusion of the sign for the thing signified. Baptism is a sign of Christ's cleansing blood and the Spirit's cleansing renewal. We should look to the reality – to the thing signified – and not to the sign for our assurance. This is the error against which the New Testament constantly warns us – presuming salvation because of external association with the gospel. Michael Horton observes, "This is what Paul and the writer to the Hebrews especially labor to make plain to Jewish Christians: You who have received the sign, beware lest you fall short of trusting in Christ and all his benefits (the thing signified)."[20] Just as Paul and the Book of Hebrews warn their Jewish readers against presuming salvation simply because they possessed circumcision (see Romans 9:6-8 and Hebrews 4:1-2), the last thing we need to tell Christian children is to rest assured on their possession of baptism, apart from a credible profession of faith in God's Word.

We may ask, "Why this fixation on baptism?" The answer we are given is that we need to ground our assurance of salvation on something objective and concrete rather than in "morbid introspection" of our inner spiritual state. Steve Wilkins, who, like his associate Rich Lusk, absolutely associates the rite of baptism with saving union with Christ, argues that this "enables us to assure Christians of their acceptance with God without needlessly undermining their confidence in God's promises by forcing them to ask questions of themselves they cannot answer with certainty."[21] He makes clear in a footnote that these needless inquiries have to do with the credibility of their profession of faith.

Another proponent argues that baptism is necessary to rescue us from "the quicksand of subjectivity: experiences of conversion, feelings of spirituality, good works, holy living, an internal sense of forgiveness, signs and traces of some immediate work of the Spirit in our souls, and

---

[20] Michael Horton, *A Better Way. Rediscovering the Drama of God-Centered Worship* (Grand Rapids: Baker, 2002), 105.

[21] Steve Wilkins, "Covenant, Baptism, and Salvation," in *The Auburn Avenue Theology, Pros and Cons: Debating the Federal Vision*, 268.

so on."[22] The problem is that it is to these very things, rightly defined, that the Bible tells us to look for our assurance.[23]

Instead of the biblically-defined marks of true and saving faith, followers of the Auburn Avenue theology are told to rely upon the fact that they were baptized, which allows them to presume their salvation until such time as they completely apostatize. But what this propounds is not an objective covenant but an externalism and formalism in religion in the place of the personal, inner spirituality of faith.

I have no doubt that this approach resonates with many people today who crave a community with substance, who want to see and touch and smell their Christianity. These are worthy ends, but this false covenant theology is the wrong means. I say this because the Bible actively discourages such an approach to one's relationship with God. Jeremiah, who spoke eloquently about taking the right turn at the crossroads, preached in the very next chapter his most potent sermon on just this theme. Jeremiah stood before not just any church, but before Solomon's temple in Jerusalem. He urgently warned them against relying on any external affiliation with even that great temple apart from true and saving faith. He cried, "Do not trust in these deceptive words: 'This is the temple of the Lord, the temple of the Lord, the temple of the Lord'" (Jer. 7:4).

God never tells us to believe that we are right with him simply because we are in the church. The community of the church is not the covenant; it is a product of the covenant. The covenant is not something we can climb into by walking up a certain set of stairs. Rather, it is the way of salvation by which God invites us into relationship with himself through Jesus Christ and only in consequence into relationship with one another.

The third feature of this new covenant theology is its redefinition of faith in such a way that faith and works are inclusive one of another. One of their mottos is that faith and obedience are the same thing. In this formula, faith is not how we enter into the covenant, but the way we

---

[22] S. Joel Garver, *Sacraments and the Solas,* at: http://www.lasalle.edu/garver/solas.htm. Accessed 2/18/04.

[23] See, for instance, 2 Peter 5:11, which says that we should "make [our] calling and election sure" by cultivating the qualities of "virtue, knowledge, self-control, steadfastness, godliness, brotherly affection, and love"; 1 John, which grounds assurance of salvation in the three tests of doctrine, holiness, and love; and Jesus' teaching that "a tree is known by its fruit" (Mt. 7:16-2), just to cite a few prominent examples.

stay in the covenant; faith means not resting on and receiving Christ's work for us, but faithfully keeping covenant with God by our own works. A consideration of this third feature will form the concluding section of this chapter.

Before moving on, let us observe again the foundation on which these revisions rest; namely, the speculative theory that covenant is defined by the inner relationship of the Trinity. This reformulation comes not from the direct teaching of Scripture, nor from good and necessary consequences, but from an argument from silence emanating from the greatest mystery of all, the relationship of Persons of the Trinity. On this unsound foundation we are called to recast covenant theology and redefine practically every soteriological term. To what end are we to do this? To assert a reliance on external rites of entry into God's blessing, and covenant-keeping works as the mode of maintaining eternal life. This is, for all the soaring rhetoric of its champions, a high order of covenant confusion indeed.

THE COVENANT OF WORKS

Along this path of exalting ecclesiology over soteriology, ritual over reality, and covenant-keeping works over covenant-receiving faith, the authors of covenant confusion have one theological fortress they must overthrow. This is the classic Reformed understanding of God's dealings with Adam as the covenant of works. Here is one point of uniformity among all those seeking to recast covenant theology and with it our doctrines of salvation: for their new ideas to be ushered in, the covenant of works must be ushered out. There is absolutely no room for it in their mono-covenantal scheme in which the law and gospel, along with faith and works, are no longer held in contrast but are meshed together in continuum. In the place of the classic view of redemptive history as overseen by two covenants in the history of God's dealing with man – the covenant of works and the covenant of grace – the two covenants to which Paul makes explicit reference in Galatians 4:24-26, the covenant of works as proclaimed from Mt. Sinai and the covenant of grace from the spiritual Mt. Zion – they posit a monolithic covenant by the keeping of which God's people may be saved. According to this view, we may only be justified in the same manner offered to our first parent Adam before sin entered into the world, and in the same manner by which Jesus himself was acclaimed righteous before God. Under this scheme, our righteousness comes not by receiving Christ's righteousness, but by following his example as empowered by his grace.

An example of this approach to justification comes from N.T. Wright in his commentary on Romans 2:13, which presents the law principle, "the doers of the law will be justified." Wright sees in this not a contrast with the gospel, as Paul so vehemently insists throughout that epistle when it comes to justification (see Romans 3:10, which tells us that no one qualifies by this standard, and Romans 3:20-28, especially verse 28, which pointedly makes the very contrast that Wright denies, "For we hold that one is justified by faith apart from works of the law"). Directly contrary to Paul, Wright sees a continuity in which law and gospel are all wrapped into one. He writes, speaking not merely of the New Covenant or the Old, but of all covenants in general, "Justification, at the last, will be on the basis of performance."[24] This aligns with the teaching of Norman Shepherd in *The Call of Grace*, which sees our justification taking place in a manner parallel to Christ's own. Shepherd writes, "Just as Jesus was faithful in order to *guarantee* the blessing, so his followers must be faithful in order to *inherit* the blessing."[25] It is difficult to avoid the inference that we are justified by being like Jesus, by our faithfulness which is *just as* Jesus' faithfulness, instead of, as Paul puts it in Romans 5:19, being made righteous by the one man's obedience, namely, Christ, who lived and died not merely as our example but first as our federal head and our substitute. Both Wright's and Shepherd's views of justification require a mono-covenantal view of redemptive history and permit no place for the biblical covenant of works.

---

[24] N.T. Wright, *The Letter to the Romans* in *The New Interpreter's Bible,* 12 vols. (Nashville: Abingdon, 2002), 10:440. A key to understanding Wright's view of justification is to realize that he down-plays the significance of "present justification" in favor of the final judgment of God at the end of history. For Wright, present justification is merely a proleptic statement that has no ultimate significance in itself apart from the future works that it assumes. We are justified by faith in the present, but justification "occurs in the present *as an anticipation of that future verdict, which is according to works*" (author's italics). In his 2003 Rutherford House lecture titled *New Perspectives on Paul*, from which the prior quote is taken (http://home.hiwaay.net/~kbush/Wright_New_Perspectives.pdf), Wright frankly said, "God's final judgment will be in accordance with the entirety of a life led – in accordance, in other words, with works." His primary support for this is Romans 2:1-16, employing the New Perspective understanding that faith and works operate in continuum in justification rather than in contrast, while present justification and final vindication work in contrast rather than in continuum. In both cases, he is at odds with the classic teaching of Reformed covenant theology, and more seriously, the Bible.

[25] Norman Shepherd, *The Call of Grace* (Phillipsburg, NJ: P&R, 2000), 19.

It is often objected that the bi-covenantal structure of the covenant of works/covenant of grace scheme should not be made an ultimate litmus test of evangelical orthodoxy. It is pointed out that many people, most notably the Lutherans, who affirm justification by faith alone, say nothing of the covenant of works. Conceding that point may help us to avoid an excessive stress on the covenant of works, but it is hardly germane to the argument at hand within the Reformed community. It is one thing not to have worked out any explicit covenant theology, while holding law and gospel in proper biblical contrast. But it is quite another to construct a divergent form of covenant theology precisely in order to merge faith and works, law and gospel. In this case, which is the situation before us, there is indeed a direct connection between our attitude toward the covenant of works and our commitment to the evangelical gospel, in which justification is, as Paul declares in Ephesians 2:8-9, "through faith... not as a result of works."

What is the covenant of works? The Westminster Confession of Faith says, reflecting on Genesis 2:16-17, "The first covenant made with man was a covenant of works, wherein life was promised to Adam; and in him to his posterity, upon condition of perfect and personal obedience" (VII.2). According to classic covenant theology, and following the clear teaching of Scripture, Adam's failure under this covenant brought all of mankind under the curse of death (see Genesis 2:17 and Romans 5:12-14). In response, "The Lord was pleased to make a second, commonly called the covenant of grace; wherein He freely offereth unto sinners life and salvation by Jesus Christ; requiring of them faith in Him, that they may be saved" (WCF VII.3). Under this bi-covenantal scheme that is foundational to the whole system of doctrine taught in the Westminster Standards, after Adam failed to fulfill the covenant of works, God sent his Son to fulfill it in our place, offering Christ's merit to us in the covenant of grace, which we receive by faith alone.

Numerous objections are made to this teaching, surprisingly from many who vow to uphold the Westminster Confession, to which clear biblical answers may be and have been presented. But the most important objection, in my view, follows from a hotly contested word I used above, that is, *merit*. Some critics consider it unseemly that man could ever stand before God on the basis of earned merit. This objection takes many forms. First is the rejection of merit as the basis for divine-human relationships on the grounds that God is Father, and fathers receive their children on the basis of fatherly love rather than on earned merit. Second, it is said that man cannot add to God's glory, nor can a creature ever put God in his debt. Third, the idea of earned merit is rejected for depicting the divine-human relationship as that between an employer and an employee.[26]

Fourth, it is objected that God's dealing with Adam was, in fact, gracious. This is so because God was not obligated to offer any covenant to man, and especially because the promised reward offered to Adam – eternal life – was far out of proportion to the value of his obedience, which Adam already owed to God apart from reward. This complaint was made famous by John Murray and is advanced today by many. Murray also complains that the word *covenant* is not used in the Bible for God's dealings with Adam.[27]

Last are objections leveled by Norman Shepherd, in addition to the above objections. He complains that the covenant of works stands in direct opposition to the idea of salvation by grace alone. That God accepts us by the grace/faith principle rules out the merit/works principle. Furthermore, he protests that until we reject the idea of earned merit, "we feel threatened by passages of Scripture that speak of repentance and obedience as conditions for entering eternal life," and are forced to use "exegetical and dogmatic devices of dubious validity" to avoid legalism.[28]

The name most prominently associated with the defense of the covenant of works today is Meredith G. Kline. In his article, *Covenant Theology Under Attack,* Kline dismantles these objections to the covenant of works. First, he challenges the authority of an *a priori* objection against merit, and especially the idea that the rewarding of obedience is alien to the father-child relationship. To the idea that God's glory cannot be increased by our actions and thus no debt can be imposed on God, Kline responds that man was created to reflect God's glory, that God is pleased by this, and that his pleasure expresses itself in blessing. All of this fits safely under the rubric of reward and merit. Against the complaint that earned merit puts man in relation to God as an employee is to his employer, Kline replies that this is not necessarily the case. Fathers grant

---

[26] These arguments are made in Daniel P. Fuller, *Gospel and Law: Contrast or Continuum· The Hermeneutics of Dispensationalism and Covenant Theology* (Grand Rapids: Eerdmans, 1980), 18-64.

[27] John Murray, "The Adamic Administration," in *Collected Writings of John Murray,* 4 vols. (Edinburgh: Banner of Truth, 1977), 2:47-59.

[28] Shepherd, *The Call of Grace,* 61-62.

rewards to children, just as kings do to subjects. And, by the way, our Lord Jesus describes our relationship to God in terms of servants who receive rewards from their master.

Most credible of all the objections to the covenant of works is the one that argues that God's pre-fall dealings with Adam entailed a good deal of grace. That this was raised by a stalwart of Reformed theology, John Murray, has made this point all the more deserving of consideration. Murray writes, "The term [covenant of works] is not felicitous, for the reason that the elements of grace entering into the administration are not properly provided for by the term 'works'."[29] The question must be asked, however, whether grace is the proper term for God's favor shown to Adam in the Garden. Cornelius P. Venema argues for a distinction between God's kindness to Adam prior to his sin and the grace shown to him after the Fall. He writes, "There is a real difference between *undeserved favor* shown a sinless, obedient creature, and the *undeserved grace* granted the disobedient covenant breaker."[30]

Meredith Kline's response to Professor Murray's point is particularly significant, and our reception of it is likely determinative in our acceptance of the covenant of works. Kline writes,

> Properly defined, grace is not merely the bestowal of unmerited blessings but God's blessing of man in spite of his *demerits*, in spite of his forfeiture of divine blessings. Clearly, we ought not apply this term *grace* to the pre-Fall situation, for neither the bestowal of blessings on Adam in the very process of creation nor the proposal to grant him additional blessings contemplated him as in a guilty state of demerit... Only by this double-talk of using the term *grace* (obviously in a different sense) for the pre-Fall covenant can they becloud the big, plain contrast that actually exists between the two covenants [covenant of works and covenant of grace].[31]

Furthermore, Kline shows that most objectors to the idea of merit are responding to medieval Roman Catholic notions rather than biblical ones. This is confirmed in the case of Norman Shepherd.[32]   Medieval Rome

---

[29] Murray, "The Adamic Administration," 2:49.

[30] Cornelius P. Venema, "Recent Criticisms of the 'Covenant of Works,'" *Mid-America Journal of Theology* 14 (2003), 194.

[31] Meredith G. Kline, "Covenant Theology under Attack," *New Horizons*, Feb. 1994.   Published   without   abridgement   at   http://upper-register.com/ct_gospel/ct_under_attack.html, 2.

[32] See Shepherd, *The Call of Grace*, 59-61.

taught that merit must normally be based on the intrinsic value of an act (condign merit, associated with Thomas Aquinas), though God has assigned to certain acts a merit they do not otherwise possess, but which God has sovereignly and graciously decided to give them (congruent merit, associated with Duns Scotus). Condign merit refers to God's strict justice towards those already in a state of grace (which is impossible for sinners whose works are never perfect), while congruent merit approaches God through works made meritorious by God's grace.

Kline shows that merit in the covenant of works was based on neither of these suppositions: not on the supposed intrinsic value of obedience, nor by some sacramental formula, but on the basis of God's covenant stipulation. It was merit under the stipulations of the covenant of works. We operate this way all the time. My seven year old daughter has no instrinsic right to come to me demanding an allowance. But if I freely stipulate that she will receive an allowance on the condition of cleaning her room to a certain standard, no one raises abstract objections. Once it has been established that I have the right to impose such a covenant on my daughter and that I have made the stipulation, then her fulfillment of it merits the promised reward. Nor is there an objection based on this appeal to my sense of justice; the covenant is necessarily a revelation of my standards and expectations and generosity. Some may think I am paying her too much; others may thing I am paying her too little. None of that matters once the covenant of works has been made: her fulfillment merits the promised reward. In God's case, the stipulation of his covenant with Adam was determined by and was a revelation of the perfections of all his attributes, and we should all be cautioned against standing in judgment over them. Cornelius Venema summarizes the main point: "The fact is that God has, by entering into covenant with man, *bound himself by the promises and as well the demands/obligations of that covenant...* In the covenant itself, God bound himself to grant *as in some sense a reward well-deserved,* the fullness of covenant fellowship into which Adam was called."[33]

As for Shepherd's complaint that merit makes the idea of grace impossible, the answer is found in the covenant of grace, which precisely offers us the meritorious obedience of Jesus Christ, the second Adam, who fulfilled the covenant of works in Adam's and our place and imputes his righteousness to us by grace and through faith (see Romans

---

[33] Venema, "Recent Criticisms of the 'Covenant of Works,'"195. Author's italics.

5:12-21). Without the covenant of works, there is nothing for Christ to offer us in the covenant of grace. Kline puts it this way: "All the arguments employed... to prove that Adam could not do anything meritorious would apply equally to the case of Jesus, the Second Adam... The parallel which Scripture tells us exists between the two Adams would require the conclusion that if the first Adam could not earn anything, neither could the second. But, if the obedience of Jesus has no meritorious value, the foundation of the gospel is gone... There is thus no justification-glorification for us to receive as a gift of grace by faith alone."[34]

Some respond that justification involves nothing more than forgiveness. But clearly, the verbs "to forgive" and "to justify" are not the same. The former is necessary to the latter, but the latter means "to declare righteous," something that happens as we stand before the bar of God's perfect justice. We must therefore have a perfect righteousness before God, and it comes as his gift through Jesus Christ as he imputes his righteousness achieved under the covenant of works to us via the covenant of grace (2 Cor. 5:21).

Finally, Shepherd complains that the idea of merit means that we are trying to justify ourselves by our works or, if not, that sanctification has no value. But we do not argue that justification by works is impossible in the abstract, only that Adam by his sin failed to do so, and now it is impossible to us. Furthermore, the covenant of works/covenant of grace bi-covenantal scheme does not dig a chasm between justification and sanctification; instead, it protects us from confusing them as Shepherd does under his own scheme.

In the end, we must let Scripture decide. So clear is the biblical testimony as to creation and fall, involving a covenant of works between God and Adam, that Neo-Orthodox objectors like Karl Barth and James B. Torrance simply rejected the testimony of Genesis chapters 2 and 3 as mythological. They realized that they could not object to the covenant of works and still accept the teaching of those chapters. While those within the Reformed community today who object to the covenant of works certainly have a stronger view of Scripture than Barth and his followers, nonetheless their treatment of God's covenant with Adam fails to do justice to the plain teaching of the Bible. To see no difference between God's pre-Fall dealings with Adam in the Garden and his post-Fall dealings with Adam and Eve, with Abraham, and with New Cove-

---

[34] Kline, "Covenant Theology under Attack," 3-4.

nant believers in Christ is to miss both the forest and the trees of the biblical testimony regarding creation, fall, and redemption.

As classic covenant theology has recognized, God's dealings with Adam possessed all the elements of a covenant. Furthermore, John Murray's demurral aside, the Bible does refer to it as a covenant (Hosea 6:7).[35] Moreover, it is indisputable that God's covenant with Adam was based on the condition of the recipient's obedience, and in this it differs from all the post-fall redemptive covenants that follow.[36] The logic of God's covenant with Adam was that obedience produced righteousness, righteousness received justification, and justification received life. Apart from our desire to note God's goodness in the Garden (which Kline helpfully reminds us to keep distinct from God's grace towards sinners), this covenant reflected God's justice, not his grace. Complaints against non-biblical, medieval vows and teachings of merit do not change the fact that the pre-Fall covenant was conditioned on Adam's obedient works and that acting as our federal head he failed to meet the stipulated condition. As Paul so meticulously works out in Romans 5:12-21, Adam's disobedience produced guilt, guilt received condemnation, and condemnation yielded the bitter curse of death. Likewise, we can see that Jesus achieved our righteousness by fulfilling the covenant of works. Paul points out this very progression as accounting for our justification through faith in Christ; in Romans 5:18-19 he clearly spells out that Jesus' obedience produced righteousness, righteousness gained justification, and justification receives the blessing of life.

It is noteworthy that John Murray, though rejecting the term *covenant of works*, treats what he calls the Adamic administration as possessing all the features of a covenant. His discussion is organized around the headings *the condition, promise,* and *threatening,* the very features common to biblical covenants. In this, he affirms one of the strongest arguments for calling God's dealings with Adam a "covenant", namely

---

[35] Venema sagely points out that Murray's concern for biblical terminology does not keep him from coining his own non-biblical term, the Adamic Administration. He considers Murray's language decidedly inferior, writing, "This terminology is not only alien to the biblical descriptions of the pre-fall state but also to the biblical descriptions of God's communion with man in general." Venema, 193. See Benjamin B. Warfield, "Hosea 6:7: Adam or Man?," in *Selected Shorter Writings of Benjamin B. Warfield,* 2 vols., ed. John E. Meeter, (Nutley, NJ: Presbyterian and Reformed Publishing Co., 1970), 1:116-129.

[36] Except as the covenant of works is re-published in the Mosaic covenant, which itself is an administration of the covenant of grace.

that it contains all the features found in all other covenants identified as such in the Bible. This is why Murray's soteriology was safeguarded from the debilitating effects commonly resulting from a denial of the covenant of works. While objecting semantically, he retains all its important features, thus safeguarding the doctrine of justification in his thinking. Writing of God's dealings with Adam, Murray lays out the very progression I noted above, saying, "Righteousness, justification, life is an invariable combination in the government and judgment of God. There would be a relation that we may call perfect legal reciprocity."[37] Therefore, Murray observes that in the covenant of grace God does not set aside his justice, but rather satisfies it through the substitutionary atonement and the imputed righteousness of Jesus Christ, offered to us by faith alone.

Again, it is one thing to overlook the covenant of works, while retaining justification by faith alone. It is quite another deliberately to reject the covenant of works in order to reject the contrast between faith and works, the gospel and the law. Lutherans do not have, properly speaking, a covenant theology. But when one deliberately jettisons the covenant of works, the only possible result is a gospel different from that which proclaims justification by faith alone.

Only the classic bi-covenantal structure of redemptive history provides a proper place for both faith and works in our justification. We are justified by works before God's justice – not works that we performed or that Adam performed, but works that Jesus performed in our place under the covenant of works, credited to us in the covenant of grace, and we received by faith alone. In the mono-covenant scheme proposed in place of this, we receive God's covenant by grace but keep it by faith/works in combination. Those who deny the covenant of works end up turning the covenant of grace into an implicit covenant of works that Adam did not keep in the state of his mutable perfection, and by which none of his corrupted offspring can ever hope to be justified before a holy God.

A THEOLOGY OF COVENANT CHILDREN

When you ask those who are trying to rewrite covenant theology what concerns are driving them, as I have had the opportunity to do first-hand with some of them, you will inevitably hear them address the subject of covenant children. This is where many of us will most resonate with

---

[37] Murray, "The Adamic Administration," 2:47.

them, because of our shared concern about non-covenantal views of children that seemingly dominate today. For many evangelicals, until children have had a dramatic conversion experience, they are considered pagans within their own Christian homes. Some Christian children are taught not to say the Lord's prayer and not to call God "our Father." In many churches, children are not allowed in the worship service until they "come of age."

It is in response to such things that many turn to covenant theology for a vastly more positive view of children growing up in Christian homes and in the church. Douglas Wilson writes, "In a very real way, this debate is a debate over the theology of children. This is important because in the American church our theology of children is overwhelmingly baptistic, even in paedo-baptist communions." He cites the attitude of nineteenth century Southern Presbyterian theologian, Henry Thornwell, who said the Church must treat her children "precisely as she treats all other impenitent and unbelieving men – she is to exercise the power of the keys, and shut them out from the communion of the saints."[38]

To this attitude, the response is made that children are members of God's covenant and are holy, that is, are saints, by virtue of their parents (1 Cor. 7:14). To this we should agree, although we must be careful of the sense in which we mean this. Rightly, it means that children are part of the community of God's people and have been given God's Word. In their baptism they have God's mark of ownership placed upon them and are called to faith. The prayers of the church belong to them, and they have the privilege of oversight from the church's shepherds. These things we must insist upon as the right of our children by birth. What we must not do, however, is presume regeneration or salvation. While the children of believers are blessed with great privileges, salvation itself is not by heredity; saving grace does not pass on, as some have suggested, through the sperm and ovum of parents.[39]

When it comes to covenant succession, we should not presume or assume regeneration in our children, but instead hold a trusting confidence in God combined with a prayerful attention to duty as Christian parents. Here, the emphasis varies. Douglas Wilson writes, "When we have faith that works its way out in love, which is the only thing that

[38] Douglas Wilson, *Reformed Is Not Enough*, 183.
[39] See Joseph Pipa's chapter on "Covenant Children"in this volume.

genuine faith can do, then the condition that God set for the fulfillment of His promises has been met. Can we fulfill our covenant responsibilities (by believing) and yet have God fail to fulfill His promises? It is not possible."[40] The problem with this is an "automaticity" that does not square with lived experience or with the whole biblical picture. Children can be raised in the church by faithful parents, yet turn away from faith in Christ. Wilson considers this observation a disbelieving of God's promises on account of the testimony of men. In fact, his position is an example of standing on only a few select and favored promises in such a way that fails to account for the whole counsel of God. Wilson's teaching wrongfully accuses already grieving parents of damning their unfaithful children by not having been faithful enough. This is just one place in which the new covenant theology turns biblical, decretal theology on its head. Instead of God's election controlling the covenant, Wilson and others have the covenant controlling God's election. But, as Paul points out in Romans 9:10-12, "Though they were not yet born and had done nothing either good or bad – in order that God's purpose of election might continue," God said, "Jacob I loved, but Esau I hated." It was not God's sovereign purpose either for Ishmael, the first son of Abraham, or Esau, the son of Isaac, to enter into eternal life. The reason is not the faithlessness of these fathers, but the plan of God, whose promises all are "Yes" only in Christ (2 Cor. 1:20).

Wilson's is a moderate view among those trying to recast covenant theology. For many, the concern to be certain of the salvation of infants who die becomes the controlling factor in their entire doctrine of salvation. Unwilling to rest upon the silence with which Scripture treats the exceptional issue of *how* elect infants are saved (in contrast with *that* they are saved, of which Scripture is clear), they concoct a theology of salvation that recasts the normal situation of children that do not die in infancy. Some insist that infants of Christian parents must be presumed regenerate on the basis of their possessing faith – the example of John the Baptist leaping in the womb is given to prove that infants can believe. Asserting that infants can believe, while granting that infants cannot understand biblical teaching, some go so far as to redefine faith in such a way that biblical understanding plays no necessary part. For others, John the Baptist's evidence that an unborn infant can believe is combined with a presumption of regeneration in the case of all covenant

---

[40] Wilson, *Reformed Is Not Enough*, 187.

infants. Still others over-exegete passages like Matthew 18:14, where Jesus had the covenant children brought to him, "for to such belongs the kingdom of God." This is taken as a blanket declaration that all covenant children are saved until such time as they should apostatize.

On these grounds, objection is made to the idea that we must lead our children to Christ and evangelize them, longing for the day when they make a credible profession of faith. This is not treating them as pagans, as though they have no standing or privilege in the church until such time as they show faith. Nor does it mean we try to engineer some revivalistic crisis so that our children can be converted, as has been charged. Yet another over-reaction, as we have seen, is so to emphasize the significance of infant baptism that it practically supplants the place of personal faith. Baptism is indeed more than a wet dedication of our children, yet it grants no grace apart from our children's personal embrace of the gospel in saving faith; for all our gratitude for what baptism means for our children, only credible evidence of their faith in Christ should assure us of our children's salvation. As Charles Hodge wrote, we receive God's promised salvation "not by birth, nor by any outward rite, nor by union with any external body, but by the gospel, received and appropriated by faith."[41]

Overall, the confidence with which advocates of this recast covenant theology approach the status of our children before God is the most attractive feature of their writings. It has been for many a potent corrective to the effects of revivalism within their homes, which has had so many look upon their children as utter pagans until they have had a crisis conversion to Christ, the engineering of which can dominate entire childhoods. The problem, however, is that many writers simply go too far in their zeal for the status of covenant children, failing to be rightly balanced by the whole counsel of God. We have no reason to presume regeneration – a dangerous conception if there ever was one – nor should we fail to mark a difference between covenant children who have not made profession of faith and those who have. I am speaking in the latter case of the growing practice of paedo-communion, which on the basis of presumed regeneration admits little children to the Lord's Table, totally neglecting the apostle Paul's warnings in 1 Corinthians 11:28-31 against partaking of Communion without personal faith in that which it signifies.

---

[41] Charles Hodge, *A Commentary on Ephesians* (Edinburgh: Banner of Truth, 1964), 114.

In other words, from the excesses and emotional manipulations of the revivalistic mentality, we may return to a more biblically balanced position regarding our children without the excesses of hyper-covenantalism. We may prayerfully long for our children to be able to declare what David wrote in Psalm 22:9-10, without presuming that this happens in an automatic fashion: "You made me trust you at my mother's breasts... From my mother's womb you have been my God." That should not be read as a technical statement by the great Psalmist, but as a poetic expression of God's life-long faithfulness to him. We can and should have a very high view of the spiritual situation of Christian children without an unbalanced view of their covenant position that warps our whole doctrine of salvation.[42] One example of this balance comes from G. Campbell Morgan, hardly an advocate of overblown covenant theology, who taught his congregation:

> Our first business is to bring the child into a recognition of its actual re-lationship to Christ, and a personal yielding thereto. Let it be done eas-ily and naturally. Do not be anxious, if indeed your home is a Christian home, that your child should pass through any volcanic experience; but as soon as possible the little one should be able to say, Yes, I love Him and I will be His. It is as simple as the kiss of morning upon the brow of the hill, as the distilling of the moisture in the dew, or it ought to be. Thank God for men who, having wandered far away, have come back by volcanic methods, but thank God for the little ones who have been led to the point of yielding and finding their Lord before any other lord has had dominion over them.[43]

FAITH ALONE

In concluding our assessment of the covenant confusion about us today, we must consider the distinction between faith and works. This is of vi-tal important because the previous forks in the road have all led here, to a view of faith that cannot meaningfully be described as *faith alone*. I said earlier that the prominent features of this recast covenant theology are the replacing of soteriology with ecclesiology, the emphasis on the external rite of baptism, and, finally, the merging of faith and works in

---

[42] For a fuller treatment of this subject, see my "Jesus and the Little Children" in Richard D. Phillips, *Encounters with Jesus: When Ordinary People Met the Savior* (Phillipsburg, NJ: P&R, 2002).

[43] G. Campbell Morgan, *The Westminster Pulpit*, 10 vols. (Grand Rapids: Baker, 1995), 2:120-121.

what amounts to a new legalism. This is what happens when one deliberately rejects the bi-covenantal structure taught in the Bible – covenant
of works and covenant of grace – in order to escape the contrast between
law and gospel in salvation. The result is that faith no longer consists of
believing and trusting on Jesus Christ and his saving works. Instead, our
obedient works are included in the very definition of faith, so that faith
and obedience are considered as the same thing.

The problem with this is that the apostle Paul deliberately contrasts
faith with works, writing in Romans 3:28, "We hold that one is justified
by faith apart from works of the law." The same is seen in Ephesians
2:8-9, where faith and works are not in continuum but in opposition: "By
grace you have been saved, through faith... not by works." It is on this
reasoning that the Westminster Confession defines the principle acts of
saving faith as "accepting, receiving, and resting upon Christ alone"
(XIV.2).

It is clear from the writings of this new view of the covenant that a
major objective they share is to combat the easy-believism that grips the
evangelical movement today and which has resulted in such ridiculous
controversies as the so-called "Lordship Salvation" uproar of several
years ago. They find it troubling in the extreme that Christians could believe and proclaim that one can have Jesus as Savior without having him
as Lord. I whole-heartedly agree in this concern. The difference is that
these hyper-covenantal writers blame not superficial Christians and
pragmatic church-growth models, but the Bible's own doctrine of justification for this situation, because in their view it promotes faith without
works.

For this reason, those of us who emphasize faith alone in justification must strongly assert the absolute necessity of works to salvation.
Let me say that again: works are absolutely necessary to salvation, the
term "salvation" being understood here more broadly than simply the
matter of justification. You cannot be saved without works. Similarly,
we must stress that sanctification is neither optional nor is it an add-on
that may come some time after justification. You cannot be justified
without also being sanctified, just as Christ himself cannot be split, but
must be accepted whole.

While we must insist upon the necessity of sanctification that follows justification, and that faith produces good works if it is true and living faith, we must also give works their proper place and function in salvation. One way I put it is that works are necessary to salvation not as a

condition, but as a *consequence*. We are not saved *by* works, but we are most definitely saved *to* works, which includes repentance from sin and active obedience to the Lord's commands. Without these no one can consider himself to be saved, just as the writer of Hebrews warns that "without holiness no one will see the Lord" (Heb. 12:14). Paul says we were "chosen in Christ to be holy and blameless before [the Lord]" (Eph. 1:4). Therefore, without any signs of holiness no one should be convinced of his or her election.

To emphasize the necessary relationship between faith and works is to stand squarely within the Reformed tradition. The problem is that many today are going much further, merging faith and works so that they are one and the same, and in that way smuggling the idea of works into the definition of justifying faith. Most prominent in this is Norman Shepherd. One of his stated goals is to rescue the Book of James from the supposed ghetto into which it has been exiled by the fans of Paul. To this end, Shepherd defines justifying faith as believing, penitent, and obedient faith, thus merging faith, repentance, and subsequent obedience all into one. He points to James' teaching, "Was not Abraham our father justified by works when he offered up his son Isaac on the altar? You see that faith was active along with his works, and faith was completed by his works; and the Scripture was fulfilled that says, 'Abraham believed God, and it was counted to him as righteousness'... You see that a person is justified by works and not by faith alone" (Ja. 2:21-24). Shepherd interprets this as advocating a faith/works combination in justification.

Shepherd connects this to Paul by means of passages like Galatians 5:6, which says, "For in Christ Jesus neither circumcision nor uncircumcision counts for anything, but only faith working through love." On the basis of this passage, he writes, "Justifying faith is obedient faith, that is, 'faith working through love' (Gal. 5:6), and therefore faith that yields obedience to the commands of Scripture."[44] Were the distinction between faith and works maintained, even while their necessary relationship is emphasized, Shepherd would not be altering the Reformed understanding of faith. But he goes on to say, "The Pauline affirmation in Romans 2:13, 'the doers of the Law will be justified,' is not to be under-

---

[44] Norman Shepherd, "Thirty-four Theses on Justification in Relation to Faith, Repentance, and Good Works," presented to the Philadelphia Presbytery of the Orthodox Presbyterian Church, Nov. 18, 1978. Thesis 11.

stood hypothetically in the sense that there are not persons who fall into that class, but in the sense that faithful disciples of the Lord Jesus Christ will be justified."[45]

The problem here is not an ambiguity in terminology, as has often been said in Shepherd's defense, but a clear refutation of a definition of faith that is distinct from works. He is asserting that justifying faith is not merely "shown" by its works, as James 2:18 says and as the whole flow of James' argument indicates, but that justifying faith and its works are one and the same thing. For this reason, Shepherd has been able to say simultaneously that we are justified by faith alone and that we are justified by works. Faith, repentance, and the new works of obedience that follow are not merely joined in salvation, but are meshed together in what Shepherd calls "the obedience of faith," wrongly applying Paul's use of that expression in Romans 1:5. Furthermore, Shepherd's intent becomes clear when he adds that justification ultimately takes place at the final judgment and that the obedient believer may lose his or her justification by failing to continue in faithful obedience.[46]

Shepherd's definition of faith does not direct us to look to and rely upon Christ and His work, but ourselves and our work. In the circles in which his teaching is followed and where these new views of covenant flourish, one often hears that we are saved "by our faithfulness to the covenant." This is a far cry from the Reformed understanding of faith alone as the condition of the covenant of grace, that is, faith as trusting in what Jesus Christ has done for us. Instead, avowedly in the interest of grace, Shepherd has us looking to our repentance and our obedience not to assess our sanctification, but as the instrument of our justification. This is what Meredith Kline meant when he warned against the merging of law/gospel and works/faith: "The irony of all this is that a position that asserts a continuum of 'grace' everywhere ends up with no genuine gospel grace anywhere. An approach that starts out claiming that a works principle operates nowhere ends up with a kind of works principle everywhere. What this amounts to is a retreat from the Reformation and a return to Rome."[47]

Kline's assertion is confirmed with particular clarity in the case of Ralph Smith, with whose book *Eternal Covenant* I began this study of

---

[45] Ibid., Thesis, 20.

[46] Ibid., Thesis 19. Here is where Shepherd's thought on justification and that of N.T. Wright intersect so clearly. See earlier discussion of Wright's view of justification.

[47] Kline, "Covenant Theology under Attack," 4.

covenant confusion. Smith's book follows essentially the same outline used in this paper, but he reaches far different conclusions. Starting with his speculations on covenant as the ontological basis of Trinitarian union, he moved forward to redefine covenant not as a pact but as a gift of relationship. As I have done, he then moved forward to consider the covenant of works, which he assailed, making God's covenant with Adam no different from any other redemptive covenant presented in the Bible.

Where does this lead him? Smith posits, without qualification or embarrassment, that God's covenant with Adam in the Garden is the same covenant God offers to sinners today for their salvation, without modification since the Fall. This is the mono-covenantal scheme in full bloom. Where Adam failed, despite his sinless state, we sinners are now to succeed if we are to be declared just by God. Like Adam we have received God's covenant favor and must simply maintain it "by being faithful, living out his faith in God by doing works that correspond with it... The basic situation is still similar. We are required to be faithful to the covenant by having a living faith in God, one that works by love."[48] As Kline foretold, having removed the covenant of works, what Smith actually has abolished is the covenant of grace.

What about Christ's saving blood? Smith allows that we need to be forgiven through Christ "when we sin," which one gains the impression is not likely to be very often for a faithful covenant-keeper. But we are justified by works, that is, by our works, at least so long as we continue to do them. One wonders what was the effect of the Fall; it must have been very slight if the view of Smith and Shepherd and others in their camp is correct. Perhaps here more than anywhere else, in its low view of the consequences of the Fall, this new theology of covenant intersects with Roman Catholicism, along with sharing an approach to justification which depends on the grace of God working *in us* rather than the alien righteousness of Christ imputed *to us* by grace and through faith alone. What Cornelius Venema wrote about the Barthian rejection of the covenant of works fits here equally well, and is worthy of quoting at some length:

> The difference between man's situation before the face of God before and after the fall into sin is flattened out, even obliterated... In this revision there is no place any longer for a historical fall from favor with

---

[48] Smith, *Eternal Covenant*, 70.

God through the sin and disobedience of our first parent and covenant representative, Adam. Nor is there any place for a subsequent cove- nanting between God and his people in the covenant of grace, by means of which fallen man is restored to renewed covenant fellowship with God in Christ, the second Adam.[49]

What, then, are we to make of James chapter 2, to which Smith, like Shepherd makes appeal? First of all, we should observe that while James certainly emphasizes that only a living faith justifies -- a faith that goes on to perform works and is proved only by works -- he also clearly distinguishes between the two: "I will show you my faith by my works," he says (2:18). Works show and prove faith. Furthermore, the best han- dling of this book in the Reformation tradition is not Luther's dismissal of James from the canon, which Shepherd sets forth as practically the only alternative to his own position. Instead, Reformed teachers have rightly understood the different purposes to which Paul and James were addressing themselves. William Premble explained it well in his 1635 treatise on justification:

> [Paul] speaks of that faith which is true and living, working by char- ity... [James] disputes against that faith which is false and dead, without power to bring forth any good works. So that the apostles speak no contradiction, because Paul teaches that we are justified by a true faith and James affirms that we are not justified by a false faith... Paul severs works from our justification, but not from our faith. James joins works to our faith, but not to our justification.[50]

Paul's view of faith and works is made explicit in Romans 4:4-5, in the heart of his teaching on justification in that great epistle: "Now to the one who works, his wages are not counted as a gift but as his due. And to the one who does not work but trusts him who justifies the ungodly, his faith is counted as righteousness." The faith that is counted as right- eousness is distinct from works, though it goes on to do good works. Such a faith does indeed justify us by works, but those works are not our own but Christ's perfect obedience imputed to us, for what Paul de- scribes in Philippians 3:9 as "not a righteousness of my own that comes from the law, but that which comes through faith in Christ, the right- eousness from God that depends on faith." One fears for those who seek

---

[49] Venema, "Recent Criticisms of the 'Covenant of Works,'"187.

[50] William Premble, *The Justification of a Sinner. A Treatise on Justification by Faith Alone* (1635 edition, reprint, Morgan, PA: Soli Deo Gloria, 2002), 200-203.

to stand justified before God on the basis of their own covenant-keeping faithfulness. Indeed, I fear that the words once written by Paul speaking of works-reliant Jews might be said of many today, that they did not achieve righteousness "because they did not pursue it by faith, but as if it were based on works... For, being ignorant of the righteousness that comes from God, and seeking to establish their own, they did not submit to God's righteousness" (Rom. 9:2, 10:3).

In a recent article on this topic, Stefan Lindblad writes words that I find a fitting conclusion to our discussion of saving faith as faith alone:

> Justifying faith is inseparable from the other graces of salvation, and yet faith is the alone instrument of justification. There is no other way, no other instrument whereby a sinner receives Christ for justification. Repentance does not justify. Our good works do not justify. Our obedience does not justify... God declares a sinner righteous by grace alone, through faith alone, on account of Christ alone. The church must gain a renewed appreciation and affection for this truth. For here is the heart of the gospel. If we lose it, or, worse, renounce it, then we will bring ruin to our churches and destruction to our own souls. May Christ grant us mercy to guard this truth against error, boldness to proclaim this truth in its fullness, and, most of all, grace for sinners to believe this truth unto justification and life.[51]

BACK TO THE CROSSROADS

What, then, are we to make of this redefined covenant theology? One essential response is for those who have an interest in it to take the time and make the effort to understand what really is being said. I have endeavored to do that, having prepared this paper after extensive personal interactions with many leading figures on the other side and having read the opposing materials with a sincere desire for charity and understanding. When people are exploring new avenues of theological configuration, it often takes a good deal of time just to figure out what they really are saying. No doubt, this is a factor in the current debate over covenant theology. What may strike our ear as heretical may turn out to be, on further investigation, something less threatening and closer to biblical orthodoxy than we thought at first hearing.

But there is one aspect of this recasting of salvation by covenant that

---

[51] Stefan T. Lindblad, "Justifying Faith and the Application of Salvation" *The Banner of Truth*, issue 479-80, Aug-Sept. 2003, 20.

causes only greater alarm the more clearly it is understood. This is the compromising of the doctrine of justification through faith alone. In surveying this recast covenant theology, which first redefines covenant so as no longer to contain the elements of a pact or agreement, and then wipes out the distinction between the covenant of works and the covenant of grace, the overall effect is to offer a gospel in which works are so intrinsic to faith that we are justified by works and not by faith alone. That is a different gospel from that taught in the Continental Reformed Confessions and the Westminster Confession of Faith.

More significantly, it is the apostle Paul who tells us in Galatians that a gospel of faith plus works in justification is no small error but is "a gospel contrary to the one you received" (Gal. 1:9). There, Paul makes explicit that faith excludes "works of the law" (see chapter 3). Despite claims of the self-styled New Perspective on Paul that seek to blunt the force of Paul's words, the overwhelming testimony of Scripture and increasingly of scholarly opinion today is that Paul does in fact intend to exclude from our definition of justifying faith the very kinds of works this recast covenant theology is trying to smuggle in. [52] To this false teaching it is Paul who assigns his apostolic anathema precisely because of its denial of justification by faith alone.

That being the case, it is urgent that all teachers in Christ's church

---

[52] For scholarly refutations of the New Perspective on Paul's understanding of "works of the law" in Galatians and Romans, see A. Andrew Das, *Paul, the Law, and the Covenant* (Peabody, Mass.: Hendrickson, 2001); Simon J. Gathercole, *Where Is Boasting? Early Jewish Soteriology and Paul's Response in Romans 1-5* (Grand Rapids: Eerdmans, 2002), 91-111, Colin G. Kruse, *Paul, the Law, and Justification* (Peabody, Mass: Hendrickson, 1996); and Mark A. Seifrid, *Christ, Our Righteousness: Paul's Theology of Justification* (Downers Grove, Ill.: InterVarsity, 2000). For an excellent treatment of the various strands running through the "New Perspective" see Guy Prentiss Waters, *Justification and the New Perspectives on Paul* (Phillipsburg, NJ: P&R Publishing, 2004).

turn back from a view of justification that relies on a combination of faith and works, or on our supposed "faithfulness to the covenant." I pray that each of us will heed Paul's warning as well as Jeremiah's exhortation, and that as needed we will retrace our steps back to the crossroads where the gospel has been compromised, finding there and taking anew the good road that leads to life. "Ask for the ancient paths," the prophet implores us, "where the good way is, and walk in it" (Jer. 6:16).

Chapter 7

Justification by Faith Alone[1]

John Carrick

It was almost five hundred years ago, at the time of the great Protestant Reformation of the sixteenth century, that the Biblical doctrine of justification by faith alone was rediscovered by, and thus recovered to, the Church of Jesus Christ. For centuries this particular doctrine, that is so pivotal to our understanding and to our reception of the gospel, had lain tragically buried out of sight under the additions, traditions, and superstitions of men in the Church of Rome. But in the sixteenth century, largely through God's work in the heart and life of an obscure monk by the name of Martin Luther, this great doctrine was rediscovered, recovered, and reestablished as the great "article of the standing and the falling of the Church."

It is, therefore, all the more tragic that within the last twenty-five to thirty years a quite remarkable and astonishing erosion of this particular doctrine has occurred—an erosion which has reached such proportions that we can almost speak of something of a landslide in this particular area. It was in 1975 that you have the beginnings of what was called the Shepherd Controversy. Professor Norman Shepherd began to teach that justification was not only by faith, but also by works, and that works and

---

[1]This a transcription of a sermon preached at the 2004 Spring Theology Conference of Greenville Presbyterian Theological Seminary.

faith ran parallel in this matter of justification. Two years later you have
the publication of *Paul and Palestinian Judaism*, the seminal work by E.
P. Sanders, the Dean Ireland's Professor of Exegesis at Oxford University. This particular work has had a colossal influence upon Pauline studies and New Testament studies in general and has led to what is now
known as the "Sanders revolution" and, indeed, "The New Perspective
on Paul". This "New Perspective on Paul," which has been gaining
ground and currency over the last twenty-five to thirty years, has been
led by E. P. Sanders himself, by James D. G. Dunn, the Lightfoot Professor at Durham University, and by N. T. Wright, who has taught at
both Oxford and Cambridge Universities and who was recently installed
as the Bishop of Durham in the Church of England. Then more recently,
in the year 2002, we have witnessed the emergence of the so-called
"Federal Vision Theology." This "Federal Vision Theology," emanating
out of Auburn Avenue Presbyterian Church,[2] emphasizes in particular
the objectivity of the covenant. It is reacting strongly against the per-
ceived individualism of much modern evangelicalism and against the
antinomiansim that is rampant in many circles, and is, therefore, reem-
phasizing, in a quite dramatic manner, the objectivity of the covenant,
even to the extent of saying that baptism saves. You can see, then, from
this brief sketch that we have here a number of different strands and a
number of different streams that have been developing and gathering
momentum and which are now converging some twenty-five to thirty
years later. There can be no question but that we live in days in which
this great Biblical doctrine of justification by faith alone is being recast,
reformulated, and undermined.

It is for that reason that I would call your attention to this great
statement in the twenty-eighth verse of the third chapter of the book of
Romans, where the Apostle Paul says, "Therefore we conclude that a
man is justified by faith without the deeds of the law."[3] Now notice the
context of this great statement. The Apostle Paul, as he unfolds this
magnificent epistle to the Romans, has been at pains to establish—
primarily in the opening chapters—the tremendous universality of sin.
He does so in the first chapter by emphasizing the sheer degeneracy of
the Gentile world. He emphasizes there that the Gentiles have broken
and shattered the commandments of God; that God eventually gave them

---

[2] Auburn Avenue Presbyterian Church is located in Monroe, Louisiana.
[3] Scripture quotations are from the Authorized Version.

up and gave them over unto all manner of wickedness, in particular, idolatry, homosexuality, and lesbianism; that the Gentiles are, in fact, to a man, "guilty before God" because they have broken and shattered God's law. Then, in the second chapter, the Apostle goes on to emphasize the self-righteousness and the hypocrisy of the Jews— how that they preach and teach one thing, and yet they themselves break and shatter the very commandments of God that they teach and preach. And then in the third chapter the Apostle brings together these two strands, namely, that of Gentile sin and Jewish sin, by emphasizing the sheer universality of sin—that both Jews and Gentiles are guilty before God. They are all under the power and the guilt of sin. Thus the Apostle has, in these opening chapters, painted in the darkest, blackest possible terms a picture of man in sin, man under the wrath of God, man in the most dire and helpless straits. That, he says, is the diagnosis; that is the human condition. Thus whether you are a Jew, or whether you are a Gentile, you are under sin.

It is, however, towards the close of this third chapter that the Apostle begins to unfold the great divine remedy for this terrible situation, which otherwise would have meant that each and every one of us would have been lost and dead for ever in our trespasses and in our sins. This divine remedy is none other than the divine method of justification. This God, with whom we have to do, is a God that justifies ungodly men and has so contrived a wonderful way of salvation that He is able to be both just and the justifier of those that believe in Jesus. Thus we see that this divine method of justification, which is the divine remedy for the human condition, is rooted and grounded in the person and the work of the Lord Jesus Christ. We see that in verses twenty-five and twenty-six: "Christ Jesus, whom God hath set forth to be a propitiation through faith in His blood, to declare His righteousness for the remission of sins that are past, through the forbearance of God: to declare, I say, at this time His righteousness, that He might be just and the justifier of him which believeth in Jesus." You will notice that this method of justification is a method that excludes boasting; it excludes boasting precisely because it excludes man's works. We see that in verse twenty-seven: " Where is boasting then? It is excluded. By what law? Of works? No, but by the law of faith." And so, in verse twenty-eight, the Apostle summarizes for us this great doctrine: "Therefore we conclude that a man is justified by faith without the deeds of the law."

This, then, is my main thesis, that *the Apostle lays it down as a fun-*

damental proposition of the gospel that the justification of the sinner is
by faith alone and that this is completely independent of the works of
the law. My first point, then, is that *the sinner is not justified by the*
deeds of the law which he himself performs. Listen again to what the
Apostle says in verse twenty-eight: "Therefore we conclude that a man is
justified by faith without the deeds of the law." That little phrase,
"without the deeds of the law," is pivotal, fundamental, and central to
this great doctrine that we are considering. It means literally, "apart
from the deeds or the works of the law." Thus the justification of the
sinner is independent of the works or the deeds or the observance of the
law of God. Now what exactly is the meaning of this term "the deeds or
the works of the law"? Well, it is very obvious that the Apostle must be
referring primarily to the moral law of God. He must be referring primarily to the Ten Commandments; and it is, in my view, quite wrong
and quite untenable to restrict, as some would fain have us do, this particular phrase "the deeds of the law," to certain aspects of the ceremonial
law, thus bypassing the central thrust of these early chapters, which are
clearly and palpably speaking of the moral law of God. It is contrary to
the natural sense of the passage to understand this phrase as referring to
the ceremonial law, or certain aspects of that, plus certain commandments. It is contrary indeed to the whole tenor of these first three chapters. So then, the Apostle is referring here primarily to the moral law of
God; and he is telling us that no man is justified in the sight of God by
observing the commandments, because he cannot do it. It is impossible,
he says. "By the law is the knowledge of sin." The purpose of the law is
to convict and to condemn. That, he says, is why God gave it. Thus the
Apostle is clearly excluding the works of the law from this divine
method of justification.

In verse twenty, the Apostle emphasized exactly the same point:
"Therefore by the deeds of the law there shall no flesh be justified in His
sight." What is so crucial here, and so vital to our understanding and our
teaching of this great doctrine, is *the Apostle's use of negatives.* Notice
that he says in our text, "*without* the deeds of the law." Notice that he
says in verse twenty, "*No flesh* shall be justified by the deeds of the
law." It is these negatives which are so pivotal in our understanding
properly this great doctrine of justification by faith. You will remember
that in Galatians the Apostle Paul does exactly the same thing; he emphasizes exactly the same point. He does not merely define the doctrine
positively. He does that; but he also defines it *negatively* with some most

remarkable emphases and repetitions. Listen to what he says: "Knowing that a man is not justified by the works of the law, but by the faith of Jesus Christ; even we have believed in Jesus Christ, that we might be justified by the faith of Christ, and not by the works of the law: for by the works of the law shall no flesh be justified." This to me is one of the most remarkable statements to be found in whole of the New Testament. The Apostle Paul goes to great lengths and great pains through his remarkable emphases and through the triple use of negatives to emphasize that, on the one hand, we are justified by faith, and that, on the other hand, we are not justified by our own works of the law. Notice then this use of negatives. Indeed I would contend strongly that what we see here is a vital principle, namely, that whenever the Apostle defines the great doctrine of justification by faith, he does not merely do so positively. He does do that. In addition to that, however, in order to safeguard the doctrine, in order to defend this vulnerable doctrine, he uses negatives time and time and time again. The reason why he does so is that this doctrine is, as Dr. J. I. Packer once put it, "very vulnerable." This doctrine is fearfully and wonderfully made. This doctrine is rooted and grounded in the propitiation that Christ is, and that He has wrought. It is rooted and grounded in "the redemption that is in Christ Jesus." It is rooted and grounded in the *solo Christo* principle. Therefore any tinkering or tampering with this doctrine will inevitably undermine the gospel of the Lord Jesus Christ. It simply is not enough to define this doctrine positively. That must be done; but it must also be defended and defined negatively just as the Apostle does, both in Romans and in Galatians.

So then I emphasize at this very point that the sinner is not justified by his own works; he is not justified by the deeds of the law; he is not justified by observing the moral law; he is not justified by observing the ceremonial law; he is not justified by repentance; he is not justified by baptism; he is not justified by holiness; he is not even justified by faith plus works. He is justified "*without* the deeds of the law." All human works are rigidly and emphatically excluded from this great doctrine of justification by faith.

Why, then, is this principle of such vital importance at the present time? Well, this doctrine is coming under increasing attack. The erosion has been taking place. We have seen this, initially, in the teaching of Professor Norman Shepherd. Shepherd was an ordained Presbyterian minister[4] and theological professor, who, in 1975, began to teach that justification is by works as well as by faith. He was not denying justification by faith; and yet he was including works, which is tantamount to a denial of justification by faith alone. He was saying that works *run parallel* to faith in the matter of justification. Shepherd spoke of "a single total response."[5] He wished to *merge* faith and works. He wished to *merge* faith and obedience. Do you not see the problem here? In the light of this great text, in the light of the tremendous negatives of the Apostle, whether he is writing to the Romans or to the Galatians, do you not see the problem of merging faith and obedience, of merging faith and works, in this pivotal doctrine of justification before God? The Apostle, notice, *excludes* works. Shepherd has been *including* works in the matter of justification. But the Apostle clearly excludes them—he rules them right out of court. Boasting is excluded because works are excluded. It is "not by the works of the law." Martyn Lloyd-Jones, who was consulted at the time of the original controversy, described Shepherd's teaching as "a subtle form of legalism and eventually 'another gospel.'"[6] I remind you, therefore, of what the Apostle Paul says: "A man is justified by faith *without* the deeds of the law."

Then in 1977 E. P. Sanders published his seminal work. This work, which has created such a tremendous stir in academic circles, was entitled *Paul and Palestinian Judaism*. It is essentially an analysis of Second Temple Judaism from the years 200 B.C. to A.D. 200 The central thesis of E. P. Sanders' work is that the Judaism of the New Testament is not a works-religion. He contends that it was a religion of grace. He contends that it was not characterized by works-righteousness or self-righteousness. It was not a religion of merit. It was, he says, a religion of grace that operated by means of election on the one hand and by means of the covenant on the other. What, then, was the significance of works for the Jew, according to Sanders? Well, according to Sanders, the significance of works did not lie in *entering into* the covenant, but rather in *staying in* the covenant. Works functioned as "boundary markers" or "badges" that one was in the covenant. Sanders has coined this

---

[4] Out of the controversy, Professor Shepherd left the Presbyterian ministry and spent several years as a minister in the Christian Reformed Church.

[5] Shepherd is cited in O. Palmer Robertson, *The Current Justification Controversy* (Unicoi, TN: The Trinity Foundation, 2003), 24.

[6] Lloyd-Jones is cited in Ibid., 48.

term, "covenantal nomism," which has become so popular in "The New Perspective." In other words, we keep the law as a sign that we are in the covenant. We keep the law as a sign and a boundary marker that we do indeed belong to God in this covenant of grace.

You will notice immediately that this position of Sanders, first promulgated in 1977, involves a complete rejection of the understanding of New Testament Judaism on the part of the Reformers. According to Sanders, what the Reformers did was simply to read back into the New Testament their own particular debate with the Church of Rome. Thus by undermining this idea of the legalism and the self-righteousness of Judaism in the New Testament, "The New Perspective" has undermined the position of the Reformers with regard to the Church of Rome as well. But the position of the Reformers was that the religion of the Jews in the New Testament was indeed legalistic, that it was indeed a religion of works-righteousness, that there was indeed this essential strand of self-righteousness, not only in man in general, but in the Jews in particular. That was their particular understanding; and I believe that they were profoundly right. But Sanders' book has had a colossal impact in academic circles and has resulted in the "Sanders revolution" and in "The New Perspective"; and it has become the reigning paradigm in academic circles.

How, then, does "The New Perspective" interpret this particular verse? Well, it limits the scope of the phrase "the deeds of the law." It limits it in a particular way. It says that the phrase "the deeds of the law" refers essentially to circumcision, certain food laws, and Sabbath observance and the observance of certain other holy days. According to "The New Perspective," these deeds were "ethnic identity markers" or "ethnic boundary markers"; they were "badges," if you like, which marked out those who were in the covenant - those who had been elected by God. According to "The New Perspective," it was not so much *Jewish legalism* that the Apostle was attacking, but rather *Jewish exclusivism*—the way in which the Jews tended to rule out the Gentiles. According to "The New Perspective" the Apostle is saying that it is *not* by these "ethnic boundary markers"; it is not by these "ethnic identity markers"; it is not by these "badges" that we are justified, but rather by faith.

What, then, is our response to this "New Perspective" which has been gathering massive momentum in recent decades? Well, it is simply not valid to limit the phrase "the deeds of the law" to circumcision, certain food laws, and Sabbath observance and the observance of certain holy days. This is totally contrary to the natural sense of the passage. It is totally contrary to the whole tenor of the first three chapters and indeed to the rest of the Epistle to the Romans. If you read carefully through the first three chapters of this great book, you will find that there is scarcely one of the Ten Commandments that is not mentioned as broken and shattered both by Jew and by Gentile alike. Therefore, it simply is not valid on the part of "The New Perspective" to limit and to restrict, as it must, this phrase "the deeds of the law" to this narrow focus. It is very evident, as the Apostle paints this dark, dark picture of mankind guilty before God, that he has in mind the works of man in general—his total inability to keep the moral law of God and the fact that he is guilty before this God before whom he stands. Not only that, but it simply is not valid to dismiss the reality of Jewish legalism. This too is one of the tenets of the "New Perspective." In order to promote their case they have to get rid of the concept of Jewish legalism and Jewish self-righteousness. But just look at Christ's scathing denunciation of the Pharisees in Matthew 23. Just look at Christ's Parable of the Pharisee and the Publican in the Temple (Luke 18:9-14). Do you remember that parable? The Lord Jesus Christ spoke that parable unto "certain which trusted in themselves that they were righteous." There you have it from the lips of the One that is the Truth Incarnate! The Lord Jesus Christ goes on to describe a certain Pharisee that "went up into the temple to pray"; and this is what the Savior says: "The Pharisee stood and prayed thus with himself, 'God I thank thee, that I am not as other men are, extortioners, unjust, adulterers, or even as this publican. I fast twice in the week. I give tithes of all that I possess.'" There we have it! This is in the Temple! This is in the Second Temple! This is "Second Temple Judaism!" Thus you see that Second Temple Judaism, as depicted and as painted by the Lord Jesus Christ, is profoundly self-righteous; it is profoundly legalistic; and it is a religion of self-justification. The problem with this "New Perspective" is that it seems to know far, far more about Palestinian Judaism that it does about the human heart; and it seems to listen to E.P Sanders far, far more than it does to the Eternal Son of God. One of the great ironies of this "New Perspective" is this, that in rejecting the concept of Jewish legalism, and in promoting the concept of "covenantal nomism," it has in fact fallen foul of the very legalism it is seeking to eradicate. I remind you, therefore, once again, the Apostle says, "*without* the deeds of the law"; it is *apart from* the works of the flesh.

But then, in the year 2002, we have another development—the emergence of the so-called "Federal Vision Theology," which is emanating out of Auburn Avenue Presbyterian Church. The great emphasis here is undoubtedly upon the objectivity of the covenant. There is, on the one hand, an understandable rejection of the individualism, the subjectivism and the antinomianism that is so often rampant in evangelical circles. At the same time, this particular theology, in emphasizing the objectivity of the covenant, has gone too far in the opposite direction. It emphasizes the objective nature of the covenant, the objective nature of the sacraments, and even alleges that "baptism saves." Now, if baptism saves, then baptism justifies; and if baptism justifies, then we are justified by a work; and if we are justified by a work, then we are not justified by faith. You can see how dangerous this assertion is. If baptism saves, we have here an undermining of the great doctrine of justification by faith alone. This "Federal Vision Theology" is, in my view, just one step removed from the sacramental principle and the sacramental system of Roman Catholicism. Any elevation of the sacraments along these lines is introducing into the doctrine of justification the principle of works and is undermining and undercutting the great principle of salvation and justification by faith. Moreover, I would remind you of that upon which the Reformers insisted so often. They insisted repeatedly on what they called "the natural popery of human heart"—the natural Pelagianism of the human heart, the natural tendency of the human heart to justify itself before God. You see it supremely in the Pharisee in the temple; and any knowledge of the human heart, and any pastoral contact with the hearts of men confirms, massively, this innate tendency in men to justify themselves before God and to imagine that they are acceptable on the basis of what they do, or of what they have done, or of what has been done unto them. "The natural popery of the human heart!" Once again I remind you, the apostle says, "*without* the deeds of the law."

Second, we see here that *the sinner is justified by faith alone.* He is not justified by his own works. He is justified by faith alone. Listen again to verse twenty-eight: "Therefore we conclude that a man is justified by faith." You will notice that what the Apostle does here is this: he expresses this doctrine positively. We have noted the importance of the negatives. We see also the importance of the positive statement that we are justified by faith. Now the crucial thing to notice here is that the apostle has deliberately isolated faith in this matter of justification. We could summarize his position in this way: works are excluded, faith is isolated. It is "by faith, without the deeds of the law."

Now, it was for this reason that Martin Luther insisted upon the word "alone" in his formulation of this doctrine. He spoke of "justification by faith alone." He has been severely criticized for so doing. We can say this in his defense, however, that if the word "alone" is absent from this great statement, then the *concept* is powerfully present. I believe that Martin Luther captured the truth perfectly when he spoke of "justification by faith alone." In other words, the great *sola fide* principle of the Reformation is absolutely correct and captures perfectly what the Apostle Paul says here in verse twenty-eight, in verse twenty, and in Galatians chapter 2, verse 16. It is by faith; and it is by faith alone that the sinner is justified in the sight of God.

Now then, how do we define this faith? What exactly is this faith? Faith here is being emphasized. It is, indeed, being isolated by the apostle. It is crucial, therefore, that we understand precisely what it is and how we should view it. The reformers emphasized classically that there were three great elements in faith: *notitia*, or knowledge; *assensus*, or assent; and *fiducia*, or trust. All three elements are present in true saving faith. In other words, it is not enough for a man to have knowledge of the gospel. It is not even enough for a man to give an assent to the gospel. It is essential that he has knowledge; it is essential that he gives his assent. But it is also essential that he puts his trust in the Lord Jesus Christ and rests upon Him, and Him alone for salvation. Knowledge, assent, *and* trust are crucial elements in saving faith. The Westminster Standards summarize this beautifully when they say that true faith "accepts, receives, and rests upon Christ alone for salvation."

But notice also the meaning of this verb "to justify." This too, is essential. What does it mean "to be justified"? Well, this term is undoubtedly a legal, judicial, and forensic term. We are dealing here with the imagery of the law court. There is the Jew, there is the Gentile, and they are all "guilty before God." They stand condemned. But God has sent His Son into the world. Christ Jesus has come down from heaven. God has sent Him forth, and God has set Him forth, and He is the propitiation for our sins upon the cross. As a result, God is able be both "just and the justifier of him that believes in Jesus." So then, the whole process, the whole activity is not contrary to law, but rather is legal; it is judicial and forensic. Thus we see from this great epistle that the great God, with whom we have to do, is a God that "justifies the ungodly." God is able to take an ungodly sinner such as you and me, and God is able, on the basis of the wonderful work of the Lord Jesus Christ, to declare and to pronounce that sinner, who is otherwise guilty, righteous in His holy sight. That is the wonder of the doctrine of justification. Notice the context: it is sin, guilt, judgment, redemption, the propitiation of Christ, the very cross of Christ itself.

Thus we can see that justification is the opposite of condemnation. To be justified is the opposite of to be condemned. Those that trust in Christ have passed from death to life, and those that trust in Christ have passed from a situation of condemnation into a status of justification. Moreover, this justification is even more than forgiveness. Forgiveness is, in and of itself, a very wonderful thing; and if the gospel simply consisted in God's forgiveness, that would have been a wonderful message from heaven. But to be justified goes beyond forgiveness in this sense, that God takes an ungodly man, an ungodly woman, and declares that ungodly person to be righteous and acceptable. He has passed from death to life; and the verdict of condemnation has been changed into a verdict of justification.

But how does this justification operate? How does this justification actually occur in practice? Well, chapter four demonstrates that it is by means of imputation. "God imputes righteousness" and he imputes it, says the apostle, "without works." Now, why do I emphasize this doctrine of imputation? I do so precisely because this aspect of the doctrine of justification is also coming under considerable attack at the present time. There can be no doubt that "The New Perspective" is very, very dismissive of this concept of imputation. N. T. Wright describes it as "a cold piece of business."[7] But the issue is not whether the doctrine or concept of imputation is a *cold* piece of business, or indeed, whether it is a *hot* piece of business, but whether it is a *true* piece of business! The Word of God teaches, quite clearly, in the following chapter, that it is a true piece of business. Look at verse six: "Even as David also describes the blessedness of the man unto whom God imputes righteousness without works." David, who was a murderer, David who was an adulterer, David who was a liar, David, who briefly lived in the gutters of this world—here is a man conducting himself in an ungodly manner. But what does God do? God takes this man and declares him righteous and pronounces him righteous; God imputes to him righteousness without

[7] N T Wright, *What Saint Paul Really Said* (Grand Rapids: William B. Eerdmans Publishing Company, 1997), 110.

works. Then look at verse eight. "Blessed is the man to whom the Lord will not impute sin." We have here in this very context the great Reformation doctrine of "double imputation." This doctrine is being rejected and dismissed at the present time by "The New Perspective" in particular; but it is there in the Word of God. Our sins are imputed to Jesus Christ. His righteousness is imputed to the believer; and David himself describes the blessedness of the man to whom the Lord imputes righteousness. He imputes that righteousness without works. That means that a man is justified without the deeds of the law. So then, I emphasize, over against the teaching of the Church of Rome, that this doctrine of imputation is not a legal fiction. The Church of Rome has always contended that that is what it is—a legal fiction. No, it is not a legal fiction; it is a legal fact, it is a legal act. The Word of God teaches here that "God imputes righteousness without works" and it teaches "the blessedness of the man to whom the Lord does not impute sin." Thus we are brought back once again to what Martin Luther described as the "great exchange"— this "admirable exchange" that occurred upon the cross of Calvary, whereby our sins are laid upon the head of the Lord Jesus Christ and His perfect righteousness is given, or credited to and reckoned to all those who put their trust in Him. The Word of God says this: "For He hath made Him, to be sin for us, who knew no sin; that we might be made the righteousness of God in Him," (2 Cor 5:21). I emphasize, therefore, that it is by faith that this righteousness is imputed; it is by faith that a man is justified.

We see, then, that faith in the sight of God is the instrument of our justification. It is, if you like, the channel through which we receive it. It is the great means by which God bestows it. When I say that faith is the instrument of our justification, I do not mean, of course, that faith is the ground of our justification. Jesus Christ is the ground of our justification. He is the meritorious cause of our justification. But faith is the channel; faith is the instrument. Faith is, if you like, the beggar's hand which reaches out and receives the gift; and faith is the sole instrument of this justification. It is *sola fide;* and the reason why it is *sola fide* is so that it might be *solo Christo,* so that it might be *sola gratia.* These great *solas* are interdependent; they stand or fall together. If you undermine *sola fide,* you undermine *solo Christo.* If you undermine *solo Christo,* you have destroyed *sola gratia.* It is by faith, by Christ alone, and by grace alone. That is the glory of the gospel and it is the glory of the great heritage of the Reformation which has been given to us in these last five hundred years. I emphasize, therefore, over against the teaching of "The New Perspective," that faith is not some mere badge. N. T. Wright says, faith "is the God-given badge of membership, neither more nor less."[8] Why does he say that? He says that because he wishes to merge faith and obedience, faith and works, justification by faith and justification by works.[9] But if faith is the badge, then how is the sinner saved? If faith is not the instrument of our justification, but is the badge or mark of our salvation, then how, exactly, is the sinner saved? And it is at this point that one finds a very real vagueness in the teaching of N. T. Wright. It is evident from our text that faith is the instrument. It is evident from our text that faith is not a badge, but rather the very instrument by which the righteousness of Christ is imputed to us. It is the very instrument by which the sinner is justified. It is the beggar's hand:

> Nothing in my hand I bring;
> Simply to Thy cross I cling.

Faith, I say, is the beggar's hand that receives the gift from Jesus Christ.

Notice, in passing, the individualism of the gospel that is implicit in this text. Notice that the Apostle says, "Therefore we conclude that *a man* is justified by faith." Now when I speak of the individualism of the gospel, I am well aware, of course, that there is a very unhealthy individualism rampant in the churches, and I wish to disassociate myself from that entirely. Any tendency to neglect the church, any tendency towards isolationism, any tendency to neglect the preaching of the gospel, the sacraments, and the discipline of the church is, indeed, an unhealthy individualism. But, I emphasize it, and I do so on the basis of this text, that there is a true and proper individualism in the gospel. The Apostle says that "*a man* is justified by faith." The individual in the sight of God, that is guilty before God, is justified freely by the grace of God; and he is justified by faith.

But why has God chosen *faith* to be this instrument, whereby we receive this salvation and this justification? Professor John Murray once made a remarkable statement: "Faith is *self*-renouncing; works are *self-*

---

[8] N. T. Wright, *What Saint Paul Really Said*, 160.

[9] The answer to "Why Tom Wright wishes to merge faith and human works?" is given in his own words when he alleges that the doctrine of justification is "the great *ecumenical* doctrine." (*What Saint Paul Really Said,* 158) Historically, that is, of course, a piece of nonsense; and it can only be described as a piece of wishful thinking. It does, however, explain a leading presupposition that drives Wright at this point.

congratulatory."[10] Faith is self-renouncing." In other words, as the sinner comes to the cross of Christ and lays hold of Jesus Christ and Him
crucified, he is conscious of his sin, but he looks unto another and is
saved. There is great concern at the present time in "The New Perspective" and also amongst "Federal Vision" theologians about "the introspective conscience of the West." But there is a proper place in the gospel for introspection. You and I need to know that we are sinners. I
emphasize this, that if the sense of sin is introspective, looking unto Jesus Christ is, as Professor Murray puts it, "extraspective"[11]—it looks
away from self and it looks unto Jesus Christ and Him crucified. I emphasize, therefore, that Jesus Christ is the great object and the great center of this faith. I do so for this reason, that we live, as I am sure that
you are well aware, in an age of pseudo-spirituality—an age of pseudo-
faith. Often you will hear men and women being interviewed on the
television; and the question is asked, "Do you have faith?" They often
respond, "Yes!" Their faith, however, might be in Mother Nature; it
might be in Mother Earth; it might be in Allah; it might be faith in faith
itself; it might even be faith in God, but apart from faith in Jesus Christ.
But the Word of God emphasizes that unless we believe in the Son, we
do not believe in the Father. Jesus Christ is, therefore, the great object
and the great center of our faith. Listen to what the apostle says here:
"Christ Jesus, whom God hath set forth to be a propitiation through faith
in His blood," (Rom 3:24, 25). My good friends, let me ask you, do you
believe in Jesus? That is the condition. God justifies those that believe
in Jesus Christ and those that believe in Him alone. I repeat the question, then: do you believe in Jesus? Do you believe that Jesus is the
Christ? Do you believe that Jesus is the Son of God? Do you believe
that He came out from God and came forth from the Father and came
down from heaven and was born of a virgin and was laid in a manger,
and lived a perfect, impeccable life, and at the age of thirty, began to
move out amongst men doing good, healing the sick, raising the dead,
teaching the people, preaching the gospel, uttering those things that had
been kept hidden from the very foundation of the world. But at the very
end of it all we find the very center of it all, namely, the cross of Calvary; for He set His face to go unto Jerusalem, there to lay down His life

---

[10] John Murray, *The Epistle to the Romans* (Grand Rapids: William B. Eerdmans
Publishing Co., 1990), 123.
[11] Ibid.

for our sins. My good friends, do you believe in Him? Do you believe in *this* Jesus? For this is the condition of our justification. It is by faith that a man is justified and by faith alone.

I come, then, to the application of my text; and my first point is *an exhortation to all that preach the Word of God and rule in the Church of Jesus Christ.* We have been dealing here with one of the cardinal doctrines of the Christian faith. It is an absolutely central, pivotal doctrine. I remind you, therefore, especially those that preach the Word of God and have the responsibility of ruling in the Church of Jesus Christ, of the words of Jude: "I exhort you that ye should earnestly contend for the faith which was once delivered unto the saints," (Jude 3). Now, when Jude uses the word "faith," he means, of course, the Christian faith in general. I emphasize that for this reason, that theologians often distinguish between two different senses of the word "faith," and validly so. They say there is "the faith *which* we believe," and there is "the faith *by* which we believe." Both are true. "The faith *which* we believe"—that is what Jude is speaking of when he urges us to contend earnestly for this faith. "The faith *by which* we believe"—that is what the Apostle Paul is speaking of when he tells us here, in our text, that "we conclude that a man is justified by faith." The faith *which* we believe, and the faith *by which* we believe. But notice there is a very, very important connection between the two. And if men tinker and tamper with the faith *by which* we believe—if men tinker and tamper with this delicate, vulnerable instrument that God has given to us, then they tinker and tamper with the faith *which* we believe—they inevitably tinker and tamper with the gospel of Jesus Christ himself. There is no doubt in my mind whatsoever that "The New Perspective" is busy mangling this great doctrine of justification. You read their writings. There is something labored, convoluted, and tortured about it all. Indeed, they are not only busy mangling the great doctrine of justification, they are in the process of mangling the very gospel which is the only message of hope we have to give to poor, lost, ruined, guilty sinners. Let me put it this way. Where, in "The New Perspective," is the biblical emphasis upon sin? Where, in "The New Perspective," is the biblical emphasis upon guilt? Where in this "New Perspective" is the biblical emphasis upon the judgment of God? And where, O where, in this "New Perspective" is the emphasis upon the Savior that we find in the blessed gospel of Jesus Christ? The whole gravitational pull of this "New Perspective" is, as Professor Donald Macleod has put it, towards "the religion of self-justification."[12]   The same is true of "Shepherdism"; and the same is true, sadly, of the "Federal Vision Theology." Each of them is a subtle form of legalism. They are subversive of the gospel; they are subversive of this great, wonderful, yet vulnerable doctrine of justification by faith alone.

This great doctrine is, as J. I. Packer once put it, like Atlas—Atlas, that bears a whole world upon his shoulders; and if Atlas stumbles, a whole world comes crashing down. We are living in days of great crisis. The last twenty-five or thirty years have witnessed an astonishing erosion of this great doctrine which is still "the article of the standing or the falling of the Church." In my view, we face potentially one of the greatest crises and one of the greatest battles since the days of the Reformation with regard to this particular doctrine. It is for this reason that I urge all those that preach the Word of God and that rule in the Church of Christ to study this great doctrine afresh, to master it, to become well acquainted with its contours and its recesses, and with the most minute points of this wonderful doctrine that God has given to sinners and to the Christian Church, to love this doctrine, to delight in it, to preach it, to proclaim it, and to uphold it. If this doctrine is destroyed, the very gospel of Jesus Christ will be destroyed with it. I urge you, therefore, those that preach the Word of God and those that rule in the Church of Jesus Christ, to contend earnestly for this great doctrine which is still "the article of the standing or the falling of the Church," to contend for it in the pulpit, and with the pen, and even in the courts of the Church. I urge you to proclaim it and to uphold it, to proclaim and uphold the old paths, and the old perspective which the reformers have so wonderfully chiseled out on the anvil of study and often of suffering, and have given to us in these last five hundred years. I exhort you to contend earnestly for "the faith once delivered unto the saints" and for this delicate instrument "by faith alone" that we find here in our text this evening.

But secondly, we have here *a consolation to all true believers in the Lord Jesus Christ.* Listen to what the Apostle goes on to say: "Therefore being justified by faith, we have peace with God through our Lord Jesus Christ," (Rom 5:1). You know, peace is always a very, very precious thing. Jonathan Edwards once said that "all happiness consists in peace"—international peace; national peace; ecclesiastical peace; do-

---

[12] Donald MacLeod, *A Faith To Live By* (Fearn, Ross-shire, UK: Christian Focus Publications, 1998), 167.

mestic peace; peace of mind; even the peace of God.[13] But towering above it all is "peace with God"—that objective status into which we enter by grace, through faith alone. "Being justified by faith, we have this peace with God," says the Apostle. It is, notice, through our Lord Jesus Christ. You see, this great doctrine is the doctrine of assurance, above all others. It may be that there is some soul here tonight that is constantly troubled by the issue of assurance. You are tossed to and fro on every wind of thought concerning your status and your condition in the sight of God. My good friends, I urge you to study afresh this great doctrine. For this doctrine is, above all, the doctrine of assurance; and you will see that this great doctrine teaches us that our assurance is rooted and grounded in the Lord Jesus Christ. For we cannot separate the doctrine of justification from the doctrine of atonement; they are interwoven, they are intertwined. They are utterly inseparable in the verses that we have considered here tonight. "We have peace with God through our Lord Jesus Christ." As a result, says the apostle, "there is now no condemnation to them that are in Christ Jesus." My good friends, have you grasped that—that you are justified freely by the grace of God, through faith? You are justified by Jesus Christ, His person and His work, appropriated and received through faith alone. As a result, "there is now no condemnation to them that are in Christ Jesus," (Rom 8:1).

Now let me emphasize and illustrate the beauty of this doctrine. There are, no doubt, some Christians here tonight that in the past have been much greater sinners than others; and there are, no doubt, some Christians here tonight who are less godly than other Christians. But I want to emphasize that there is no Christian here tonight that is any less justified than any other Christian for this reason: that although sin admits of degrees, and although godliness and holiness admit of degrees, this wonderful justification that God gives us by faith never admits of degrees. Thus every single true believer here tonight is just as much justified in the sight of God as any other Christian. This is a wonderful fact: and this is the rock of our position. Thus when we trip and fall and stumble in this life, it is to this that we must come back. I emphasize again this truth: the Christian can never, ever lose this justification. We do not go in and out of it. We do not have it one day and lose it the next. Listen to what the Apostle has to say: "And whom He justified, them He

---

[13] Jonathan Edwards, *The Works of Jonathan Edwards. Sermons and Discourses, 1723-1729,* ed. Kenneth P. Minkema (New Haven: Yale University Press, 1997), 14:130.

also glorified," (Rom 8:30). In other words, there is an inevitable connection between our justification and our glorification. If you are a true believer in the Lord Jesus Christ, then you are justified freely by His grace; and if you are justified freely by His grace, then one day God will glorify you. He has given us His word; He has given us His promise. "And whom He justified, them He also glorified." Count Zinzendorf puts it very beautifully in his hymn:

> Jesus, Thy blood and righteousness,
> My beauty are, my glorious dress;
> Midst flaming worlds in these arrayed
> With joy shall I lift up my head."

> This spotless robe the same appears
> When ruined nature sinks in years.
> No age can change its glorious hue.
> The robe of Christ is ever new.

My good friends, do you have an understanding of this great doctrine? Have you grasped that it is by faith in Jesus Christ that you are justified? Have you grasped that, though you must look inwards and see your sin, you must look outwards and behold Him in faith? Have you seen that "this spotless robe" never, ever changes? It can never, ever be taken away from you. Once you have it, you have it forever, because those that God justifies, He also glorifies.

In 1662, David Dickson lay on his deathbed. David Dickson was a Presbyterian minister in the Church of Scotland who wrote a wonderful commentary on the Psalms. He was a professor of divinity in Glasgow University and later in Edinburgh University. But at the end of his life, at the age of seventy-nine, when he was visited by his friend, John Livingstone, it was not those things to which he was looking. No, no, this is what he said: "I have taken all my good deeds and all my bad deeds, and cast them through each other in a heap before the Lord, and fled from both, and betaken myself to the Lord Jesus Christ, and in Him I have sweet peace."[14] My good friends, have you done that? Have you taken all your good deeds and all your bad deeds, and have you cast them

---

[14] David Dickson, *A Commentary on the Psalms* (reprint, Edinburgh: The Banner of Truth Trust, 1959), xxiii.

through each other in a heap before the Lord and fled from both, and be-taken yourself to the Lord Jesus Christ, and in Him do you have sweet peace? If you have not done so, I urge you here this evening to arise and to go to Him, the Savior who says, "Come unto Me!" "Come unto Me, all ye that labor and are heavy laden, and I will give you rest" (Matt 11:28) — "rest unto your souls," peace with God and a home in heaven, and glorification that nothing and nobody can take away. For whom God justifies, He also glorifies and takes to be with the Forerunner, who has gone within the veil, even Jesus Christ, our Lord. Amen.

Chapter 8

Defense of Paedocommunion

Robert S. Rayburn

I am a son of the covenant. I grew up the loyal son of a Reformed and Presbyterian home. I was taught the catechism as a boy and I believed it. As I came into young adulthood I had occasion to put some of that teaching to the test. I satisfied my mind, for example, that the doctrine of divine sovereignty, which I had been taught as a boy, was not only the unequivocal teaching of Holy Scripture, but also the necessary implication of the Bible's theology, its doctrine of God. Through my college and seminary years I examined for myself and settled my mind concerning some other doctrines that lie near the heart of that theological system that we have inherited from the magisterial reformers, the British and Dutch Puritans, and the American Presbyterians. I continue to believe that the unassailable strength of that theology and the way of life derived from it is its robust biblicism, its determination neither to fall short of nor go beyond the plain-speaking of the Word of God.

When I was ordained to the Presbyterian ministry, I took no exceptions to the *Westminster Standards*. I was well into my ministry when, for the first time, I was presented with an argument that seemed to me, on its face, to cast doubt on the biblical foundation of a part of my faith and life as a Reformed Christian. It was, to be sure, not a major part of the theological system I had been taught in home, in church, and in seminary. Indeed, I have no recollection of the question ever coming up in a seminary class, though it may have incidentally. No statement of this particular doctrine or its related practice is found in any of the great Reformed confessions, even in the most elaborate of them, and in the case of our Presbyterian standards the assertion amounts to no more than fourteen words at the tail end of a long answer to a question of the *Larger Catechism*. It was, however, the well-nigh universal assumption of our church and lay beneath a universal practice. It has to do with how the church understands the nature of the church membership of covenant children. This, in turn, has significant implications for our understanding of the way God takes with the children of the covenant and so bears on the practice of the sacrament of the Lord's Supper. Reformed churches have since the Reformation excluded baptized covenant children from participation in the Lord's Supper *until* they are of an age at which they are thought capable of professing their own faith in Jesus Christ. But now that practice and the understanding that lay beneath it was being called into question.

When I first began to doubt this practice, I turned to our Reformed authorities on the assumption that I would find what I had always found before: a careful and learned presentation of the biblical data and a persuasive argument that the Bible teaches what we had always believed and practiced. It is an understatement to say that I was disappointed by what I found. In many works of Reformed systematic theology, even in many works on the Lord's Supper and its practice, there was no mention of, much less any serious consideration of, the universal practice of excluding covenant children from the covenant meal. In the rare instances in which an argument was offered in support of our practice it was perfunctory and utterly incapable of resisting the attack that was now being mounted against our theory and our practice. The new thinking, in fact, had all the power and persuasiveness I had so long associated with theological constructions of the Reformed type, namely, that it took seriously the actual statements of the Bible and constructed from them a consistent doctrine and practice. The new understanding of the Bible's teaching regarding the place of our children at the sacramental meal was not only consistent with the biblical data themselves, but also was more consistent with Reformed definitions of the sacrament than was the traditional practice. I noticed for the first time that if one reads the chapters *Of the Sacraments* and *Of the Lord's Supper* in our *Westminster Confession of Faith* one finds not only that there is not the scintilla of an idea that our covenant children would not be welcome at the Lord's

Supper, but also any number of statements that seem to demand their participation.

Our motto in the Reformed church has long been *ecclesia reformata sed semper reformanda*. Surely we should be the last Christians to suppose that our spiritual ancestors got everything right, that they, alone among all Christians in all ages, were not distracted by the distempers of their times or did not, however unintentionally, slip into or perpetuate mistakes of thought and practice simply because, consumed by the great issues of their time, they had neither the time nor the opportunity thoroughly to consider every possible issue. Children had not participated in the Lord's Supper for centuries by the time of the Reformation. No one was clamoring for them to do so. Only a few isolated voices were raised in support of such a practice. There were many other battles to be fought. There is not, to my knowledge, a single work devoted to the question *pro* or *con* from the era of the Reformation or the generations immediately thereafter. The most one finds is a few pages here and there.[1] It is time to ask whether a mistake was inadvertently made and what better way to answer that question than to return to Holy Scripture not to defend an existing tradition but to collect the data and construct from the ground up the Bible's own doctrine and practice.

And what do we find when we come to the Bible? First, so far as Holy Scripture ever speaks to the question, it always includes covenant children in the sacramental meals of the church. A family preparing the Passover meal prepared as much food as it had mouths to feed (Exod. 12:4).[2] Explicit mention is made of the participation of covenant chil-

---

[1] See the summary of Reformed reflection on the question from the time of the Reformation through the scholastic period in Bernhardus DeMoor, Commentarius Perpetuus in Johannis Marckii Compendium, Pars V, Caput XXXI, xii, (Leiden, 1768), 643-648. That reflection amounts to a few pages here and there.

[2] It was sometimes asserted that "the Passover, the place of which has been taken by the Supper, did not admit all guests indiscriminately, but was duly eaten only by those who were old enough to be able to inquire into its meaning [Ex. 12:26]." John Calvin, Institutes of the Christian Religion, IV, xvi, 30, trans. F. L. Battles (Philadelphia: The Westminster Press, 1965). So also, for example, Walaeus in DeMoor, Commentarius, Pars V, 645. This is an unnatural and tendentious reading of the text, however, and, just as often, it is admitted by Reformed authorities that children did eat the Passover meal. So, for example, Herman Witsius, Economy of the Covenants between God and Man, vol. 2, trans. W. Crookshank (London, T.Tegg and Son, 1837), 269 and Louis Berkhof, Systematic Theology (Grand Rapids, Wm. B. Eerdmans Publishing Co., 1941), 656. The lovely rhetorical touch in 12:26 – "And when your children ask you..." – manifestly does not mean either that the children have been sitting at the table watching adults eat food

dren in other sacramental meals. The children of the priests, indeed everyone in their households, shared in the sacrifices the priests offered (Lev. 10:14; 18:11) and the children of Israelite worshipers were included as a matter of course in the various sacramental meals of Israelite worship. I would appeal to Moses when he says, "there bring your burnt offerings and sacrifices, your tithes and special gifts, what you have vowed to give and your freewill offerings, and the firstborn of your herds and flocks. There, in the presence of the Lord your God, you and your families shall eat and shall rejoice in everything you have put your hand to, because the Lord your God has blessed you (Deut. 12:6-7).

Twice more in that section of general instruction for sacrificial wor-

---

that is not permitted them or that some capacity for catechetical conversation is a prerequisite of participation in the Passover meal. 12:4 assumes their participation in the meal; 12:26 that the meal becomes an occasion for conversation about the mighty acts of God. Umberto Cassuto, A Commentary on the Book of Exodus, trans. I. Abrahams (Jerusalem: The Hebrew University, 1967), 144. Regarding the directions of 12:3-4, Brevard Childs comments, "The whole community of Israel is involved (v. 3) and the concern to include all Israel continues throughout the chapter as an essential feature.... The final phrase in v.4b offers the normal eating capacity as the criterion by which the computation of participants is made. The very young and the very old would not count in the same way as the average adult." The Book of Exodus (Philadelphia, Westminster Press, 1974), 197-198. In regard to v. 26, Childs writes, "Because this rite is to become a permanent institution within Israel, later generations must need to know its significance. How does Israel transmit its faith to the next generation? The writer poses the questions in terms of a child's query." [p. 200] That as a matter of course little children partook of the Passover meal may be said to be the consensus of the commentaries. ". . .more than two families might unite for this purpose, when they consisted simply of the father and mother and little children." C.F. Keil and F. Delitzsch, Commentary on the Old Testament, vol. ii, trans. J. Martin (Reprint, Grand Rapids, Wm. B. Eerdmans Publishing Co., 1973), 11. The phrase, "the whole community of Israel" in 12:3, 6, 19, and 47 is instructive. It is a way of speaking that emphatically includes the entire population of Israel (e.g. 16:1 and passim) while making provision for representative acts (12:6, 21), acts, that is, in which the entire community may be said to be acting through its representatives. It is manifestly not a way of speaking intended to carve up the population into participating and non-participating elements. The eating of the Passover meal itself is plainly not a representative act but the literal act of the entire community. When in 12:47 we are told that the whole community is to celebrate the Passover, it would be passing strange to suppose that the real intention of that direction was to include some of the community while excluding a substantial segment of it. It is difficult to resist the impression that the interpretation of Exod. 12:26 that takes it as a demonstration of the non-participation of covenant children in the Passover meal owes its existence to the assumption that children would not have and should not have eaten the Passover, an assumption that, in turn, owes its existence to the longstanding practice of Christian churches not to give covenant children the Lord's Supper.

ship a point is made of saying that the worshipper's "sons and daughters" are to participate with him in the eating of these sacrificial meals. (Deut. 12:12, 18) In a manner typical of the presentation of the liturgical regulations of the Mosaic law, the profile of participants is not always described, but, when it is, the children are included as a matter of course (Deut. 16:11, 14).

Second, statements such as these, artless as they are, are the more weighty for the total absence of contrary testimony. At no point do we hear that children *per se* are excluded from a certain sacrificial meal. At no point are we taught that certain qualifications must be met for participation in the sacramental meals of the covenant, qualifications that children could not meet by reason of their age or immaturity. At no point do we encounter what we surely might reasonably expect to encounter, namely, instruction concerning or the narrative of a covenant child being prepared for or granted entrance into this sacramental participation, having reached a certain age or having crossed some spiritual boundary. It is a point to be made repeatedly: the Scripture often *says* that covenant children participated in the sacramental meals of Israelite worship; it never *says* that they did not or were not to. Scripture knows how to say that certain privileges are reserved for those who reach a certain age, as, for example, it does in the case of the priesthood, but it never says anything like this regarding the participation of children in the sacramental meals of the covenant. Indeed, it says nothing remotely like this.

Third, there is nothing surprising in any of this. It is altogether what we would expect given the doctrine of covenant children in the ancient Scriptures. The participation of children in the sacramental meals is entirely consistent with the inclusion of those children in the membership of the covenant community, in the Lord's insistence upon their circumcision, in the Scripture's inclusion of them as participants in the life of the community in ceremonies of covenant renewal (e.g. Deut. 29:11; Joel 2:16), in its artless assumption of early, even infant, faith (Ps. 22:9-10; 71:5-6; 1 Kings 18:12), in its everywhere treating them as spiritually susceptible to the nurture and admonition of the Lord, and in its placing them on a continuum of development in faith and devotion from infancy to adulthood. In short, there is nothing in all this doctrine to suggest that some spiritual frontier had to be crossed before the children of the covenant were allowed to participate in its liturgical life; nothing to suggest that the sacramental meals, alone of all the means of grace, were to be withheld from them; nothing to suggest by what principle and for what reason they alone would be excluded from this part of the life of that community to which they are everywhere said to belong. On the contrary, all the teaching of these Scriptures consistently presents covenant children as members of the covenant community and so participants in its life and liturgy as they were able.[3]

The data of the New Testament present a similar picture. Children are included, as a matter of course, in the membership of the church (Matt. 18:13-15; Eph. 1:1; 6:1-3; 1 Cor. 7:14), testimony is once again given to early, even infant faith (2 Tim. 3:15; Luke 1:15),[4] the sign of the covenant is given to them (Acts 2:38-39; 16:15, 33), and, as before, there is not the whisper of a suggestion that the apostolic church practiced some adolescent rite of passage that was prerequisite to covenant children being permitted to participate fully in the liturgical life of the church. There is no liturgical regulation to this effect, there is no narrative of such a thing happening, there is no teaching of such a principle as would render such a rite expedient or necessary.[5]

---

[3] It is true that children were not required to participate in the three pilgrimage feasts, but neither were the women of the community. In fact, it is striking to note how often children and women are mentioned together in the liturgical directions. Their participation clearly is based on the same principle of membership in the covenant community.

[4] Calvin's brilliant exposition of the "seed" of faith and repentance in the infants of the covenant, part of his argument for infant baptism, seems to me a powerful justification of paedocommunion (Institutes, IV, xvi, 16-20). His insistence that covenant children are to grow into a fuller understanding of their baptism as they get older is a perfect way of describing their developing relationship to the Lord's Supper [xvi, 21]. The primary ground of infant baptism in Reformed theology is that the children of believers are subjects of the covenant of grace and members of the covenant community. However, it is also widely asserted, following Calvin, that covenant children are to be baptized as believers, if not in the same sense as an adult may be a believer, but as possessing the seed of faith. Indeed this may be said to be the most common position of Reformed theology. Henricus Eskelhoff Gravemeijer, Leesboek over de Gereformeerde Geloofsleer, 2nd ed., vol. 3 (Utrecht, H. Ten Hoove, 1894), 428-433 and DeMoor, Commentarius, Pars IV, 318-325.

[5] These observations certainly rest the burden of proof on those who wish to defend as biblical a two-tier membership in the church (communicant and non-communicant) and the practice of requiring as a rite the profession of faith on the part of covenant children as the prerequisite for entrance into the fullness of their covenant privileges. Where does the Bible say this? This is a particularly pressing question in light of the fact that the evidence suggests that in first century Judaism children regularly ate the Passover meal. This point is admitted, if reluctantly, even by paedocommunion's detractors. R. Beckwith, "The Age of admission to the Lord's Supper," Westminster Theological Journal XXXVIII No. 2 (1976) 144-148.

It is, of course, thought by many that just such a principle is provided in the Apostle Paul's admonition against the unworthy eating of the Lord's Supper in 1 Corinthians 11 and in his requirement that believers examine themselves before coming to the table. It is a fact very easy to demonstrate that this single remark is virtually the entire argument against paedocommunion in Reformed works that deal with the question. As I was growing up and for some time into my ministry, I also thought that the requirement of self-examination before participation in the Supper must exclude little children in the nature of the case. It was the only rationale I had ever heard and it satisfied a superficial consideration, which was the only sort of consideration ever given to the question in those days. I began to doubt its relevance the first time I actually thought about it! Quite apart from the unassailable facts that Paul is neither discussing paedocommunion in 1 Corinthians 11 nor addressing himself to the subject of the general qualifications for participation in the Supper, the Apostle says nothing in correcting the abuse of the sacrament in the Corinthian church that the prophets did not say before him at a time when the participation of children in sacramental meals was not only permitted but ordered by the express statements of Holy Scripture.[6]

---

[6] In other ways the application of Paul's admonition in 1 Cor. 11 to the question of paedocommunion is problematic. The assumption seems to be that little children are incapable of spiritual acts and are therefore excluded, in the nature of the case, by Paul's requirement that there be active mental and spiritual engagement with the meaning of the Supper on the part of those who participate. This point is often made as an argument against paedocommunion by Reformed authorities. But mental and spiritual life is a continuum and has very early beginnings as the Bible artlessly acknowledges when it speaks of a person "rejoicing" in his mother's womb, or trusting in the Lord at his mother's breasts, or knowing the Scripture from his infancy. A weaned covenant child should already be beginning to reckon with the meaning of Christ and his salvation and the implications of faith. Both the understanding and the practice of faith are continual and their beginning is, we are everywhere taught in Holy Scripture, ordinarily found very early in the life of covenant children. As the Word is being given to a covenant child and its truth established in his heart, the sacrament naturally comes alongside to contribute its share to the establishment and maturing of faith. Given the long-standing emphasis of the Reformed tradition on the interrelationship between Word and sacrament, an emphasis that is fundamental to its understanding of the purpose of the sacrament, the practice of teaching our littlest children to say "Our Father..." but requiring them to wait years to eat the Savior's body and blood is a practice requiring an explanation clearer and more directly related to the actual statements of the Bible than has ever been provided. The fact is, as very little children can take and eat, so very little children can believe and can begin to grow in the faith of Christ their savior. Therefore, even if one were to accept that the text requires self-examination by every participant, it would still not exclude

154 DEFENSE OF PAEDOCOMMUNION

When Isaiah or Amos or Jeremiah accuse their contemporaries of an unworthy participation in worship, including sacramental worship, and call them to self-examination and repentance (e.g. Isa. 1:10-20; Amos 5:18-27; Jer. 7:1-29; Hos. 6:6; Mic. 6:8; 1 Sam. 15:22), they were certainly not setting aside the Law's requirement that God's people eat the sacrifices with their sons and daughters. Nor were they establishing a ritual requirement of self-examination, as if a prerequisite of participation in a sacramental meal was some spiritual exercise by which certain signs of sufficiently righteous living were to be detected and assurance of salvation thereby once again confirmed. The prophets were calling the people to repentance and reminding them that not only could no one

---

weaned covenant children from the Lord's Supper. Quite the contrary. It would seem to require their faithful participation, suitable to their age and spiritual maturity, as it requires the faithful participation of all members of the church. This is a point requiring some emphasis. The typical statements in Reformed materials to the effect that the food of the Supper is not suitable for very little children or that the ritual of the Supper is beyond the means of infants often betray a failure to distinguish between a nursing infant and a weaned child or between the beginnings of spiritual life and the maturity of adult faith. It is an Achilles' heel of Reformed polemics against paedocommunion that Calvin (Institutes, IV, xvi, 30) should argue that "...the Supper is given to older persons who, having passed tender infancy [qui superata teneriore infantia...] can now take solid food;" that DeMoor should find it sufficient to exclude from the Supper covenant children who have been recently baptized [Commentarius, Pars V, 643]; that John Murray should wish to say no more than "We can readily detect that there is in the elements used and the actions involved something that is not congruous with early infancy." (Christian Baptism [Philadelphia, Presbyterian and Reformed Publishing Co., 1972], 77-79); and that Witsius should maintain that "Infants cannot examine themselves..." (Economy, vol. 2, 455). Such statements amount to admissions that very little children, that weaned children indeed, can partake of the Lord's Supper, which is, after all, all that is being argued for! These arguments may tell against the Orthodox practice of intinction by which the bread soaked in wine is given to the newborn upon his baptism, but they do not tell against the custom of children's participating in the sacramental meal as soon as they are able to eat, the pattern established in Holy Scripture itself. However, it is very doubtful we should understand Paul in 1 Corinthians 11 as actually laying down some liturgical requirement of self-examination as a prerequisite for participation in the Lord's Supper. Paul is speaking to adults about sins they were committing. He is relating the repentance he demands to their practice of the Supper. He is not thinking about the participation of children and is not addressing their case. We do not know what special directions Paul might have given for the participation of children in the Supper, for he never addressed the question; nor did any other biblical writer. More would have to be said before we could fairly take him to mean that he understood his remarks to bear directly on the participation of children. We do not draw such a conclusion when Paul tells a congregation that those who do not work should not eat or when Peter tells his hearers that they must repent in order to be baptized.

worship God aright who had no intention of serving him, but that the hypocritical worship of rebels was deeply offensive to God. They were not saying that one must have an adult-like faith in order to participate properly in the worship of God, they were not saying that a certain maturity of mental development was a prerequisite of right worship, and they were not saying that warnings addressed to adult sinners in the nature of the case excluded the little children of those who came to God in faith. The application of Paul's admonition in 1 Corinthians 11 to the general question of the participation of children in the Lord's Supper violates the universe of discourse. Making this still more clear is Paul's assertion, at the beginning of his long discussion of the Lord's Supper in the Corinthian church, that the entire community of Israel ate "the same spiritual food" and drank "the same spiritual drink" (1 Cor. 10:3). That children ate the food so described is not in dispute. Nor can it be doubted that the children, as part of the people of Israel, also ate the sacrifices of the altar, a point Paul makes subsequently (1 Cor. 10:18). Why would we then suppose that Paul was excluding children from the sacramental meal by his remarks in 1 Corinthians 11? The fact that some adults may sin against the sacrament was never before a reason to exclude the children. This is a point all the more relevant in that no one supposes that the children were excluded from participation in the agape feast that apparently regularly preceded the Lord's Supper in the Corinthian church. Paul is entirely used to the idea of the entire spiritual community participating in a meal together. His is a warning not to participate unworthily.

The fact is, the argument that Baptists use against infant baptism has precisely the same form as the argument the Reformed have long urged against the participation of little children in the Lord's Supper. If Peter says, "Repent and be baptized," and if meaningful repentance is beyond the means of very little children, then, in the nature of the case, little children are excluded from baptism. To which argument the Reformed have long rightly replied that Peter is speaking to adults in that context and, while his words certainly applied to the adults who were listening to him, in the total context of biblical teaching they do not apply to covenant children. There is another way to qualify for baptism than by an adult's repentance or an adult's profession of faith. Well, in the same way, if Paul says, "let a man examine himself and then let him eat," and if very young children cannot conduct such an examination, then we have argued that little children cannot participate in the Lord's Supper.

To which argument the Reformed should have boldly replied, with Bible in hand, there is another way to qualify for a place at the table of the Lord than by an adult's profession of faith or an adult's self-examination.

The similarity between the Baptist argument against paedobaptism and the Reformed argument against paedocommunion being what it is, it should surprise no one that the same reply the Reformed have long made to the Baptists is now being made by many among the Reformed to the argument of their own tradition that would exclude covenant children from participation in the Lord's Supper.

For better or worse, Reformed writers never pondered the possible objections to the use of 1 Corinthians 11 as an argument against paedocommunion. Their appeal to it was perfunctory at best as the literature amply demonstrates. Recent efforts to rehabilitate the argument against paedocommunion from 1 Corinthians 11 are novel and go well beyond the simple appeal to the necessity of self-examination one finds in the literature. The Reformed tradition, therefore, obliges no one to face any other objection to paedocommunion than that Paul requires that a man examine himself before he eats or drinks. If it is once admitted that it is not obvious that Paul's demand in that context has any bearing on the participation of children in the covenantal meal, there remains no serious argument against paedocommunion in the Reformed tradition. The exclusion of children from the Lord's Supper is a practice suspended in mid-air.

It is admitted by everyone that from the mid-third century onwards the practice of paedocommunion was commonplace in the church.[7] Mention is made of the practice in the *obiter dicta* of Cyprian and Augustine, among others. Some have attempted to argue that the lack of evidence for the practice earlier than Cyprian is evidence that it was an innovation in his time,[8] but their arguments are special pleading. In fact, the case is precisely similar to that of the patristic evidence for infant baptism: 1) it occurs quite early; 2) the practice is not mentioned in still

---

[7] The relevant testimonia are conveniently collected in Christian Keidel, "Is the Lord's Supper for Children?" Westminster Theological Journal XXXVII, no. 3 (1975): 301-303 and Tim Gallant, Feed My Lambs (Grande Prairie: Pactum Reformanda Publishing, 2002), 106-121.

[8] Beckwith, "The Age of Admission," 125-126 and Leonard J. Coppes, Daddy, May I Take Communion? (Thornton, CO: Leonard J. Coppes, 1988) 41-42.

earlier materials, but neither is it spoken against;[9] 3) and in the references to it there is no sense of its being either an innovation or a contro-
versial practice; indeed, it is a practice so much taken for granted that it
may be appealed to in demonstration of other things. Reformed polemi-
cists for infant baptism have regularly used this kind of evidence to
demonstrate both that infant baptism was the common practice of the
primitive church and that the most natural explanation for this practice is
that it was the inheritance of apostolic Christianity.

The fact is that even later authorities who did not approve the practice of paedocommunion, such as Calvin and, interestingly, the Council
of Trent,[10] accepted that it was the common practice of the early church.
To be sure, a rationale is sometimes provided by the fathers with which
we would not entirely agree. We encounter the same disappointment in
what the fathers sometimes said in explaining the practice of infant baptism. Nevertheless these facts seem beyond dispute: 1) the early church
widely and regularly gave the Lord's Supper to infants; 2) she assumed
the practice to conform to apostolic practice; 3) she did not regard 1 Corinthians 11 as forbidding paedocommunion; and 4) she regarded her
children as in need of the Supper fully as much as her adult members.[11]

The practice of the Reformed church in withholding the Lord's Supper from her baptized covenant children until such time as they profess
faith was, as I have said, never furnished anything but a superficial justification. The *Westminster Confession of Faith* defines the visible church
as "all those...that profess the true religion, together with their children"
(XXV, ii). It defines the sacraments as "holy signs and seals of the
covenant of grace...to represent Christ and his benefits, and to confirm
our interest in him: as also to put a visible difference between those that
belong unto the church and the rest of the world" (XXVII, i). It maintains that "The sacraments of the Old Testament, in regard of the spiritual things thereby signified and exhibited, were, for substance, the same
with those of the New" (XXVII, v). Upon those principles, manifestly
biblical as they are, is based the Reformed practice of paedobaptism. By

[9] The reference in Origen's Homilies on Judges 6.2 appealed to by Beckwith and
Coppes is ambiguous and proves nothing.
[10] The Canons and Decrees of the Council of Trent, Twenty First Session, Chapter
IV.
[11] The practice gradually disappeared in the medieval church, apparently as a result
of the rise of superstitious views of the sacramental elements By the time of the Reformation, paedocommunion had not been practiced for several centuries.

no application of those same principles can paedocommunion be invalidated. Quite the contrary. Paedocommunion is as much the necessary consequence of this ecclesiology as is paedobaptism. Perhaps this explains why a practice, so visible and consequential in its effect on the life of the church, is finally provided justification not in the *Confession of Faith* but in a few words of the Larger Catechism (L.C. 177).

We can, therefore, put the theological challenge of paedocommunion in terms of this question: where does Scripture ever suggest and by what principle does Reformed theology assert that a participant in the benefits of the covenant of grace is to be denied the sign and seal of those benefits?[12] It is not, after all, obvious why the Word and one sacrament should be given to covenant children at the headwaters of their lives, but the Lord's Supper, the meal of the covenant, should await some unnamed spiritual development characteristic of adolescence or young adulthood. One thing newborns need above all is nourishment.[13]

That is the argument for paedocommunion. It can be elaborated in greater detail, to be sure, but the argument is elegantly simple and strikingly similar to the argument the Reformed are accustomed to offering for the practice of paedobaptism: 1) the covenant meals were enjoyed by covenant children in the ancient epoch; 2) the ancient Scriptures teach comprehensively and emphatically that the participation of children in the sacramental meals was by virtue of their membership in the

---

[12] "Withholding of the Supper from children deprives them of not one benefit of the covenant of grace." H. Bavinck, Gereformeerde Dogmatiek, (Kampen: J. H. Kok, 1918), 4:642. The great Bavinck is deserving of the highest respect, but that statement is, on its face, preposterous. The means of grace are supreme benefits of the covenant of grace!

[13] While in this case John Murray is speaking of infant baptism, the following words intriguingly seem still more appropriate in reference to paedocommunion. "It is objected that infants cannot understand the meaning of that which is dispensed. Of course they cannot. But that they derive no benefit from baptism or that it is not the divine method of signifying and sealing blessings to them is by no means a proper inference. The same objection would apply to circumcision and would impinge upon the wisdom and grace of God who instituted it. The same objection, if valid, would apply to Christ's blessing of little infants. This objection, in fact, rests upon the iniquitous assumption that all blessing is contingent upon conscious understanding of its import on our part. Are we to say, for example, that it is of no avail to an infant to be born and nurtured in a Christian family simply because the infant has no conscious understanding of the great blessing that belongs to him in the care, protection, devotion, and nurture of Christian parents? ...The means of grace are channels along which the saving and sanctifying grace of God flows. To be in the channel of grace by God's appointment is of deepest consequence. It is only worldly-wise calculation and not reasoning inspired by the recognition of the methods of divine grace that can find force in this type of objection" (Christian Baptism, 74-75).

covenant community and answered their need to participate in its life and ritual from the very headwaters of their lives; 3) the theology of covenant children and of God's way of grace with them taught comprehensively in the Old Testament is reiterated in the New Testament; there is no new doctrine of the children of the covenant in the last twenty-seven books of the Bible; 4) the argument against paedocommunion typically drawn from 1 Corinthians 11 and Paul's demand for self-examination on the part of those who had abused the Supper is an instance of the failure to interpret statements contextually; and 5) the evidence of patristic Christianity lays the burden of proof squarely on those who would assert that the practice of paedocommunion was not early Christianity's inheritance from apostolic Christianity.

Defenders of the tradition nowadays tend argue for it primarily in two ways. First and foremost they reassert the traditional argument drawn from 1 Corinthians 11,[14] often as if it remains self-evident. It is the power and the danger of tradition that it can create a paradigm of understanding and interpretation so compelling and satisfying that it renders many minds oblivious to problems and incapable of imagining another viewpoint. We have, not surprisingly, encountered this reality many times in the debate about infant baptism. Second, the defenders of the Reformed tradition attempt to weaken, if not break altogether, the historical/typological connection between Passover and the Lord's Sup-

---

[14] The corollaries of that argument, really the same argument in other forms, are, first, the distinction between baptism as the sacrament of initiation and the Lord's Supper as the sacrament of nutrition and, second, the supposed distinction between the passive role of the individual in baptism and his active role in the Lord's Supper. Such distinctions, tendentious inferences at best, are plainly instances of petitio principii and, as arguments against paedocommunion, are worthless. Nevertheless, that the supposed distinction between baptism as a sacrament of initiation and the Lord's Supper as a sacrament of nutrition, common in earlier Reformed materials, should be used as an argument against paedocommunion seems to me both passing strange and powerful evidence of how uncritical the Reformed argument really was. Covenant children are to be nourished with the Word from their earliest days. By what principle would they not be given another mean of their spiritual nourishment? This is a difficult question to answer for the Reformed who make a great deal of the intimate relationship between word and sacrament and are often prepared to say that the sacrament is the Word of God in another form. By what principle, then, are our children to be given the sacrament that is the "seal of the righteousness that is by faith" and to be given the Word of God (Gen. 18:19; Deut 6:6-9; Psalm 78:1-8), but are not to be given the visible word, the second sacrament, the sacrament that supposedly provides the nourishment of faith, especially since the spiritual feeding of children is a major theme in covenantal ethics?

per. Some, to be sure, attempt to demonstrate that covenant children did not eat the Passover meal. The more sophisticated accept that if the case against paedocommunion is left to rest on that claim it is doomed.[15] A better approach, therefore, is to weaken the force of the connection between the Passover and the Lord's Supper and correspondingly weaken the implication for paedocommunion of the participation of little children in the Passover meal. The problem the defenders of the tradition face at this point is that arguments to that end are not part of the Reformed polemic against paedocommunion. These arguments in the new literature, these constructions of the nature of Old Testament ritual or of the relationship between those rituals and the Lord's Supper are novelties.[16] None belongs to the tradition of Reformed teaching on the Lord's Supper and, in my opinion, that fact is some evidence that they are too hurriedly and somewhat desperately conceived, being run into the breach in hopes of stemming the full-scale retreat now underway from the position established at the Reformation. This new theology of Old Testament ritual has not been found persuasive and, from the side of the opposition, none of this thinking so far broached has come at all close to providing adequate justification for setting aside the weighty arguments that have been advanced for paedocommunion and against our long-standing practice of withholding from Christian children the sacramental meal of the covenant.

There are some dangers in developing novel arguments to defend a tradition under attack. The greatest of these is that the sturdiest form of the tradition, the form most impervious to fatal injury from the assault being made upon it, is that form at furthest remove from the position being advanced by the rebels. It would be a Pyrrhic victory if the Reformed practice of withholding the Lord's Supper from covenant children until their profession of faith in adolescence or young adulthood should be maintained at the price of the diminishment of that part of the

---

[15] It is telling that in the recent deliverances of Reformed Churches critical of paedocommunion (the majority report of the Presbyterian Church in America and the minority reports of the Orthodox Presbyterian Church and the Christian Reformed Church) it is admitted that covenant children ate the Passover meal. The argument in these papers instead takes the form that there is some reason why, though children could partake of the sacramental meals of the Mosaic ritual, they cannot partake of the sacramental meal instituted by Christ.

[16] Such is the nature of Coppes' argument against paedocommunion in *Daddy, May I Take Communion?*

tradition held in common by detractors and defenders alike, namely, the matchless privilege and solemn responsibility of bringing children into the world and raising them in the confidence that the God of the covenant is their God and the faith of the covenant is their inheritance (Gen. 17:7; Ps. 78:1-8; Ezek. 16:20). The debate should remain what it has always been: an argument about the meaning of the participation of children in the sacramental meals of the Old Testament and the bearing of 1 Corinthians 11 on present practice. The Reformed tradition rests on very little. That little is either enough or it is not. Multiplying arguments is sure to cause mischief as it always has when efforts are made to buttress a position not made sufficiently strong by the plain statements of the Bible.

Sniping attacks may comfort those unsettled by the suggestion that our beloved Reformed theology may be in significant error at one point, but they will do nothing to satisfy the growing number of ministers and people who are now persuaded that a mistake was made and has been perpetuated these five hundred years. What is needed is not some new and arcane theory of the Mosaic ritual that has some presumed bearing on the question of paedocommunion. What is needed is a persuasive argument as to why, 1) though children participated in the sacramental meals of the church in the ancient epoch; 2) though there is no teaching anywhere in the Bible to the effect that children are not to participate and no rationale provided according to which they would be excluded from the sacramental life of the community of which they are members and members who participate in all the other means of grace; 3) though in all the pages of Holy Scripture there is no mention of covenant children beginning to participate in the sacramental meal they had not shared before nor instruction as to their preparation for taking such a step; 4) though there is no evidence in the Bible of our ritual of the profession of faith by covenant children; 5) though the New Testament reiterates the ancient theology of covenant children and introduces no new principle that might be applied to the question of the participation of covenant children in the Lord's Supper; 6) though the early church practiced paedocommunion so far as the evidence goes; and 7) though the Reformed doctrines of church and sacrament furnish principles that would seem to require paedocommunion, *nevertheless* our children, members of the church and the objects of her nurture, should not be given this one means of grace.

One can always defend a tradition. One can find a reason, if reasons are needed, to continue to do what we have always done. The question is not whether we can think of reasons for our traditional practice. The question is whether anyone with our theology of covenanted grace and a mind unprejudiced by the custom of centuries would ever read the Bible and conclude that covenant children were positively excluded from participation in the sacramental meal. The Bible never *says* that they were excluded and it often *says* that they did participate. I am a Reformed Christian. I want biblical authority for what I believe and for what I practice. It is precisely that desire that has made me an advocate of paedocommunion.

Chapter 9

Pauline Communion
vs. Paedocommunion[1]

Kenneth L. Gentry, Jr.

In 1975 the *Westminster Theological Journal* published Christian L. Keidel's article "Is the Lord's Supper for Children?" That article sparked a debate that smolders still today in Reformed circles.[2] Despite Roger T. Beckwith's quick and effective response to Keidel, published the following year in the same journal, paedocommunionism developed a life and following of its own.[3] Though widely practiced in liberal ecclesiastical circles, the doctrine has been adopted more recently by numerous ministers within conservative communions. Nevertheless, three leading conservative Presbyterian denominations have declared against it: the Presbyterian Church in America, Orthodox Presbyterian Church, and Reformed Presbyterian Church, United States.[4]

---

[1] Unless otherwise noted the New American Standard Bible is used throughout this paper.

[2] Christian L. Keidel, "Is the Lord's Supper for Children?," *Westminster Theological Journal* 37, no. 3 (Spring 1975): 301-341

[3] Roger T. Beckwith, "The Age of Admission to the Lord's Supper, *Westminster Theological Journal* 38, no. 2 (Winter 1976): 123-51.

[4] Orthodox Presbyterian Church, "Reports of the Committee on Paedocommunion: Majority and Minority Reports," *Minutes of the General Assembly* (1986, 87, 88). Presbyterian Church in America, "Report of the Ad-Interim Committee to Study the Question

The debate before us is between paedocommunionism and the historic Reformed practice of communion. The paedocommunionist argues that both new covenant sacraments belong to the whole Church, including her baptized young children; some include infants. Paedocommunionist Peter Leithart writes: "All those who are baptized are united with Christ under the covenant . . . ; all who have not been cut off should be admitted to the Table that seals and strengthens that union."[5] He insists that "nothing more than the rite of baptism is required for access to the Lord's table."[6] Reformed theology disagrees. For instance, Greg L. Bahnsen discountenances paedocommunion with these words regarding Leithart's point: "many (like myself) do not affirm . . . James Jordan's stance on automatic infant communion (without sessional examination)."[7]

THE REFORMED TRADITION

A proper beginning for my response to the paedocommunionist challenge will be from within my theological frame of reference. As a creedal faith, Presbyterian and Reformed theological reflection commences within a well-defined doctrinal tradition, and that tradition is almost universally opposed to paedocommunion.

As Reformed paedocommunionist Robert S. Rayburn has confessed, "the authorities of Reformed theology render an almost unanimous judgment that covenant children before the age of discretion ought not to be brought to the Lord's Table."[8] Indeed, he is well aware of the traditional forces set against him: "Surely after four and one-half centuries of virtual unanimity on the question of paedocommunion it is natural to be suspicious of what amounts to a charge that virtually without exception

---

of Paedocommunion," in Paul R. Gilchrist, *PCA Digest: Position Papers, 1973–1993* (Atlanta: Presbyterian Church in America, 1993).

[5] Peter J. Leithart, *Daddy, Why Was I Excommunicated?: An Examination of Leonard J. Coppes, Daddy, May I Take Communion?* (Niceville, Fla.: Transfiguration, 1992), 44.

[6] Peter Leithart, "A Response to '1 Corinthians 11:17-34: The Lord's Supper," in E. Calvin Beisner, ed., *The Auburn Avenue Theology, Pros and Cons· Debating the Federal Vision* (Fort Lauderdale, FL · Knox Theological Seminary, 2003), 298.

[7] Greg L Bahnsen, *Theonomy in Christian Ethics*, 3rd ed. (Nacogdoches, TX.: CMP, 2002), xxix.

[8] Robert S. Rayburn, "Minority Report" in the "Report of the Ad Interim Committee to Study the Question of Paedocommunion," *Minutes of the Thirteenth General Assembly of the Presbyterian Church in America* (St. Louis, June 17-21, 1985), 338.

our theologians and our fathers and mothers in the faith have all these generations been deaf to the Lord speaking in the scriptures concerning the place of our children at his table."[9] Fellow Reformed paedocommunionist Keith A. Mathison concurs: "There can be no question that the traditional confessional position of the Reformed churches has been opposed to paedocommunion."[10] Nevertheless, Rayburn regards the "common opinion of the Reformed church on this matter" as "ill-considered."[11]

Paedocommunionists are certainly correct regarding the overwhelming and continuing Reformed resistance to paedocommunion. Consequently, as I begin a Pauline critique of paedocommunionism, I must emphasize to the Reformed Christian the alien nature of the revival of this ancient theological error.[12]

The great Reformer John Calvin specifically denounced paedocommunion in several places in his writings. In his commentary on Exodus we read: "Since, then, the Paschal Lamb corresponds with the Holy Supper, we may gather from hence, that none can be duly admitted to receive it, but those who are capable of being taught."[13] In his commentary on the Gospel of John he writes: "With respect to young children, the ordinance of Christ forbids them to partake of the Lord's Supper; because they are not yet able to know or to celebrate the remembrance of the death of Christ."[14]

In his *Institutes of the Christian Religion*, Calvin directly considers the alleged incongruity of offering baptism but not the Lord's Supper to children. He writes (in part):

The Supper is given to older persons who, having passed tender in-

---

[9] Rayburn, "Minority Report," 342.

[10] Keith A. Mathison, *Given for You: Reclaiming Calvin's Doctrine of the Lord's Supper* (Phillipsburg, NJ: P & R, 2002), 315. Ironically, Mathison argues for paedocommunion — a position he shows to be contrary to Calvin — in a book sub-titled: "Reclaiming Calvin's Doctrine of the Lord's Supper." See also, Peter Leithart, *Daddy, Why Was I Excommunicated?*, 41.

[11] Rayburn, "Minority Report," 338.

[12] David Holeton, *Infant Communion — Then and Now* (Toronto: Grove, 1981).

[13] John Calvin, *Commentaries on the Four Last Books of Moses Arranged in the Form of a Harmony*, trans. Charles William Bingham, (reprint, Grand Rapids: Baker, 1979), 1:465.

[14] John Calvin, *The Gospel According to St John*, in *Calvin's New Testament Commentaries*, ed. David W. Torrance and Thomas F. Torrance, trans. T. H. L. Parker (Grand Rapids: Eerdmans, 1959), 1:169 (at John 6:53).

fancy, can now take solid food. This distinction is very clearly shown in Scripture. For with respect to baptism, the Lord there sets no definite age. But he does not similarly hold forth the Supper for all to partake of, only for those who are capable of discerning the body and blood of the Lord, of examining their own conscience, of proclaiming the Lord's death, and of considering its power. Do we wish anything plainer than the apostle's teaching when he exhorts each man to prove and search himself, then to eat of this bread and drink of this cup [1 Cor. 11:28]? A self-examination ought, therefore, to come first, and it is vain to expect this of infants . . . . If only those who know how to distinguish rightly the holiness of Christ's body are able to participate worthily, why should we offer poison instead of life-giving food to our tender children? . . . Circumcision, which is known to correspond to our baptism, had been appointed for infants. But the Passover, the place of which has been taken by the Supper, did not admit all guests indiscriminately, but was duly eaten only by those who were old enough to be able to inquire into its meaning [Ex.12:26]. If these men had a particle of sound brain left, would they be blind to a thing so clear and obvious? (*Inst.* 4:16:30)

As a result of his strong convictions, "The Register of the Company of Pastors" in Calvin's Geneva required (in 1541) that: "On the Sunday before its celebration an announcement shall be made that no child is to come to it before having made profession of faith in accordance with what is taught in the catechism."[15]

All of the Reformed creeds and confessions follow this approach. The Belgic Confession (1561) notes in Article 35 that "Judas, and Simon the sorcerer, both indeed received the sacrament, but not Christ, who was signified by it, of whom *believers only* are made partakers." It continues a few sentences later: "Therefore no one ought to come to this table without *having previously rightly examined himself.*" The Heidelberg Catechism (1563) in answer to Question 75 reads: "Christ has commanded me and *all believers*, to eat of this broken bread, and to drink of this cup, in remembrance of him." The Scots Confession (1560) states in Chapter 21 that "we confess and believe without doubt that *the faithful* in the right use of the Lord's Table, do so eat the body and drink the blood of the Lord Jesus that he remains in them and they in him."

Question 177 in the Westminster Larger Catechism (1648) answers

---

[15] Philip E. Hughes, ed., *The Register of the Company of Pastors of Geneva in the Time of Calvin* (Grand Rapids: William B. Eerdmans Publishing Co., 1966), 44.

forthrightly: "The sacraments of Baptism and the Lord's Supper differ, in that Baptism is to be administered but once, with water, to be a sign and seal of our regeneration and ingrafting into Christ, and that even to infants; whereas the Lord's Supper is to be administered often, in the elements of bread and wine, to represent and exhibit Christ as spiritual nourishment to the soul, and to confirm our continuance and growth in him, and that only to such as are of years and ability to examine themselves."

Not only are these (and other) Reformed confessions and catechisms opposed to paedocommunion, but so also are the Reformed scholars from the 1600s to the present, including such notables as Herman Witsius, Charles Hodge, R. L. Dabney, B. B. Warfield, Louis Berkhof, Herman Bavinck, John Murray, and Morton H. Smith (to name but a few).[16] One could list one Reformed scholar after another, from one generation after another, in confirming the Reformed resistance to paedocommunion.

Paedocommunionist Tim Gallant objects to the Reformed tradition rooted in Calvin: "It may be rightly questioned whether there is sufficient biblical analysis here [in Calvin] with which to sustain an entire tradition."[17] Mathison, Rayburn, Gallant, and other paedocommunionists argue that Calvin (and the other Reformers) "never gave this issue the deep exegetical and theological reflection that they gave to so many other issues."[18]

However, the paedocommunionists' objection to Reformed ecclesiology has more of a polemical than a substantial force, for throughout his ministry Calvin was deeply engaged in study of the sacraments. His positive contributions are so compelling that a negative critique of the question is not needed. As Calvin scholar J. K. S. Reid observes: "a great deal of Calvin's attention was devoted to the right statement of

---

[16] See for example: Herman Witsius, *The Economy of the Covenant Between God and Man* (reprint, Phillipsburg, N.J.: P & R, n.d.), 2:267ff; Robert L. Dabney, *Lectures in Systematic Theology* (reprint, Grand Rapids: Zondervan, 1973), 727ff; 801ff; Louis Berkhof, *Systematic Theology* (Grand Rapids:William B. Eerdmans Publishing Co., 1941), 656-57; Herman Bavinck, *Gereformeerde Dogmatiek* (Kampen: 1918), 4:641ff; John Murray, *Christian Baptism* (Phillipsburg, N. J.: Presbyterian and Reformed, 1972), 76-79; Morton H. Smith, *Systematic Theology* (Greenville, S.C.: Greenville Seminary Press, 1994), 2:688ff.

[17] Tim Gallant, *Feed My Lambs: Why the Lord's Table Should be Restored to Covenant Children* (Grand Prairie, Canada: Pactum Reformanda, 2002), 20.

[18] Mathison, *Given For You*, 320.

what ought to be believed concerning the nature of the Holy Communion of Holy Supper."[19] John W. Nevin notes of Calvin:

> his profound, far-reaching and deeply penetrating mind drew forth the doctrine [of the Lord's Supper] from the heart of the Church, exhibited it in its proper relations, proportions and distinctions, gave it form in this way for the understanding, and clothed it with authority as a settled article of faith in the general creed. He may be regarded then as the ac-credited interpreter and expounder of the article, for all later times. . . His instructions and explanations here are very full and explicit. He comes upon the subject from all sides, and handles it under all forms, didactically and controversially; so that we are left in no uncertainty whatever, with regard to his meaning, at a single point.[20]

Even Mathison admits, "Calvin's doctrine of the Lord's Supper is one of his greatest contributions to Christian theology,"[21] for "his writings on the subject span the entire course of his career as a reformer and are found in sermons, tracts, commentaries, and theological treatises."[22] Indeed, "one of [Calvin's] greatest contributions to theology, [was] his doctrine of the Lord's Supper" which came "after years of studying the Scriptures and the writings of the church fathers."[23]

THE ECCLESIASTICAL QUESTION

The question of paedocommunion is a significant issue from not only a creedal and historical perspective, but also the ecclesiastical and theological. After all, the sacraments help define the church, by serving as one of her "marks." The Westminster Confession of Faith reads: "Sacraments are holy signs and seals of the covenant of grace, immediately instituted by God, to represent Christ and His benefits; and to confirm our interest in Him: as also, to put a visible difference between those that belong unto the Church and the rest of the world; and solemnly to engage them to the service of God in Christ, according to His Word,"

---

[19] J. K. S. Reid, *Calvin. Theological Treatises. The Library of Christian Classics* (Philadelphia: Westminster, 1954), 18.

[20] John Williamson Nevin, *The Mystical Presence: The Vindication of the Reformed or Calvinistic Doctrine of the Holy Eucharist* (1846; reprint, Eugene, OR.: Wipf & Stock, 2000), 50.

[21] Mathison, *Given for You*, 272.

[22] Ibid., 3.

[23] Ibid., 15.

(27:1; see also Larger Catechism 162). Not only so, but another mark of the church is discipline, which potentially involves exclusion from the Lord's Supper. The Westminster Confession 30:2 and 4 state that church officers hold the "keys of the kingdom of heaven" which includes administrative power to suspend and excommunicate members of the church (see also Larger Catechism 173).

My narrow purpose here will be to show the objections to paedocommunion that can be clearly inferred from Paul's writings. If we can demonstrate that Paul's sacramental theology disallows paedocommunion, then we will have dealt a fatal blow to paedocommunion.[24] We shall see that Paul's regulations in 1 Corinthians 11 demonstrate the error of the assertion that baptism alone qualifies one for participation in the Lord's Supper. Although this is not the place for specifying my own understanding of the meaning and function of the Lord's Supper, my views on the sacrament are well known: they are found in the venerable Westminster Standards which I adopted in my ministerial ordination vows. My views are those of almost 500 years of Reformed teaching and practice.

As we begin our inquiry, we must recognize that the two sacraments do not exhibit the same truths. As noted above in LC 177, baptism points to our once-and-for-all ingrafting into Christ and is, therefore, administered to a passive recipient, is appropriate to an infant, and must necessarily precede the Lord's Supper, whereas the Lord's Supper provides ongoing feeding upon Christ which is appropriate only to one of age,[25] is

---

[24] Though I will be criticized for not considering the broader case for paedocommunion, my reader must understand that within the Reformed tradition, the burden of proof is on the paedocommunionist. My focus on the counter evidence is theologically appropriate. For instance, no matter how broadly we might seek to prove the deity of Christ from Scripture, if the words of the angel of Revelation 19 were found on the lips of Jesus, our efforts would be in vain: "I fell at his feet to worship him. And he said to me, 'Do not do that; I am a fellow servant of yours and your brethren who hold the testimony of God; worship God.'"

[25] Whereas baptism (and circumcision) can be and are applied to the newborn infant, the Lord's Supper (and Passover) cannot physically be consumed until the child has grown sufficiently to not choke on or spit out the elements. Interestingly, weaning in biblical days was a noteworthy event in the life of a child (Gen. 21:8; 1 Sam. 1:22_24; 1 Kings 11:20; Ps.131:2; Isa. 11:8; 28:9; Hos. 1:8). It generally occurred around age three, 2 Macc 7:27. When Samuel was weaned, he was old enough to be left with Eli to serve in the tabernacle, 1 Sam. 1:24. See: "*gamal*" in the *Theological Dictionary of the Old Testament*, 3:26-27. This is not to say that the age of weaning defines the age of communion (either in the Passover or the Lord's Supper). Rather I note this simply to point

actively engaged by the recipient, and requires baptism as a prerequisite. In some ways these sacraments' spiritual implications are pictured in Christ's statement in John 13:10a: "He who has bathed [picturing once-for-all baptism] needs only to wash his feet [picturing the ongoing sanctification exhibited in the Lord's Supper]."

Interestingly, many Reformed paedocommunionists draw back from the full implications of their rhetoric (e.g., the historic Reformed tradition spiritually "starves" covenant children by denying them the food of the Supper)[26] and their theological principles (e.g., arguing that the Supper is open to *all* members of the church).[27] That is, they do not commonly press their rhetoric or theology so far as to urge *infant* communion as paralleling *infant* baptism (although some do). Gallant, for example, pulls back somewhat by saying, "I would not encourage infant communion, since it is both unnecessary and can lead to unhealthy superstition. . . . Such communion was apparently never considered necessary in connection with the old covenant meals, and biblically speaking, nothing suggests it should be considered necessary now."[28] They often urge that the sacrament be withheld until the child is weaned and able to partake of bread and wine.[29]

---

out that the feeding sacraments were not designed with a view to infants and very young children's partaking.

[26] Paedocommunionists try to employ family meals as illustrations of the necessity of sacramental meals for the young: "A household illustration will help. A child is born. . . . he has one basic privilege, and that is access to the food on the family table. . . . Feed God's children." Leithart, *Daddy, Why Was I Excommunicated?*, 74. Gallant: "The table of the Lord belongs to the family of the Lord. The family of the Lord includes believers and their children." *Feed My Lambs*, 23. Even the title of Gallant's book attempts to play on this heart-string.

[27] Most paedocommunionists in Reformed circles do not insist upon communion for newborns, infants, and very small children. They do not practice intinction, yet they vigorously assert that the Lord's Supper is open to *all* in the church. Peter Leithart writes: "All those who are baptized are united with Christ under the covenant; . . . all who have not been cut off should be admitted to the Table that seals and strengthens that union." Leithart, *Daddy, Why Was I Excommunicated?*, 44. Mathison: "According to those who advocate paedocommunion, all baptized members of the church are entitled to partake of the Lord's Supper, including baptized infants and young children." Mathison, *Given for You*, 313.

[28] Gallant, *Feed My Lambs*, 192.

[29] Keidel, *"Is the Lord's Supper for Children?"*, 305-06. Gallant, *Feed My Lambs*, 34, 154-55. Mathison, *Given for You*, 318. Keidel, for instance: "By the word 'infant' this article will mean those who are physically capable of eating the Lord's Supper. Thus we are not advocating a strict return to the ancient practices of forcing food and wine

These introductory issues aside, I will now undertake my task by surveying the Pauline objection to paedocommunion.[30] Paul provides us with the most direct and extended teaching on the sacrament in all of Scripture, for he not only cites the words of institution (1 Cor. 11:23-25) in the context of rebuking the Corinthians for their abuse of the Supper (1 Cor. 11:18-22, 30-33), but he also applies the words of institution in order to demonstrate regulations for proper partaking (1 Cor. 11:23-29).

THE SETTING OF THE PAULINE POSITION

1 Corinthians has two closely related passages that undermine the paedocommunionist theology: 1 Corinthians 10:16-21 (within its immediate context of 10:1-33 and its overall topical setting of 8:1-10:33), and 11:18-33. In chapter 10 the Lord's Supper is mentioned only as an example; in chapter 11 it appears as a major topic in itself.[31] Paedocommunionists mistakenly allege that 1 Corinthians 10 supports their position, whereas they generally seek to re-interpret chapter 11 in order to reduce its usefulness as negative evidence. The brief summary of chapter 10 that follows shows that it does not help their case; my primary focus will be on chapter 11, since it disables their practice.

In 1 Corinthians 8:1–11:1 Paul provides a "unified argument"[32] wherein he considers the issue of Christian liberty, especially as applied to the question of food offered to idols. He opens this major section thus: "Now concerning [*peri de*] things sacrificed to idols...." (1 Cor. 8:1a). The *peri de* signals the beginning of one of Paul's responses to questions from a letter the church had sent to him.[33]

We see this idolatry-focus especially in Paul's statements in 1 Corin-

---

down the throat of a child, or of intinction. By 'children' it will mean those youngsters who have not yet reached an 'age of discernment.'"

[30] I confine my comments to these texts knowing that I will be accused of being a "Baptist" for not considering the Old Testament feasts (cf. Leithart, "Response," 301 and Rayburn, "Minority Report," M13GA, 342). However, I would point out that one chapter limits the scope of my argument, and the fact remains that if Paul condemns a practice in the New Testament, that practice in the Old Testament feasts is irrelevant.

[31] Anthony C. Thiselton, *The First Epistle to the Corinthians* (NIGTC) (Grand Rapids: William B. Eerdmans Publishing Co., 2000), 750.

[32] Thiselton, *1 Corinthians*, 717.

[33] Gordon D. Fee, *The First Epistle to the Corinthians* (NICNT) (Grand Rapids: William B. Eerdmans Publishing Co., 1987), 365 (cf. 267–68); David E. Garland, *1 Corinthians* (Baker Exegetical Commentary on the New Testament) (Grand Rapids: Baker, 2003, 364; Simon Kistemaker, *1 Corinthians* (NTC) (Grand Rapids: Baker, 1993), 262.

thians 8:10 and 10:1-22, where he expresses his alarm regarding their actually "dining in an idol's temple"(8:10) during a pagan worship service. "Going to the [pagan] temples is the real issue," according to Fee.[34] As Witherington puts it, "in v. 14 Paul gives the directive that all of chs. 8–10 has been arguing for: Flee from idolatry."[35] Paul eventually admonishes them quite directly when he declares: "you cannot drink the cup of the Lord and the cup of demons; you cannot partake of the table of the Lord and the table of demons" (10:21).

The Greeks at Corinth were enamored of a "knowledge" that bordered on Gnosticism, functioning as something of a Christian proto-Gnosticism. We must note that as Paul introduces this new section he highlights the matter of knowledge: "we *know* that we all have *knowledge*. *Knowledge* makes arrogant, but love edifies. If anyone supposes that he *knows* anything, he has not yet *known* as he ought to *know*" (8:1b-2).[36] The Corinthians apparently felt that their superior knowledge protected them from being charged with sin because they attended pagan worship feasts.[37] According to Fee, "in their minds being spiritual meant to have received *gnosis* . . . special knowledge."[38] Interestingly, Paul must assert even his own apostolic authority (1 Cor. 9; see esp. 9:1-2, 5) as he confronts their supposedly superior "knowledge" which led to their abuse of Christian liberty.[39]

Then in 1 Corinthians 9:24–11:1 Paul issues severe warnings while adducing dramatic examples demonstrating the real spiritual danger they are courting — *despite their knowledge*. He does so in remarkable ways — ways that render the passage useless for paedocommunionists.

---

[34] Fee, *1 Corinthians*, 300.

[35] Ben Witherington, *Conflict & Community in Corinth: A Socio-Rhetorical Commentary on 1 and 2 Corinthians* (Grand Rapids: William B. Eerdmans Publishing Co., 1998), 224.

[36] Their proto-Gnostic approach encouraged some to ignore concerns about sexual immorality (because it involved only the flesh, 1 Cor. 6:12-20) and others to deny sexual obligations in "carnal" marriage (7:1-6). Paul cites their thinking in this regard: "Now concerning the things about which you wrote, it is good for a man not to touch a woman" (1 Cor. 7:1). That is, *they* argued, "it is good for a man not to touch a woman," denying their obligation to have marital intimacy. See Fee, *1 Corinthians*, ad loc.

[37] They actually held true principles, but employed or applied them in sinful ways. They declared that an idol is nothing (8:4-6) and food is inconsequential (8:8); therefore, they thought they could attend idol festivals.

[38] Fee, *1 Corinthians*, 366.

[39] Paul's apostolic reference is an "integral part" of the unity of 8:1–11:1. Thiselton, *1 Corinthians*, 718.

In 1 Corinthians 9:24-27 Paul issues a warning regarding the danger of catastrophic failure in the unexamined Christian life. He points out that even *he himself as an apostle* must "buffet my body and make it my slave, lest possibly, after I have preached to others, *I myself* should be disqualified" (9:27).[40] After asserting his apostleship and his ministerial rights in the preceding verses, this is quite a dramatic warning to the proud, self-sufficient, knowledge-boasting, supposedly super-spiritual members of the Corinthian church. The great apostle himself could fail of the high prize of God's calling: *autos adokimos genōmai* ("I myself may become disqualified"). If Paul were to fail to control himself,[41] this lack of self-restraint would prove that he did not stand the test, and he himself would be declared a counterfeit in the end,[42] a "reprobate."[43] He would fail to receive the "imperishable crown" (9:25), of final salvation itself. "What an argument and what a reproof is this!"[44] (Of course, this argument was hypothetical; Paul does pass the test (see 2 Cor. 13:6; 2 Tim. 4:7-8.)

After using himself as an example of self-examination, Paul exposes the Corinthians' error at the Table by drawing the parallel between them and Israel of old.

1 CORINTHIANS 10

In the next passage, beginning at 10:1, Paul drives the point home to these Corinthians who are so confident in their "knowledge": "For I do not want you to be *ignorant* of the fact, brothers" (NIV). The explanatory *gar* ("for") connects the following material with the preceding. He says he does not want those knowledge-glorifying Christians to be "ignorant."[45] In 9:24-27 he presents himself as an example of one striving

---

[40] Paul will return to a thought in verse 27 (*adokimos*) and apply it to regulations regarding the Lord's Supper in 1 Corinthians 11:19 (*dokimoi*) and 11:28 (*dokimatzeto*). See my exposition there.

[41] In the phrase "buffet my body [*soma*]," *soma* stands for the *whole of life*. For he mentions he does *"all things* for the sake of the gospel" (9:24) and seeks "self control in *all things"* (9:25). Thiselton, *1 Corinthians*, 716. See also: Charles Hodge, *Commentary on the First Epistle to the Corinthians* (1857; reprint, Grand Rapids: Eerdmans, 1994), 169.

[42] R. C. H. Lenski, *The Interpretation of St Paul's First and Second Epistle to the Corinthians*, 2nd ed (Columbus, Ohio: Wartburg, 1946), 388.

[43] Hodge, *1 Corinthians*, 169. Kistemaker, *1 Corinthians*, 315-16.

[44] Hodge, *1 Corinthians*, 169.

[45] "Ignorant," *agnoein*, related to *gnosis*, "knowledge," 8:2.

for self-mastery with a view to passing the test, whereas in Chapter 10 he points to *Israel* in the wilderness as an historical example of failing the test on a massive scale.[46] In Chapter 10 he emphasizes his deep concerns with admonitions regarding the issues raised in chapters 8–9: "Therefore let him who thinks he stands take heed lest he fall" (10:12). "Therefore, my beloved, flee from idolatry" (10:14). "You cannot drink the cup of the Lord and the cup of demons; you cannot partake of the table of the Lord and the table of demons" (10:21).

The allusions Paul makes to Old Covenant parallels to baptism and the Lord's Supper in 10:1-4,[47] the citing of the Israelites' failures as "examples for us" (10:6, 11), the warning against the Corinthians' self-confident pride (10:12), followed by mentioning the nature of the Lord's Supper over against pagan feasts (10:16-17), clearly imply that the Corinthians "think their participation in the Christian sacraments has placed them above danger."[48] In fact, "the nature of this argument strongly suggests that those 'think they stand' (v. 12) do so on the basis of a somewhat magical view of the sacraments. Otherwise one can scarcely make sense of the present paragraph. Therefore, their argument with Paul most likely included some reference to their own security through the sacraments, which so identified them as Christians that attendance at the idol temples was of no consequence since those 'gods' did not exist (8:4-6)."[49] Thus, "they believed that the Christian rites of Baptism and the Supper secured them from any possible harm."[50] They prided themselves in their advanced knowledge and sacramental "inoculations"; like Israel they "test the Lord" by accepting his covenantal gifts, then flaunt-

---

[46] Fee and Thiselton both recognize resonances with Psalm 78 and Deuteronomy 32 in 1 Corinthians 10:1-13. These press upon the Corinthians the call to self-control given in chapter 9. Thiselton, *1 Corinthians*, 723.

[47] Paul is not referring to these Old Testament illustrations as sacraments themselves. Hodge, *1 Corinthians*, 173; Thiselton, *1 Corinthians*, 726; Garland, *1 Corinthians*, 449; Kistemaker, *1 Corinthians*, 326; Fee, *1 Corinthians*, 445, n. 18.

[48] Ibid., 459.

[49] Fee, *1 Corinthians*, 443.

[50] C. K. Barrett, *The First Epistle to the Corinthians* (BNTC) (Peabody, MA: Hendrickson, 1968), 220, 275. Witherington: "Possibly the Corinthians had a magical view of the Christian sacraments and thought that since they had partaken of the Christian initiation rite (baptism) and the Christian communion rite (the Lord's Supper) there were immune to spiritual danger at pagan feats. They seem to have held to some form of an 'eternal security by means of sacraments' view." Witherington, *Conflict & Community in Corinth,* 234, see 220; see also, Leon Morris, *1 Corinthians,* Tyndale New Testament Commentary (Grand Rapids: William B. Eerdmans Publishing Co., 1985), 138.

ing their covenantal standing (10:9).

In 10: 1-2, Paul draws an analogy between Israel's "sea baptism" (10:1-2) and Christian baptism, and between Israel's "spiritual food and drink" (10:3-4) and the Lord's Supper. The paedocommunionist presses these parallels into service to prove that children should partake of the Lord's Supper. They point out that "all" those "baptized" (10:1-2) received "the same spiritual food; and all drank the same spiritual drink" (10:4). Certainly we know that small children came out of Egypt and were thus "baptized" early in the exodus. Therefore, claim the paedocommunionists, Paul's theology allows children at the Lord's Table.

This argument, however, is exegetically fallacious and theologically vacuous for a variety of reasons: First, it presses the illustration beyond Paul's design and intent. This is an occasional, *ad hoc* letter wherein he confronts proud *adult* Christians about *their* specific sins. He is not considering the place of children in the covenant (he never mentions children); nor is he giving a general theological argument regarding the Lord's Supper (as he does later, in chapter 11). Rather, he highlights *adult* sins from the Old

Testament illustrations (which he sets forth as "an example for us," v. 6, 11): "Do not be idolaters, as some of them were" (v. 7); "do not act immorally, as some of them did" (v. 8); "let us not try the Lord, as some of them did" (v. 9); "nor grumble, as some of them did" (v. 10).[51]

Second, the context deals with their abuse of Christian liberty evidenced by dining at pagan worship feasts (8:10; 10:7, 14, 21, 28); it does not consider the question of general church practice. Again, "going to the [pagan] temples is the real issue," according to Fee.[52] The Corinthians deemed themselves above reproach and free from danger to their souls because they had partaken of the "immunizing" Christian sacraments; hence Paul draws parallels between the Old Testament's divine provisions and the Christian sacraments (see comments above). Nevertheless, Paul's focus remains on the question at hand: *idolatry by adults within the Corinthian church* — not on general truths regarding the Lord's Supper.

Third, the point of Paul's drawing out Old Testament examples has a singular lesson: *Divine blessings and privileges for covenant members*

---

[51] The "some" was really all but two: Aaron and Caleb, Num. 14:30, 38; 26:65; 32:12.
[52] Fee, *1 Corinthians*, 300.

do not insure them against sin and failure. The Corinthians thought they stood firmly in covenant grace (10:12); their overconfidence led them to "test God" (10:9). Therefore Paul rebuked them by warning that "knowledge makes arrogant" (8:1b).

To strengthen his rebuke Paul declares that "all" Israel passed through the sea, and "all" did eat the "spiritual food."[53] "Nevertheless" (*alla,* 10:4), they *so miserably failed* that God was *not* pleased with them (10:5a) and he scattered their bodies in the wilderness (10:5b; see also vv. 8-10). Again, what is Paul's point? "Therefore let him who thinks he stands take heed lest he fall" (10:12). Paul repeats "all" five times in 10:1-4 "to emphasize the enormity of their corporate sin"[54] despite the marvelous blessings and provision of God. Do the Corinthians trust in their sacramental partaking? They should recall the virtually complete failure of Israel despite similar divine blessings! Are they proud of their "knowledge"? Even the Apostle Paul himself must live carefully (9:27).

The paedocommunionists wrongly press Paul's emphasis on "all" here in their attempt to demonstrate that *both* of the sacraments should apply even to very small covenant children. Paul is not concerned, however, that toddlers may be going into the pagan festivals. He is simply showing that despite "all" Israel's having undergone a baptism of sorts and having been sustained by the miraculous provision of food, God nevertheless laid them waste for their sins against his requirements (Num. 32:11; Josh 5:6). That is *all* Paul is arguing. In 10:7 "he specifically links the rebellious people in Israel and some of the Corinthians."[55] The sins Israel committed, writes Paul, are an admonitory example "for us" (10:6, 11), i.e., the adult Corinthians (8:10; 10:14, 21, 22, 28). Rather than exercising self-control (9:27), "they stood up to play" (10:7).

---

[53] "Spiritual food" means *miraculous,* Holy Spirit supplied, material food. "Spiritual" indicates the source of the miraculous provision, i.e., from the Holy Spirit. It speaks of its "supernatural character," A. T. Robertson, *Word Pictures in the New Testament* (Nashville: Broadman, 1930), 4:151. Paul nowhere speaks of the Lord's Supper as "spiritual food,"and he often uses *pneumatikos* ("spiritual") in the sense of "provided by the Holy Spirit": 1 Cor. 9:11; 12:1; 15:44, 46; see also Gal. 4:29. Thiselton, *1 Corinthians,* 726; Hodge, *1 Corinthians,* 172-72. The Old Testament does not view the manna as sacramental, but as ordinary food (Exod. 16:2-4; Neh. 9:15, see also John 6:27, 31-32, 49, 58). Furthermore, the "spiritual drink" of water was consumed by animals, as well (Num. 20:8). Nor was the "baptism" a sacrament, for it included animals and a "mixed multitude" (Exod. 12:38), not covenant people alone.

[54] Fee, *1 Corinthians,* 444.

[55] Kistemaker, *1 Corinthians,* 329.

Their "play" contrasts to self-control, in that *paizein* (which is a cognate of *paidia*) speaks of unthinking, unrestrained abandon.[56]

After describing the horrendous examples of flesh-oriented (i.e., sinfully rebellious) Israel (10:18, *Israel kata sarka*[57]), Paul declares that the Corinthians' problem is their failure to understand the spiritual implications of religious communal meals (as in pagan temples). He shows them that despite their supposed superior knowledge (8:1-7), partaking of meals as part of pagan worship effects a "participation" (10:16, *koinōnia*[58]) and "sharing" (10:17, *metechein*) in the object of religious devotion, whether it be the true God (10:16-17) or idol-demons (10:19-20). Therefore, he proclaims, "you cannot drink the cup of the Lord and the cup of demons; you cannot partake of the table of the Lord and the table of demons" (10:21).

The paedocommunionist believes one of his strong arguments lies in the principle established in 10:17: "since there is one bread, we who are many are one body; for we all partake of the one bread." Gallant (following Leithart and others) argues on the basis of this text, "The Lord's Supper is for the body as a whole. The universal participation is so taken for granted that Paul argues from the evident fact to the implication of the real oneness of those who partake." That is, "Paul here makes the body of Christ and the table of the Lord coextensive."[59]

But this most certainly is not "taken for granted." In fact, the verse is wrenched from its context to assert something Paul does not intend. One

---

[56] The word derives from *pais* and signifies "to act in childlike or childish fashion." Gerhard Kittel, ed., *Theological Dictionary of the New Testament* (Grand Rapids: William B. Eerdmans Publishing Co., 1967), 5:625. Children are known for unthinking abandon (1 Cor. 14:20).

[57] I agree with Kistemaker, Garland, and others that "Israel according to the flesh"(10:18b) speaks of the *sinful* Israel shown in unrighteous conduct in 10:1-10 (Kistemaker, *1 Corinthians*, 343; Garland, *1 Corinthians*, 478-79). This phrase does not refer to righteous Israel at God's altar, but rebellious Israel at the golden calf (Ex. 32:6; see 1 Cor. 10:7, 14). Verse 19 mentions the idols again. The word "gentiles" does not occur in the best Greek texts of 10:20; rather the simple pronoun "they," i.e., sinful Israel. In fact, Paul cites Ex. 32:16 from the Song of Moses when he declares here that "they made sacrifices to demons, not God." He is clearly referring to Israel. Those mentioned in 10:18 almost certainly do not include children because the sins committed are those of adults (Deut. 32:17), and only the adults died because of their conduct (Num. 32.11; Josh 5:6).

[58] Calvin writes of this verse of this verse that Paul is discussing "the spiritual union between Christ and believers " Calvin, *1 Corinthians*, 216.

[59] Gallant, *Feed My Lambs*, 32, 33.

must bear in mind that he is instructing and chastening the *Corinthians who are dining at both the table of Jesus and at the table of demons.* He is telling *them* that those who partake of the Lord's table (whoever they are, which leaves open the question of *who* partakes of the Supper) are sharers in the body of Christ. Likewise, those (whoever they are) who partake of the idol's table are sharers in the idol. That is his point, and nothing more. He is demonstrating the solidarity of the one dining at a worship meal with the god venerated in that meal. He is not stating positively that all covenant members without exception *should* partake, but that those who *actually do* partake are sharers in the body of Christ-- which leaves open the question of who else shares in the body of Christ. Therefore, those particular Corinthians who attend pagan feasts are, likewise, guilty of *sharing in demonism.*[60] As Kistemaker puts it: "Here, then, is Paul's purpose for stressing the fact that believers partake of the one loaf: Christianity and paganism are mutually exclusive."[61]

Thiselton well argues regarding 10:16-17 that the vertical and theological relationships to Christ have priority over the horizontal and social relationship in the church.[62] Indeed, the former is foundational to the other. As Leithart notes, but for the wrong reason, Paul can move easily from the sacral body (v. 16) to the ecclesial body (v. 17).[63] Paul is therefore urging the Corinthians to reflect upon the theological meaning and implications of the Lord's Supper so that it will affect their social conduct in it, discouraging them from partaking of pagan meals. This theology will also encourage a proper "body life" within the church in the later context of 11:17ff.

Despite the frequent references to 1 Corinthians 10 by paedocommunionists, and despite its seeming support of paedocommunion, the chapter is not at all conducive to this sacramentalist approach.[64] We now

---

[60] Besides this, the paedocommunionist argument fails even on its own terms, because for the most part they confess that infants and very small children do not take the Lord's Supper even though they are part of the body of Christ. The traditional Reformed view does the same thing: it withholds the Lord's Supper from covenant children *for a time.*

[61] Kistemaker, *1 Corinthians*, 343.

[62] Thiselton, *1 Corinthians*, 762.

[63] Leithart, "Response," 303

[64] Paedocommunionists attempt a similar defense in employing Gal. 3:27· "For all of you who were baptized into Christ have clothed yourselves with Christ." Paedocommunionists point out that this verse indicates that *our baptized children* should partake of the Lord's Supper because they are "clothed" with Christ. This exegetico-theological attempt

turn to the key impediment to the theory for paedocommunion: 1 Corinthians 11:17-34. Here Paul's direct teaching undercuts the entire paedocommunionist argument.

1 CORINTHIANS 11:17-34

In this section I will be following the outline provided by Knight (who follows Fee rather closely).[65] Although space does not allow a full exegesis of the details of the passage here, I will emphasize aspects of Paul's material that have a more direct bearing on the subject of paedocommunion.

THE STATEMENT OF THE PROBLEM: (1 COR. 11:17-22)

As an occasional epistle, Paul's letter deals with specific issues that have arisen in the first century church at Corinth, responding to questions sent to him from the church (e.g., 1 Cor. 7:1; 16:17). Beginning at 1 Corinthians 11:17, he confronts their egregiously errant behavior at the Lord's Table. After having praised them somewhat a little earlier (11:2), he opens this new section withholding any praise because of the unloving pride of social status evidenced by some in their conduct at the Table: "But in giving this instruction, I do not praise you, because you come together not for the better but for the worse" (11:17, see also v. 22).

    I agree with Rayburn and other paedocommunionists that "as the context makes clear and as the commentators confirm, Paul's remarks are specifically directed against an impious and irreverent participation (a true *manducatio indignorum*)."[66] But I disagree with the implication Rayburn draws from this fact and will argue that the way Paul responds to the specific abuse contravenes paedocommunion. Paul counters the Corinthian error not only by direct rebuke of their conduct (11:17-22),

---

fails on three accounts: (1) This verse explains the preceding verse (note the explanatory *gar*), which reads: "you are all sons of God *through faith* in Christ Jesus" (v. 26). Paul is strongly emphasizing *the role of personal faith* throughout the epistle (2:16; 3:2, 5, 7, 14, 23-25; 5:5-6). (3) Galatians is dealing with *adults* in danger of apostatizing from the faith (Gal 1:6; 3:1-4; 4:10-11; 5:2-4); he is confronting *them* with an argument based on *their* baptism.

  [65]George W. Knight III, "1 Corinthians 11:17-34: The Lord's Supper: Abuses, Words of Institution and Warning, with an Addendum on 1 Corinthians 10:16-17" in *The Auburn Avenue Theology, Pros & Cons: Debating the Federal Vision*, ed. E. Calvin Beisner (Fort Lauderdale, FL: Knox Theological Seminary), 282-83.

  [66] Robert S. Rayburn, "Minority Report," 340. See also: Gallant, *Feed My Lambs*, 77-81. Keidel, "Is the Lord's Supper for Children?," 323ff. Leithart, "Response," 301ff

but also by correcting them, (1) *reminding* them of the important theological truths in the words of institution (vv. 23-26), and (2) drawing from those well-known interpretive words general sacramental regulations (27-32). These two procedures govern the particular first century approach to the Lord's Supper — and all other approaches that may arise.[67]

Contrary to his brief illustrative allusion to the Lord's Supper in 1 Corinthians 10:16-17, 21 (of which paedocommunionists make much), Paul here rigorously focuses his attention directly on the sacrament. In this troubled church, some among them are disrupting their community by asserting themselves in a self-centered manner (see also 8:1-11:1). We will see that he explains the meaning of the sacrament and the regulations governing it in such as way as to preclude paedocommunion.

Paul opens his discussion of the Lord's Supper by noting that the Corinthians' holy convocation has collapsed into unholy confusion: "in giving this instruction, I do not praise you, because you come together not for the better but for the worse. For, in the first place, when you come together as a church, I hear that divisions exist among you; and in part, I believe it" (1 Cor. 11:17b-18). The Corinthian fellowship is being torn by a schism rooted in the pride of the wealthy who separate themselves from and neglect the poor during the very administration of the Lord's Supper (vv. 21, 22, 33, 34). This deserves and receives Paul's scathing rebuke (vv. 17, 20, 22, 34). It also elicits his dire warning (vv. 27, 29-31) on the basis both of theological principle (Christ's body was given for all of them, v. 24) and sacramental reality (it is the "Supper *of the Lord*," v. 20).[68]

Paul notes the divine irony regarding these proud schismatics: "For there must [*dei*] also be factions [*haireseis*] among you, in order that those who are approved may have become evident among you" (11:19). Their lamentable, sinful schisms are actually necessary, divinely-governed sorting devices, for as Calvin notes, "in this way hypocrites are brought to light" and "the sincerity of the faithful is proved."[69] Hodge observes of Paul that "this is the reason why he believed what he had

---

[67] This is similar to the situation with the Old Testament case laws. They illustrate judicial principles through specific cultural examples *while expecting wider application* (cf. LC 99).

[68] "Supper of the Lord" (*kuriakon deipnon*) is an unusual expression emphasizing that it belongs to Christ, and not to the privileged. Kistemaker, *1 Corinthians*, 389.

[69] Calvin, *1 Corinthians*, 238.

heard. He knew that such things must happen, and that God had a wise purpose in permitting them."[70] As Kistemaker argues, Paul counsels against factions (*schismata*, v. 18) within the church, but acknowledges that dissensions (*haireseis*, v. 19) providentially must occur. [71] Even though infiltration of unbelievers into the Corinthian church is a major concern for Paul,[72] he is confident that God sovereignly employs dissension within the church to make clear who are truly believers.[73]

Paul, therefore, warns the Corinthians that their social behavior in this sacramental context arises from an underlying spiritual problem of enormous consequence (hence, vv. 27, 29-31): "that those who are *approved* [*hoi dokimoi*, "the approved ones"] may have become evident among you" (v. 19b). The *dokimos* word group is common in Paul,[74] and even in this sense of "approved as truly redeemed" (1Cor. 9:27; 2 Cor. 2:9; 13:5-7). Indeed, a very important representative of this word group appears in our very context at verse 28.

The root concept of the *doki-* group signifies something that is "genuine on the basis of testing, approved (by test), tried and true."[75] For instance, in 2 Corinthians 13:5-7 he commands the Corinthians: "Test yourselves to see if you are in the faith; examine yourselves! Or do you not recognize this about yourselves, that Jesus Christ is in you — unless indeed you fail the test? But I trust that you will realize that we ourselves do not fail the test. Now we pray to God that you do no wrong; not that we ourselves may appear approved, but that you may do what is right, even though we should appear unapproved." In part, this is precisely the issue Paul raised earlier in 1 Corinthians 9:27 where he declared, "I buffet my body and make it my slave, lest possibly, after I have preached to

---

[70] Hodge, *1 Corinthians*, 218. See also: A. T. Robertson, *Words Pictures in the New Testament* (Nashville: Broadman, 1930), 4:163.

[71] Kistemaker comments that Paul uses the term *haireseis* in a good sense, as in Acts 24:5. Consequently, they are "necessary," not reprehensible. Kistemaker, *1 Corinthians*, 387-88.

[72] 1 Cor. 5:11, 13; 10:12; 2 Cor. 2:17; 6:14-18; 11:4, 12-15; 12:21; 13:2.

[73] Christ had earlier warned of corruption through infiltration, e.g., Matt. 7:15-23; John 8:31 (see vv. 37, 40).

[74] See: *dokimazo*: Rom. 1:28; 2:18; 12:2; 14:22; 1 Cor. 3:13; 11:28; 16:3; 2 Cor. 8:8, 22; 13:5; Gal. 6:4; Eph. 5:10; Phil. 1:10; 1 Thess. 2:4; 5:21; 1 Tim. 3:10. *Dokimo*: Rom. 5:4; 2 Cor. 2:9; 8:2; 9:13; 13:3; Phil. 2:22. *Dokimos*: Rom. 14:18; 16:10; 1 Cor. 10:18; 11:19; 13:7; 2 Tim. 2:15.

[75] F. Wilbur Gingrich and Frederick W. Danker, *A Greek-English Lexicon of the New Testament and Other Early Christian Literature*, 2nd ed. (Chicago: University of Chicago Press, 1979), 256. See also: *TDNT*, 2:259.

others, I myself should be *disqualified* [*adokimos*]." The context in chapter 9 shows he is speaking of being disqualified from *eternal salvation* (9:25), from redemption itself. Surely if someone is so disqualified, he may not partake of the *Lord's* Supper.

In 1 Corinthians 11:20 Paul continues presenting his reasons for rebuking them: "Therefore when you meet together, it is not to eat the Lord's Supper." They are coming together ostensibly as a church (*sunerchomenon*, v. 20; see also vv. 17-18) to feast, caring nothing for the less privileged among them (v. 21), and thereby despising the "church of God" (v. 22). As noted above, in verse 20 Paul refers to the sacrament in an unusual and emphatic way: the supper *of the Lord, kuriakon deipnon*.[76] He contrasts it with "each one" taking "his *own* Supper" (*hekastos to idion deipnon*, v. 21). Whose Supper is to be the focus in their gathering of the church? Paul's expression lays special emphasis on the sacrament as *belonging to the Lord*.[77] This is something anyone partaking must understand, but which is forgotten by the Corinthians. As we shall see more fully in working our way through the passage, the communicant must recognize the theological significance of the meal and his spiritual obligations during the meal.

Significantly for our response to the paedocommunionist, Paul does not here rebuke the entire church, as if everyone were involved in this sin of prideful schism. As Kistemaker points out, Paul rebukes some, but not others (vv. 21, 22); he distinguishes those being rebuked from "the approved" (v. 19); he poses questions on their conduct designed to convict them (v. 22). Later (in v. 28) when Paul urges men to examine themselves, he makes it clear they must do so *individually*: "let a man examine himself" (*dokimazetō anthrōpos heauton*) to see whether they are subject to disapproval and rebuke. As we shall see, individual self-examination is an essential requisite for partaking of the Lord's Supper, which applies in the Corinthian situation and all others, whenever Christians gather to commune at the Table.

---

[76] See the only other occurrence of the adjectival use of *kurios* in Rev. 1:9: "the Lord's day."

[77] Earlier Paul speaks of the "Lord's cup" (*potērion kuriou*) and "Lord's table" (*trapezēs kuriou*), 1 Cor. 10:21.

THE BASIS FOR HIS RESPONSE (1 COR. 11:23-26)

In 1 Corinthians 11:23-25 Paul again sets before them the very words of institution from the Savior himself. Commentators too seldom relate these words to Paul's contextual flow,[78] yet they actually provide extremely important, context-specific information. Paul links Christ's words to the problem he has just described, when he writes: "For [*gar*] I received from the Lord . . . . (v. 23)" Having set their specific conduct in bold relief in the preceding verses, Paul now provides theological instruction to demonstrate the perversity of their ecclesiastical behavior (despite their supposed superior knowledge on spiritual matters).

He introduces the words of institution by *reminding* them that he "received from the Lord that which I also delivered to you" (v. 23a). This is not *new* information for them; he is not subjecting them to *ex post facto* legislation. They already knew the *Lord's* instruction, for he had delivered it to them. It was an authoritative, universal teaching flowing directly from the Master himself. He refers to this well-known tradition in order to highlight the attitudinal and behavioral obligations demanded by the *Lord's* purpose in the sacrament.

With a poignant play on words Paul drives his point home: "I received from the Lord that which I also delivered [*paredōka*] to you" – just as the Lord was "delivered" [*paredidoto*] by Judas to death (11:23). Paul's point (evidenced as a major concern in this letter[79]) is: Should you not then give up the prideful self-centeredness displayed in your sinful conduct toward your brothers in Christ? Do you not hear "the Lord Jesus" (v. 23b) graciously declaring: I gave up "my body" specifically "for you" (v. 24b)? The Lord's Supper speaks of grace conferred in Christ's vicarious, substitutionary atonement: "this is my body for [*huper*, "in behalf of"] you." By its very nature then, the sacrament is extended lov-

---

[78] See discussion in Anders Eriksson, *Traditions as Rhetorical Proof: Pauline Argumentation in 1 Corinthians*, CBNT 29 (Stockholm: Almqvist & Wiksell, 1998), 4ff.

[79] Thiselton (p. 885) notes that the broader context of 8:1–14:40 has as a major theme our *forgoing rights* for the *good of others*. See especially: 1 Cor. 8:9-13; 9:1, 12, 14-15, 19-23; 10:23-24, 28-29, 32-33; 11:33; 12:15-26; 13:1-3; 14:1-5, 12, 19, 31, 34-35. Christ's covenant love (11:25) is exhibited in his giving up his rights (his very life) for his people. After all, "the Son of Man did not come to be served, but to serve, and to give His life a ransom for many" (Matt. 20:28; see also 2 Cor. 8:9; Phil. 2:7; 1 Tim. 2:6: Titus 2:14; Heb. 9:28).

ingly to his people (cf. 1 Cor. 10:17). Therefore the Corinthians must understand that their self-seeking behavior at the Supper is proscribed in principle by the very words of institution and Christ's example.

According to Paul, the Lord commanded "this do this in remembrance of Me" both after he broke the bread *and* after he presented the cup (1 Cor. 11:24, 25). The paedocommunionist argues for the objective, communal character of this "remembrance," that is, that the sacrament is a *memorial* that exists objectively by means of the church's corporate act in keeping Christ's sacrifice before the congregation as a whole when they celebrate the Lord's Supper. For the paedocommunionist it is an objective, symbolic re-enactment of the crucifixion of Christ that exists irrespective of the individual's personal, subjective, or mental recollection of the historical circumstance of Christ's vicarious death. Mathison chides the "subjectivism" of "those who reduce the Lord's Supper to an act of mental recollection" in that they "are imposing modern modes of thought on the text of Scripture."[80] Likewise, of verse 26 he notes that to "proclaim the Lord's death" is a "visible sermon" presented in the objective act of breaking the bread.[81]

Gallant points to such texts as Numbers 10:10 and Leviticus 24:7 as presenting objective memorials that function whether or not the individual subjectively reflects on the historical events themselves.[82] Leviticus 24:7 reads: "You shall put pure frankincense on each row that it may be a memorial portion of the bread, even an offering by fire to the Lord." Numbers 10:10b reads: "they shall be as a reminder of you before your God." Inconveniently for Gallant, these particular examples are rituals that stir *God's* memory "leading him to participate in covenant fellowship with his people."[83] They differ in purpose from the "remembrance" feature of the Lord's Supper which calls upon the *individual* participants

---

[80] Mathison, *Given for You*, 232. This charge of "imposing modern modes of thought" is perplexing for two reasons: (1) Were not the ancients required to mentally reflect on events of the past? How is this a modern issue? (2) Do not we as moderns erect memorials and even engage in memorial acts (for instance, at the changing of the guard at the Tomb of the Unknown Soldier)?

[81] Oddly, Mathison uses a *non sequitur* and contradicts himself in his next paragraph where he notes: "The Lord's Supper is a visible sermon in which Christ's death is vividly proclaimed." Mathison, *Given for You*, 233. Does not a sermon on "Christ's death" — even a "visible" one — demand "mental recollection"?

[82] Gallant, *Feed My Lambs*, 84.

[83] John H. Hartley, *Leviticus*, WBC (Dallas: Word, 1992), 401.

themselves to remember its significance.[84]

Thiselton provides a way around the subjective/objective debate over the Lord's Supper. He points out that exhortations to "remember God's mighty acts" or "remember the poor" do not refer to our merely calling these matters to mind. Rather, in calling them to mind he obliges one to "assign to them an active role within one's 'world.'"[85] In the Old Testament, to "remember God" requires one to engage in worship, to serve him diligently, to faithfully obey him, whereas to "forget God" implies the opposite response. Likewise, the call to remembrance in the words of institution remind us of the psalmist's words in Psalm 105:1, 5: "Oh, give thanks to the Lord, call upon His name; make known His deeds among the peoples," which effectively calls us to "remember His wonders which He has done, His marvels and the judgments uttered by His mouth." Remembering his works is not a passing mental state, but is a spark to elicit praise and proclamation. This and other such "remember" commands require "transforming attitude and action."[86] Therefore, to "remember the poor" means to bring to mind the need of the poor *so as to take action* to relieve their necessity, not simply to subjectively reflect on their problems or to objectively memorialize their circumstances.

Thus, when Christ commands, "this do in remembrance of me," he is laying upon the participant a *covenantal responsibility*: He calls us to remember his redemptive labor *so that* we should act upon our consequent spiritual duty of Christ-likeness (which is what the Corinthians were most certainly *not* doing). [87] In fact, "remembrance of me" is here expressed as *tēn emēn anamnēsin*, where the "presence of the possessive adjective *my* between the definite article and the noun expresses emphasis. It is the act of remembering Jesus' person and word."[88] This

---

[84] Jeremias made a notable attempt to demonstrate that the Lord's Supper calls upon God to remember his covenant with us: Joachim Jeremias, *The Eucharistic Words of Christ*, trans. by Norman Perrin (Philadelphia: Fortress, 1966), 244–55. His work has been powerfully rebutted by many commentators, who observe its contradiction of Paul's main point in the text. Consequently, it finds little currency today, despite Leithart's attempt to revive it (Leithart, "Response," 302).

[85] Thiselton, *I Corinthians*, 879.

[86] Thiselton, *I Corinthians*, 879.

[87] The Gospel record of the words of institution even provide clear interactive commands to which the very young child cannot respond as *an act of obedience*: "take, eat ye" (Matt. 26:26b) and "drink ye" (Matt. 26:27b).

[88] Kistemaker, *I Corinthians*, 399.

responsibility is beyond the capacity of the unconverted, as well as the precious child of the covenant, who does not yet spiritually understand the saving action of Christ *or* its holy implications for us.

This inability to be spiritually engaged is even true of the narrow, culture-specific application made by Paul in the Corinthian situation: the little child cannot share with others or refrain from greediness. That is, they have yet to learn not only the proper behavior (which can be mimicked), but also the *theological reason* and the *spiritual motive* for that behavior *in the name of Christ,* that is, as a distinctly Christian duty.[89] After all, "good works" are only such actions as are performed in accordance with God's command (the deontological aspect of ethics) with a view to His glory (the teleological aspect of ethics) and out of love to and faith in Him (the motivational aspect of ethics).[90] Each partaker of the Lord's Supper must do this individually, knowingly, lovingly, responsibly; he must do so as a holy obligation. (Covenantal actions require vows; see Psa. 50:5; 56:12.) This is the essence of Paul's rebuke: some are remembering neither the crucified one and his self-sacrificial love in redemption (the specific focus of the Lord's Supper), nor, consequently, have they been responding appropriately to the Lord's Supper.

In 11:26 Paul again inserts *gar* as he continues explaining the Corinthians' failure: We must "do this in remembrance of Me," he writes, "for [*gar*] as often as you eat this bread and drink the cup, you proclaim the Lord's death until He comes." Here he highlights the recurring character of and continual obligation entailed in the Lord's Supper: "*as often as you eat this bread and drink the cup.*" As Knight observes, this "remembrance" is personally to engage us "as often as you partake," that is, each and every time -- which the Corinthians had forgotten, v. 21. Thus, the sacrament continually calls the communicant to Christ-likeness, repeatedly requiring that we remember him in all of his grace toward us, that is, that we partake in gratitude.[91] Interestingly, only in Paul do we find

---

[89] See: Matt. 18:5, 20; Mark 9:41; John 14:13-14; see also 1 Cor. 5:4; Col. 3:17; 2 Thess. 3:6.

[90] WCF 16:7: "Works done by unregenerate men, although for the matter of them they may be things which God commands; and of good use both to themselves and others: yet, because they proceed not from an *heart purified by faith*; nor are done in a right manner, *according to the Word*; nor to a *right end*, the glory of God, they are therefore sinful and cannot please God, or make a man meet to receive grace from God: and yet, their neglect of them is more sinful and displeasing unto God."

[91] Knight "1 Corinthians 11:17-34," 285. See also: Thiselton, *1 Corinthians*, 880.

"in remembrance of me" attached to the giving of *both* the bread *and* the cup. This is another means whereby Paul emphasizes responsible partaking in "remembrance" of Christ.[92]

But there is more in 11:26: The Lord's Supper links the past gracious act of Christ to his future judgment in his second coming. "For as often as you eat this bread and drink the cup, you proclaim the Lord's death until He comes." Thus, not only are participants in the sacrament required appropriately to "remember," but they must also recognize that they will be held *accountable*: Christ is coming again — *in judgment*. Moule has powerfully demonstrated the eschatological judgment theme in the Lord's Supper.[93] He points out that upon declaring Christ's coming (v. 26b), Paul in rapid succession throws out one judgment term after another: *dokimazetō* (v. 28), *krima* (v. 29), *diakrininōn* (v. 29), *diekrinomen* (v. 31), *ekrinometha* (v. 31), *krineomenoi* (v. 32), *katakrithōmen* (v. 32), and *krima* (v. 34). The apostle does so (as we shall see) while also underscoring the Supper's *present-day* effect in temporal judgments: chastenings by means of sickness and death (v. 30). Thus, personal, sacramental remembering appropriates "the sacramental verdict" wherein faithful partakers recognize their own guilt and cast themselves upon Christ who makes them right.[94]

Of course, having a non-Romanist sacramental perspective, we insist that the Word of God surround and interpret the sacrament. How else would anyone know what the bread and the wine represent, since they are *appointed* signs, not *natural* ones?[95] How else would one realize that the Supper proclaims the coming judgment of Christ? Although the faithful communicant partakes in full knowledge of Christ's coming and of his own responsibility before the Lord, small children, by reason of their undeveloped understanding, cannot so partake; the Supper service was not designed for them. Not only are infants and very young children physically unable to partake of the bread and the wine, but (even when

---

[92] Thiselton, *1 Corinthians*, 880

[93] C. F. D. Moule, "The Judgment Theme in the Sacraments," in W. D. Davies and D. Daube, eds., *The Background of the NT and Its Eschatology. In Honour of C H Dodd* (Cambridge: Cambridge University Press, 1956), 464ff.

[94] Thiselton, *1 Corinthians*, 881.

[95] "The water, the bread, and the wine in the sacraments are not *by nature* the signs and seals of Christ and His benefits. No one could see them there if God had not categorically declared it to be so." Pierre-Charles Marcel, *The Biblical Doctrine of Infant Baptism: Sacrament of the Covenant of Grace*, trans. Philip E. Hughes (Cambridge: James Clarke, 1953), 40.

they have acquired the physical ability) neither can they—or other covenant children who are too young to manifest evidence of conversion— engage in the sacramental actions with the requisite responsible, interactive involvement. An infant may be held in the arms of the pastor and baptized, but he cannot respond to the command to "take," "eat," "drink," — all while responsibly remembering and applying the Lord's death and his coming judgment to his own condition.

The Lord's Supper engages the communing Christian in the story of redemption, underscoring covenantal responsibility. Such holy partaking is unlike that of many of the Corinthians, and contrary to the example of fleshly Israel (1 Cor. 10:18) in the wilderness (1 Cor. 10:1-10). The Lord's Supper demands the "logic of self-involvement" in redemption.[96]

THE GENERAL APPLICATION OF THE INSTITUTIONAL WORDS (1 COR. 11:27-32)

Paul has carefully highlighted the theological foundation of the Lord's Supper in Christ's words of institution (which must be heard, for the words are interpretive and they come with commands to participate)[97] and sacramental actions (which must be understood, for they require specific responses to those commands).[98] From those foundational words he now draws out *general* regulations in verses 27-32: he signals this applicatory intent with *hōste* ("therefore," "for this reason").[99] He immediately presses the *universal* applicability *beyond* the specific situation at Corinth by speaking of "whoever" (*hos an*).[100] He also underscores this universal obligation by highlighting *future* partaking *beyond* their current circumstances: he employs the future tense "shall/will be" (*estai*, future middle indicative). The general future applicability follows clearly upon the principle "as often as you eat this bread and drink the cup" (v. 26), which itself covers all later partaking.

---

[96] Thiselton, *1 Corinthians*, 880.

[97] WCF 29:3: "The Lord Jesus has, in this ordinance, appointed His ministers to *declare His word of institution to the people*, to pray, and bless the elements of bread and wine, and thereby to set them apart from a common to an holy use."

[98] LC 169: "the communicants . . . are, by the same appointment, to *take* and *eat* the bread, and to drink the wine, *in thankful remembrance* that the body of Christ was broken and given, and his blood shed, for them."

[99] Knight, "1 Corinthians 11:17-34," 286.

[100] Gingrich and Danker, *A Greek-English Lexicon*, 56.

His general instructions continue in 11:27-32, which link the words of correction that follow (vv. 33-34) with the rebuke (vv. 17-22) and words of institution that precede (vv. 23-25). These instructions apply to each individual participant on any given sacramental occasion: "let a man examine himself" (dokimazetō de anthrōpos eauton, singular). Here, before he instructs the Corinthians so they may overcome their culture-specific failure (vv. 33-34), he shows that the regulations of the Lord's Supper have general applicability (vv. 27-32). We cannot limit these directives to the Corinthians in the first century; nor, as we shall see, may we narrowly interpret the general regulations as if they were mere "table manners." As Calvin observes, "Some people make it apply only to the Corinthians, and to the corruption which had got such a hold in their midst. But my own view is that Paul, as he usually does, moves from the particular suggestion to general teaching, or from one example to a whole class."[101]

The crucial verse now before us reads: "Therefore whoever eats the bread or drinks the cup of the Lord in an unworthy manner, shall be guilty of the body and the blood of the Lord" (1 Cor. 11:27). The paedocommunionist is convinced that this verse is irrelevant to the historic Reformed practice. Mathison provides a succinct paedocommunionist interpretation of this reference to "unworthy" partaking: "Identifying oneself with the body of Christ by partaking of the Supper, while showing contempt for other members of that body, is partaking of the Supper in an unworthy manner."[102] Keidel agrees: "The important thing to determine is to whom these statements and warnings are specifically addressed. If his specific audience includes infant and child members of the Corinthian church, . . . they should certainly be excluded from the Lord's Supper."[103] Rayburn asserts that "as the context makes clear and as the commentators confirm, Paul's remarks are specifically directed against an impious and irreverent participation (a true *manducatio indignorum*)."[104]

The paedocommunionist is certainly correct in pointing out the adverbial limitation of the command ("unworthy manner, unworthily" =

---

[101] Calvin, *1 Corinthians*, 251.

[102] Mathison, *Given For You*, 233.

[103] Keidel, "Is the Lord's Supper for Children?," 323.

[104] Robert S. Rayburn, "Minority Report," 340. See also, Gallant, *Feed My Lambs*, 77-81; Keidel, "Is the Lord's Supper for Children?," 323ff; Leithart, "Response," 301ff

anaxiōs[105]): Paul focuses directly on the *manner* of the participant's *action,* not his *person.* Does that, however, save the paedocommunion hypothesis from objection?

As we approach the statement in 11:27 we should keep in mind that the Lord's Supper differs from baptism in an essential respect quite germane to our debate: In baptism, the baptized is altogether passive during its application,[106] whereas the Lord's Supper requires the communicant's full knowledge, attention, and interaction. Certainly the adverbial form of *anaxiōs* dissuades us from attributing unworthiness to the communicant's person (i.e., implying that the communicant himself is an unworthy person and may therefore not partake). Nevertheless, given Christian anthropology and biblical ethics, we know that iniquitous conduct arises from spiritual failings (Matt. 15:19; Rom. 14:23b; Gal. 5:19-26). Specifically applicable to the situation at Corinth, does not John teach, "But whoever has the world's goods, and beholds his brother in need and closes his heart against him, *how does the love of God abide in him*" (1 John 3:17)?[107]

In fact, in several specific ways Paul's context throws a revealing light on the nature of the "unworthy manner" of participating:

1. He rebukes them for partaking of the Lord's Supper while disdaining fellow communicants. This specific behavior that Paul confronts (11:22, 31-32) is a defiance of his teaching regarding the nature of fellowship within the church (10:17) and the interdependence of members of the body (12:13-27).

2. He urges them to avoid unworthy partaking by requiring each communicant to examine ("test for approval") himself (11:28). This matter

---

[105] The adverb *anaxiōs* is a hapaxlegomenon. Its noun form is quite common; in fact, *anaxios* (*an* = negative; *axios* = worthy) is found in 1 Cor. 6:2, where it speaks of the person himself being "unworthy."

[106] Oftentimes the paedocommunionist muddles the Reformed argument by pointing out that adults must actively express their faith and repentance before becoming subjects for baptism. However, this is not the issue. Rather we are speaking of the interactive character of the Lord's Supper *during* its administration over against the passive reception of baptism. As an anecdotal aside, I would note that not only are infants passive parties in covenantal baptism, but in my twenty-seven years of ministry I dare say that most of them were *asleep* during its administration! And though this may also hold true for many congregants during my sermons, it never is so in their partaking of the Lord's Supper.

[107] See also: John 13:34, Rom. 13:18; 1 Thess. 4:9; Jas. 2:1-10; 1 Peter 1:22; 1 John 2:10; 3:10; 4:11, 20.

of "approving" is a recurring issue in the Corinthian corpus (e.g., 1 Cor. 9:27; 2 Cor. 2:9; 8:8; 9:13; 13:5-7).

3. He requires a communicant to "discern" (NRSV) or "judge" (NASB) the body (11:29). This reiterates the essence of the Lord's call to take it in "remembrance" (11:24-25).

Consequently, we must recognize that "Paul's primary point is that attitude and conduct should *fit* the message and solemnity of what is proclaimed."[108] This requirement is beyond the understanding and capacity of the young child who has not yet professed faith in Christ before those who hold the keys of the kingdom, the elders of the church.[109]

Before considering the obligations to examination oneself and judge the body, we should note a general adverbial qualification incumbent upon the Christian that is relevant here: The Christian must do all things "by faith" (Heb. 11). Although employed for a different end, Paul's comments in Romans 14:23 may also be apposite to our reflection: "But he who doubts is condemned if he eats, because his eating is not from faith; and whatever is not from faith is sin." In summary, because of the Communion service's obligation-laden words of institution declared to participants, its accepting, communal character expressing true *koinōnia*, its commands for interactive, discerning sacramental action, and its regulatory obligations pointed out by Paul, the historic Reformed approach to participation has always required that this sacramental eating be actively undertaken in a worthy manner, that is "by faith."[110] We must recall that Paul has uniquely emphasized the "remembrance" character of the Lord's Supper by recording "this do in remembrance of me" *twice*,[111] and he plainly declares this obligation in light of the Corinthians' failure — and the potential for unworthy participation in the future.

Considering this "by faith" requirement in Christian action, John 6

---

[108] Thiselton, *1 Corinthians*, 889.

[109] Calvin writes: "As far as young children are concerned, Christ's ordinance forbids them to participate in the Lord's Supper, because they cannot yet try themselves or celebrate the remembrance of the death of Christ," (Calvin, *John*, 1:169).

[110] As Kistemaker muses: "the adverb itself can be understood in various ways. . . . Perhaps Paul intended [it to] be interpreted as broadly as possible." Kistemaker, *1 Corinthians*, 400.

[111] This differs from the gospel accounts which mention this statement only with the giving of the bread, and that only in Luke at 22:19.

becomes most relevant. Contrary to some paedocommunionists,[112] commentators generally agree with Calvin's sentiment: "this sermon does not refer to the Lord's Supper, but to the continual communication which we have apart from the reception of the Lord's Supper."[113] After all, the sacrament was put into practice after Christ's death and resurrection: how would his original audience have understood his words when he spoke them? Furthermore, "the words 'bread,' 'give,' and 'for the life of the world' all echo what has been said earlier (vv. 27, 32, 33) and have nothing to do with the eucharist."[114]

In this sermon, Christ uses the term *sarx* for his "body," (John 6:51, 53-56) rather than *sōma,* which is the word used in the Lord's Supper (Matt. 26:26; Mark 14:22; Luke 22:19; 1 Cor. 11:24). *Sarx* points to his incarnational experience (John 1:14; 3:13; 6:38; see also Phil. 2:7-8; Heb. 2:14) in physical crucifixion and death which secures redemption. Elsewhere in the gospel, *sarx* speaks of human nature (1:13; 3:6; 8:1 5). The same is true in other places in the New Testament when flesh and blood occur together (Matt. 16:17; John 1:13; 1 Cor. 15:50; Gal. 1:16; Eph. 6:12; Heb. 2:14).[115] The incarnation motif and the obligation to believe in the proper saving object are firmly established in John 6, not sacramental worship.

Nevertheless, as Calvin comments: "in the sixth chapter of John, He discourses copiously and professedly on that mystery of sacred conjunction of which He afterwards held forth a mirror in the sacraments"[116] and "that there is nothing said here that is not figured and actually presented to believers in the Lord's Supper. Indeed, we might say that Christ intended the holy Supper to be a seal of this discourse."[117] Thus, though

---

[112] For example, see: Gallant, *Feed My Lambs*, 39ff. and James B. Jordan, "Theses on Paedocommunion," *The Geneva Papers* (Tyler, TX: Geneva Divinity School, 1982), 1.

[113] Calvin, *John*, 1:169. See also: Herman Ridderbos, *The Gospel of John: A Theological Commentary*, trans. John Vriend (Grand Rapids: William B. Eerdmans Publishing Co.,, 1997), 238; Leon Morris, *The Gospel According to John* (NICNT) (Grand Rapids: William B. Eerdmans Publishing Co.,, 1971), 376-77; Merrill C. Tenney, "The Gospel of John," in Frank E. Gaebelein, ed., *The Expositor's Bible Commentary*, (Grand Rapids: Zondervan/Regency, 1981), 9.78.

[114] Ridderbos, *John*, 238.

[115] Morris, *John*, 374, n; Ridderbos, *John*, 238.

[116] Cited from *Corpus Reformatorum* in Ronald S. Wallace, *Calvin's Doctrine of the Word and Sacrament* (Eugene, OR: Wipf and Stock, 1997), 198. Morris (and others) agree; see Morris, *John*, 377.

[117] Calvin, *John*, 1:170.

Christ does not speak here *of* the Lord's Supper, he does lay down theological foundations *for* it: his teaching here serves as a pre-interpretive word. The Lord's instruction here (as his words of institution later) establishes an important foundation for Paul's concerns and directives in 1 Corinthians 11, and serves as counter-evidence to paedocommunion (as we shall see).[118]

Continuing with Calvin's thoughts guiding us, the Reformed tradition recognizes what Christ teaches here in John: "faith alone is the mouth—so to speak—and the stomach of the soul."[119] Corresponding to this, in "the sacred Supper" the Lord "offers himself with all his benefits to us, and we receive him by faith."[120] Therefore, in John 6:53 we read: "Jesus therefore said to them, 'Truly, truly, I say to you, unless you eat the flesh of the Son of Man and drink His blood, you have no life in yourselves.'" Many of the early church fathers asserted on the basis of this passage that *partaking of the sacrament* was necessary for salvation.[121] But as Morris warns, since the Lord here declares without qualification that eating and drinking are the means for securing eternal life, "are we to say the one thing necessary for life is the sacrament?"[122]

Christ's assertion in John 6:53, however, relates to his earlier calls to personal faith in him and serves as a metaphor for believing assimilation of him into one's life:

> "Jesus answered and said to them, 'This is the work of God, that you believe in Him whom He has sent'" (John 6:29).

> "Jesus said to them, 'I am the bread of life; he who comes to Me shall not hunger, and he who believes in Me shall never thirst'" (John 6:35).

> "For this is the will of My Father, that everyone who beholds the Son and believes in Him, may have eternal life; and I Myself will raise him up on the last day" (John 6:40).

> "Truly, truly, I say to you, he who believes has eternal life. I am the bread of life" (John 6:47-48).

---

[118] Interestingly, his commentary on John 6 is one of the three places in Calvin's writings where he directly refutes paedocommunion. Calvin, *John*, 1·169.

[119] Calvin, *John*, 1:171.

[120] Calvin, *Institutes,* 4:17:5.

[121] See: Keidel, "Is the Lord's Supper for Children?," 305; Calvin, *John*, 1:169. See also: Holeton, *Infant Communion*

[122] Morris, *John*, 376.

Later in John 6:57 Jesus reiterates this concept: "As the living Father sent Me, and I live because of the Father, so he who eats Me, he also shall live because of Me." Thus, the command to eat Christ and drink his blood is a figurative way of declaring they must *appropriate Christ through faith*, which is a central theme of the Gospel of John (John 20:31, cf. 1:7; 3:15, 36; 5:24; 6:40, 47; 11:25).[123] Of John 20:31 Calvin comments: "John here repeats the chief head of his teaching, that we obtain eternal life by faith."[124]

Jesus' Bread of Life discourse is foundational to his subsequent institution of the Lord's Supper, and his teaching demonstrates that faith is required as the means of eating his flesh and drinking his blood. This faith, then, surely is required in the Lord's Supper so that it is not "unworthily" taken. If a participant cannot partake "by faith," then he may not partake at all.

Having highlighted the call to the faithful manner of partaking, we now return to 1 Corinthians 11. At verse 27 we read Paul's warning that unworthy partaking makes one "guilty" (*enochos*): "Therefore whoever eats the bread or drinks the cup of the Lord in an unworthy manner, *shall be guilty* of the body and the blood of the Lord." What does Paul mean when he warns that "unworthy" partaking makes one "guilty" of "the body and blood of Christ?"

The *guilt* resulting from partaking in an unworthy manner can be either one of two things: (1) one becomes "guilty of profaning" (ESV) the sacrament itself (sacrilege),[125] or (2) one becomes *liable* for the death of Christ.[126] Though the second option is preferred, with either meaning the necessity of proper, mature, spiritual conduct at the Lord's Supper is clear, and the significance of regulations is underscored: "His exposition of the meaning of the service shows that it is a most solemn rite, instituted by the Lord himself, and charged with deep and sacred meaning. It should accordingly be observed with unfailing reverence."[127] After all, the Lord's Supper focuses on the substitutionary death of the Lord Jesus Christ for our sin, which requires our remembrance (1 Cor. 11:24-25)

---

[123] Morris, *John*, 381, 377; Ridderbos, *John*, 652-53; D. A. Carson, *The Gospel According to John* (Grand Rapids: William B. Eerdmans Publishing Co., 1991), 663.

[124] Calvin, *John*, 2:214.

[125] Hodge, *1 Corinthians*, 230; Robertson, *Word Pictures*, 4:165.

[126] Fee, *1 Corinthians*, 559, 561; Garland, *1 Corinthians*, 550; Thiselton, *1 Corinthians*, 890.

[127] Morris, *1 Corinthians*, 160.

and communing in his death (1 Cor. 10:16) by means of interactive participation.

Regardless of which meaning of "guilty" Paul intends, this guilt against "the body and the blood" clearly does not speak metaphorically of sinning against the *church* as the body of Christ. This cannot be, for he speaks of both "the body and the blood," which is never used of the corporate church. Besides, the words of institution, speaking of his broken body and shed blood are still ringing in the Corinthians' ears. (11:23-24).

So then, what shall the communicant do? How shall he avoid partaking of the Lord's Supper "unworthily" so that he not incur "guilt"? Paul provides the directive for proper participating in the next verse: "But let a man examine [*dokmiazetō*] himself, and so let him eat [*esthietō*] of the bread and drink [*pinetō*] of the cup" (1 Cor. 11:28). Examine, eat, and drink are all in the imperative mode and are therefore commands. Furthermore, not only is each verb cast in the singular so that it applies to each *individual* communicant, but each appears in the present tense, indicating a repeated, ongoing action (we must always examine ourselves before the Lord's table).[128] Paul introduces this directive with the adversative *de* ("but"); he requires that the communicant must not commune unworthily (v. 27), *but* (*de*), to the contrary, he must "examine himself" (v. 28). As Thiselton summarizes it: The communicant must examine himself to confirm that his "understanding, attitude, and conduct are *genuine* in sharing . . . in all that the body and blood of Christ proclaims—both in redemptive and in social terms."[129]

Since Paul "gives no specific details for examining oneself," one must analyze his contextual clues in order to properly determine the nature of this requirement.[130] The lack of specifics for self-examination given in the immediate context strongly suggests (as all the other indicators in the text affirm) that examination is applicable *beyond* the specific failure of the Corinthians. That is, Paul is not requiring *only* that we examine ourselves to determine whether we properly respect our brothers while taking the Lord's Supper.

As noted previously, the verb *dokimazō* is a cognate of the adjective *dokimoi* found in 11:19 (to which 11:28 must refer[131]). The word group

---

[128] Kistemaker, *1 Corinthians*, 401.
[129] Thiselton, *1 Corinthians*, 891.
[130] Knight, "1 Corinthians 11:17-34," 187.
[131] Barrett, *1 Corinthians*, 273.

means "to make a critical examination of someth[ing] to determine genuineness, *put to the test, examine,*"[132] that is, "to prove, test, verify, examine prior to approval, judge, evaluate, discern."[133] In an earlier section of his larger context (8:1–14:40[134]), Paul showed that he himself must pass the test, lest he be *adokimos*, "disapproved" (9:27) and fail of eternal salvation. To be proven faithful he must exercise "self control in all things" (9:25). Thus, self-examination requires that the "would-be participant"[135] in the Lord's Supper "should be applying moral scrutiny to his life and behaviour"[136] as the sign of new life (e.g., Matt. 7:17; Eph. 2:10; Jas. 2:24).[137]

In our immediate context he employs the noun *dokimos* to indicate that some are true followers of Christ ("the approved ones"), thereby strongly implying that others are not (11:19; see also 1 John 2:19; Acts 20:30). Paul's command at 11:28 demands a moral-spiritual self-examination regarding one's understanding and motives in coming to the table,[138] so that he might partake in full "remembrance" and "worthily." In 2 Corinthians 13:5 Paul uses this same verb: "Test yourselves to see if you are in the faith; examine yourselves [*heautous dokimazete*]! Or do you not recognize this about yourselves, that Jesus Christ is in you — unless indeed you fail the test?" *Baur, Arndt and Gingrich* associates 1 Corinthians 11:28 and 2 Corinthians 13:5 because of syntactic similarity (verb followed by pronoun).[139] This would indicate the profound responsibility involved in self-examination, fitting with 9:27 and 11:19. One must engage in self-examination, and a little child cannot do this. The Lord's Supper is the one New Testament sacrament that is continually repeated *and* requires self-examination.

As lexicographer Walter Grundmann explains 1 Corinthians 11:28: "In virtue of the immediate presence of Christ in the Lord's Supper,[140]

---

[132] *BAGD*, 255. 1 Corinthians 11:28 is listed an example of this definition.

[133] Ceslas Spicq, *Theological Lexicon of the New Testament*, trans. and ed. James D. Ernest , 3 vols. (Peabody, Mass.: Hendrickson, 1994), 1:353.

[134] Thiselton, *1 Corinthians*, 885.

[135] Barrett, *1 Corinthians*, 273.

[136] Barrett, *1 Corinthians*, 273.

[137] See my *Lord of the Saved: Getting to the Heart of the Lordship Debate* (Phillipsburg, N. J.: P and R, 1992).

[138] Thiselton, *1 Corinthians*, 891.

[139] *BAGD*, 255.See: Knight, "1 Corinthians 11:17-34," 287-88.

[140] For Calvin's view on the presence of Christ in the Supper, see: Mathison, *Given for You*, 3–48 and Wallace, *Calvin's Doctrine of the Word and Sacrament*, ch. 13.

the Corinthians who celebrate it in an undisciplined and unworthy manner are challenged. . . . Christ cannot be approached in a careless and
disorderly way."[141] Furthermore, "before taking communion, people
must examine their conscience in order not to partake unworthily (*anaxiōs*)."[142] Here in verse 28 *kai outōs* indicates that the self-examination is
to *precede* partaking: *houtos* clearly can suggest temporal sequence,
even though this is not its fundamental meaning. Note in this regard that
as competent a Greek scholar as F. F. Bruce declares: "it should suffice
to point out the well attested use of *houtos* ('so,' 'thus') in a temporal
sense."[143] Indeed, many noted commentators accept the outright temporal significance of the term.[144] Therefore, the NIV translates this verse:
"A man ought to examine himself *before* he eats of the bread and drinks
of the cup." The NRSV renders it: "Examine yourselves, and *only then*
eat of the bread and drink of the cup."[145] Temporal sequence seems
clearly intended in other texts, as well (Acts 17:33; 20:11; 1 Cor. 14:25).

We come now to 1 Corinthians 11:29: "For he who eats and drinks,
eats and drinks judgment to himself, if he does not judge the body
rightly." Fee correctly notes that one of Paul's purposes in the whole
section is to urge the Corinthians to conduct themselves as a redeemed
community rather than as a hierarchical social club.[146] He therefore interprets "the body" as the church, the corporate body of Christ. Paedocommunionists take this route in interpreting verse 29, as well. For
example, Gallant says, "It is precisely the Corinthians' failure to discern
the church-body, that has led to these comments in chapter 11. What
Paul is teaching, in view of 10:16-17, is that when one fails to discern
that body which we have become (i.e., the church), he is thereby prone

---

[141] Walter Grundmann, "*dokimos*," in Gerhard Kittel, ed., *Theological Dictionary of
the New Testament*, trans. by Geoffrey W. Bromiley (Grand Rapids: William B. Eerdmans Publishing Co., 1964), 1:260.

[142] Spicq, *New Testament Lexicon*, 356n.

[143] F. F. Bruce, *The Epistle of Paul to the Romans* (Grand Rapids: William B.
Eerdmans Publishing Co., 1963), 222. H. A. W. Meyer (*ad loc*) lists the follow examples
from classical writings: Thucydides 3:96:2; Xenophon, *Anabasis* 3:5:6; Democritus
644:18; 802:20. See also: Knight, "1 Corinthians 11:17-34," 287.

[144] Moses Stuart, C. K. Barrett, Ernst Käsemann, B. Corley; O. Michel, J. D. G.
Dunn, R. Schmitt, A. Feuillet. Noted in Douglas Moo, *The Epistle to the Romans* (Grand
Rapids: William B. Eerdmans Publishing Co., 1996), 719, fn 38.

[145] See also: The New Testament in Modern English (Phillips); The New Testament
in the Language of Today (Beck); The New English Bible; The New Testament in Modern Speech (Weymouth)

[146] Fee, *1 Corinthians*, 559.

to act precisely in the way in which the Corinthians have been acting (i.e., schismatically), and will become guilty of the body and blood of the Lord (v. 27)."[147] Gallant then reminds us of the judgment mentioned in chapter 10: "It was the *mature* generation that all fell in the wilderness, while the next generation entered Canaan. The fact is that it is *we* who are mature who are in *much* greater danger of polluting the sacrament, and thereby eating and drinking judgment to ourselves, than those who are young."[148] Leithart agrees with Gallant: "It is *sin* that profanes the table, not youth and immaturity."[149] Thus, in their view, Paul is concerned about only one specific, overt sin (which infants/children apparently cannot commit).

However, Fee's contextual understanding of the passage does not require that we interpret 11:29 as a reference to "the body" of the church. Paul goes to great lengths to establish the theological principles contained in the Lord's Supper so that he can conclude with believers' communal obligation in his application. Let us review the flow of the context in order to see the error of interpreting "the body" (v. 29) as the church.

Paul continues to emphasize the necessity of self-examination, and once again he provides a clear link in his argument, that being, as Barrett explains, "*gar*, introducing the reason, or a further statement of the reason already given in verse 27, why a man should test himself."[150] Each and every communicant must examine himself [*anthropos heauton*] before [*kai houtōs*] he eats of the bread and drinks of the cup (11:28) "*for* [*gar*] he who eats and drinks, eats and drinks judgment to himself, if he does not judge the body rightly" (11:29). This is a solemn warning to "the one who eats" (*ho esthiōn kai pinōn*), that failure at the Table results in judgment in the end. The *gar* shows that self-examination is concerned with judging the body (*diakrinōn to sōma*). The singular "the one who eats" shows this applies to any individual who partakes.[151]

---

[147] Gallant, *Feed My Lambs,* 97. See also, Leithart *"Response,"303-04.* Gallant laments that this option (body=church) "has not been taken seriously enough by traditional interpreters, in terms of the context." Gallant, *Feed My Lambs,* 96. Kistemaker comments "almost all commentators understand this verse" in a way different from the paedocommunionist option. Kistemaker, *1 Corinthians,* 402.

[148] Gallant, *Feed My Lambs,* 99.

[149] Leithart "Response," 304

[150] Barrett, *1 Corinthians,* 273.

[151] Kistemaker, *1 Corinthians,* 402.

Let us now recall the larger context and Paul's rationale in this section of his letter. Early on he reminded the Corinthians of the words of institution (vv. 23-25) for this very purpose: to warn participants against partaking "unworthily" (v. 27a), so as not be "guilty of the body and the blood of the Lord" (v. 27b); he then required that every partaker "examine himself" (v. 28) so that he not "drink judgment to himself" (v. 29a) by profaning Christ's "body" (and blood) represented in the sacrament (v. 29b). The seriousness of the situation is highlighted by his words about judgment: "For he who eats and drinks, eats and drinks judgment [*krima*] to himself, if he does not judge [*diakrinōn*] the body rightly."[152]

This call to "judge the body" must refer to judging *the body of Christ exhibited in the Supper*, not the church as the corporate body of Christ (as the paedocommunionist avers), for the following reasons:

First, Paul laid the foundation for his rebuke by reminding them of the words of institution. He pointed out that those words require us to understand that the broken bread represents "*My body* which is for you" (v. 24). The broken body which effected substitutionary atonement and which is represented in the sacrament must be properly "judged" or discerned.

Second, according to the words of institution, the bread in the sacrament is to be consumed in "remembrance of me" (vv. 24-25). Christ gave his body for us and signifies and seals this to us in the Lord's Supper. This glorious fact lays a holy obligation upon us to "judge the body" of which we partake sacramentally.

Third, our eating "this bread" (and drinking the cup) points to the Lord's coming in judgment (v. 26). His body is not lying lifeless in a tomb; he will return again in that very body as judge. We do well to recall the eschatological judgment motif in the Lord's Supper so perceptively expressed by Moule (see above). The broken body of Christ anticipates the final judgment, and our assimilating it in the sacrament prepares us for that day.

Fourth, when a communicant eats the sacrament "unworthily," he becomes "guilty" of "the body and the blood of the Lord" (v. 27). This "guilt" is a forensic term strengthening the implication of the judgment that will occur at Christ's Second Coming. "Shall be guilty" in verse 27

---

[152] Many manuscripts, including the majority text, add *tou kuriou* ("of the Lord") after *to sōma* ("the body"). This shows an effort by scribes to clarify that Paul was referring to Christ's body (rather than the church).

parallels "drinks judgment" in verse 29. To "discern/judge the body" in verse 29 refers to the body (and blood) involved in the unworthy partaking in v. 27.[153] We can perceive a structural parallel between the two verses:

27: Therefore whoever eats the bread or drinks the cup of the Lord in an unworthy manner, shall be guilty of the body and the blood of the Lord.	**29**: For he who eats and drinks, eats and drinks judgment to himself, if he does not judge the body rightly.

Observe the points of parallel between the verses; note also that "the body and blood" become simply "the body":

27	29
Therefore	For
eats the bread or drinks the cup	eats and drinks
shall be guilty	drinks judgment
unworthy manner	not judge rightly
body and the blood of the Lord	Body

Thus, the "body" of verse 29 stands pars pro toto for "the body and the blood" of verse 27, and does not refer to the church as the body of Christ.[154] The body on the Table is in view, not the body at the Table.

Fifth, Paul requires that "a man examine himself" before he "eat of the bread" (and "drink of the cup"), which represents the body (and the blood) of the Lord (v. 28). This immediately precedes the verse in question and surely helps us interpret it.

Sixth, such unworthy eating of the bread (and drinking of the cup) brings judgment, a legal result flowing from the "guilt" incurred for "the body and the blood" (v. 27), when one does not "judge the body rightly"

---

[153] Barrett, *1 Corinthians*, 273.

[154] Note how Paul economizes expressions by dropping words in 1 Cor. 9:25: the athlete seeks a "perishable crown" we an "imperishable" (the verb and "crown" are assumed).

(v. 29). The judging of the body of the Lord in the bread[155] is foundational to establishing and promoting the social transformation in the church. He sets forth the foundational theological issues in order to secure God-honoring social conduct — the hortatory culmination in verses 33 and 34: "So then, my brethren, when you come together to eat wait for one another. . ." (11:33). In verse 29, though, he is fleshing out the serious matter of their sin as it relates ultimately to the cross of Christ. By doing this, Paul "reminds them of their dependence on Christ."[156] They must, therefore, "judge the body" of Christ represented in the sacrament.

Seventh, equating the "body" with the "church" would "require a genitive with *body,* and strains the meaning of the verb (*diakrinein*)."[157] These grammatical requirements add to the complications obstructing the paedocommunionist argument.

Eighth, we may not reach back to 1 Corinthians 10:17 and draw "the (church) body" from that context. It is too far removed from the present argument (being separated from it by the lengthy discussion of women's head coverings, 11:1-16), whereas in the immediate context Paul has been writing about Christ's physical "body" (vv 24, 27) and has spoken of the bread which represents his physical body (vv. 23, 26, 27, 28). Such a transition from speaking of Christ's own body to the church within the space of a few words would be abrupt, unexpected, and confusing.[158] To avoid just such a potential misunderstanding, in 10:16-17 he provided an unmistakable textual indication of a shift of sense: his use of plurals. In 10:16 he spoke of the "blood of Christ" and "the body of Christ," but in verse 17 he stated: "*we* who are *many are* one body." Though the transition there is *rapid*, it is nevertheless *clear*.

For these reasons, Paul's reference to "the body" cannot signify the corporate body, the church. Rather he is concluding his theological argument about the nature, meaning, and significance of the Lord's Supper, purposing to discourage their reprehensible attitudes and conduct.

In 11:30-32 Paul applies the general truths (indicated by "whoever" / "he who," 11:27-29) to the Corinthian community and their specific sin.

---

[155] We should note that the "bread" in the sacrament tends to be highlighted, for in Acts 2:42, 46 and 1 Cor. 16:2 the Lord's Supper is called simply "breaking bread."

[156] Garland, *1 Corinthians*, 553.

[157] Barrett, *1 Corinthians*, 275; Thiselton, *1 Corinthians*, 892; Garland, *1 Corinthians*, 552.

[158] Morris, *1 Corinthians*, 161.

He draws attention to the temporal chastening of the Lord that they have been experiencing, observing that this need not happen, but for their sin: "For this reason [*dia toutou*] many among you are weak and sick, and a number sleep. But if we *judged ourselves rightly*, we should *not* be judged. But when we are judged, we are disciplined by the Lord in order that we may not be condemned along with the world" (11:30-32).

Thus, before the Lord's Table we must "judge ourselves" [*heautous diekrinomen*] so that we not be judged by God [*ouk an ekrinometha*] (v. 31). Judging ourselves correctly (v. 31) parallels our worthy partaking (v. 27) and reiterates his call to self-examination (v. 28) so that we will not have to face God's anger at Judgment Day.

THE PARTICULAR APPLICATION TO THE MALFEASANTS (1 COR. 11:33-34)

In Paul's conclusion, he urges two correctives for their conduct during the sacrament: "For this reason" (*hōste*), he commands them, (1) "wait you [plural] for one another" when "you [plural] come together at church" (v. 33), and (2) if "anyone [singular] is hungry, let him eat at home" (v. 34). Paul has laid out sure foundations for rebuke; he concludes by giving practical instructions for their rectification.

Interestingly, Paul's Christian anthropology surfaces in 1 Corinthians, where he expresses his disapproval of childish (or even infantile) understanding and behavior among adults. He warns of the dangers of immaturity that precludes one's approaching the *Lord's* Table. His first comparison of adults to children is in 1 Corinthians 3:1-3, where he also deals with problems of schism in the church (1 Cor 1:10, *schismata*), just as he does in 11:18: "And I, brethren, could not speak to you as to spiritual men, but as to men of flesh, as to *babes* in Christ. I gave you milk to drink, not solid food; for you were not yet able to receive it. Indeed, even now you are not yet able, for you are still fleshly. For since there is jealousy and strife among you, are you not fleshly, and are you not walking like mere men?" Thiselton comments on 1 Corinthians 3:1: Paul's image here is of "the self-centered competitive naiveté which characterizes young children who have not yet learned to respect the interests of the other."[159] This well characterizes the Corinthians, especially as they are depicted in 11:18, 21a, and 33.

---

[159] Thiselton, *1 Corinthians*, 291.

In chapter 4 the Apostle expresses his sense of shame elicited by the Corinthians, lamenting that he has to "admonish [them] as my beloved children" (1 Cor. 4:14). Since they act like children, he must treat them as such, beloved though they are.

In chapter 13 he speaks of a child's immaturity beyond which he himself, as their example, has moved: "When I was a child, I used to speak as a child, think as a child, reason as a child; when I became a man, I did away with childish things" (1 Cor. 13:11). He could aptly have said the same of godly conduct in the Lord's Supper. (The author of Hebrews 5:12-14 also heaps shame upon his readers, reproving them for being like babies "not accustomed to the word of righteousness.")

In chapter 14 Paul expresses frustration with the Corinthians' immature understanding: "Brethren, do not be children in your thinking; yet in evil be babes, but in your thinking be mature" (1 Cor. 14:20).[160] Here he continues his reprimand for their inordinate interest in the more conspicuous charismata (1 Cor. 13:1-2, 8-9; 14:9, 18-20), which is very childish on their part (see also 13:8-11). In 14:21 he cites Isaiah 28:11, since its context also mentions the problem of childish foolishness: "To whom would He teach knowledge? And to whom would He interpret the message? Those just weaned from milk? Those just taken from the breast?" (Isa. 28:9). This is akin to God's concern expressed in Jeremiah: "For My people are foolish, they know Me not; they are stupid children, and they have no understanding. They are shrewd to do evil, but to do good they do not know" (Jer. 4:22).

In concluding the epistle to this troubled church, Paul urges the Corinthians: "Be on the alert, stand firm in the faith, *act like men*, be strong" (16:13). Again he employs images of proper conduct and faith characteristic of maturity.

All of this imagery highlights Paul's perception of children's immaturity in word, thought, and deed. Elsewhere Paul points out the well-known practice of keeping children under oversight until they have been properly taught: "Now I say, as long as the heir is a child, he does not differ at all from a slave although he is owner of everything, but he is under guardians and managers until the date set by the father" (Gal. 4:1-2). Children must put away childish thought patterns and become mature

---

[160] In Ephesians 4 he also expresses his concerns about childish immaturity in thinking, exhorting his readers to overcome it: "As a result, we are no longer to be children, tossed here and there by waves, and carried about by every wind of doctrine, by the trickery of men, by craftiness in deceitful scheming" (Eph. 4:14).

(1 Cor. 13:11). By clear inference, this fits precisely with the historic Reformed teaching regarding children: young baptized children are in the family, but not yet ready for coming to the Table until properly instructed.[161]

SUMMARY OF RELEVANT PRINCIPLES

Paul's teaching is clearly a stumbling block to the paedocommunionist. His treatment of the Lord's Supper leaves no place for paedocommunion —despite attempts at re-orienting the textual directives. We have refuted the positive paedocommunionist argument from 1 Corinthians 10, and have demonstrated Paul's negative appraisal of any such attempt in 1 Corinthians 11.

The Corinthians were engaging in a prideful, self-centered separation during the Lord's Supper. They were "despising the church of God" and shaming "those who have nothing" by their actions at the Table (1 Cor. 11:22). Paul corrects them not only by direct rebuke (11:20-22) and by practical exhortation (11:30-34), but he also links rebuke and exhortation by instructing them in biblical theology and Christian ethics (11:23-29).

He opens his theological observation by citing the words of institution for the Lord's Supper. He then drew from those words basic principles of ethical conduct at the Table, principles that must govern during every administration of the sacrament. The principles he propounded have formed the basis of almost 500 years of Reformed ecclesiastical practice. I will summarize several of his regulations that have a direct bearing on the paedocommunion vs. Reformed theology debate. As noted above, these regulations apply in the particular circumstances of the Corinthians, *because* they are rooted in the underlying theology of the sacrament and are designed to govern in *all* sacramental partaking. The regulations pointed out by Paul require that the church delay participation for covenant children until they come to a spiritual understanding of the faith demanded in the sacrament and are able to profess their faith.

1. The sacrament belongs to Christ. It is appropriately called "the

---

[161] This is somewhat similar to the situation in biological families where the family gathers to eat while the infant sleeps. The infant will be brought to the family table in due time. In the meantime, he is fed milk (I Cor. 3:2; Heb. 5:12; 1 Peter 2:2).

Lord's Supper (11:20). It is not a common meal (vv. 22, 34).[162] It speaks with great solemnity of the cruel betrayal and vicarious death of Christ (v. 23b). Therefore, we expect rules and regulations to govern its administration and reception. Common meals cannot control our understanding of the Lord's Supper.

2. The words of institution (11:23-25) contain the seeds of the sacrament's regulation. The Lord's Supper is not a common meal, but a sacrament expressing vicarious, substitutionary atonement. As such it marks out the believer who has appropriated Christ spiritually (see also John 6:53). In the words of institution we hear the promise of Christ to believers: "This is My body which is *for you*" (v. 24).[163]

3. The words of institution require the participant to hear and understand Christ's words, "This is My body which is for you" (v. 24); the elements must be taken "in remembrance of me." Paul uniquely emphasizes this command to remember by applying it to *both* elements (vv. 24, 25). "Remembrance" entails personal understanding and reflection *with a view to* communal response and action. Remembrance is neither a mere mental state nor a lifeless memorial.

4. The Lord's Supper is a recurring element in the worship of the church: we are to partake of it "often" (11:26). As such it serves as a repeated and conscious covenant renewal for all participants, urging continued growth in grace. It links God's gracious judgment of Christ in our behalf with his coming judgment where we shall all stand before him (v. 26b). This heightens the necessity of spiritual knowledge and covenantal duty.

5. The high and holy nature of the sacrament requires that we partake of it in a worthy manner. Paul expressly warns that "unworthy" partaking results in legal (i.e., covenantal) "guilt" (11:27). The proper manner of partaking is with reflection, by faith, reverently in Christ's name,

---

[162] 1 Corinthians 10:16 Paul emphasizes the uncommon nature of the meal when he refers to "the cup of blessing that we bless." Syntactically this verb + relative pronoun indicates a specifically blessed, meal that is part of worship. Knight, "1 Corinthians 11:17-34," 292.

[163] The grace of baptism may be conferred later, but the grace of the Lord's Supper is to those who believe. For instance, the Westminster Confession of Faith teaches: "The efficacy of Baptism is not tied to that moment of time wherein it is administered; yet, notwithstanding, by the right use of this ordinance, the grace promised is not only offered, but really exhibited, and conferred, by the Holy Ghost, *to such (whether of age or infants) as that grace belongs unto, according to the counsel of God's own will,* in His appointed time" (WCF 28:6).

and with Christian concern for others in the fellowship of the saints. Potential "guilt" necessarily implies a covenantal vow which cannot be taken by those too young to understand.

6. Worthy partaking is expressly defined as an obligation to "examine oneself" (11:28) before taking the elements. Approval before God is a recurring theme in the context (e.g., 9:27; 11:19) and is the result of proper, faith-based self-examination.

7. Worthy partaking involves rightly "judging/discerning the body" (11:29). That is, the incarnational body of Christ represented in the sacrament must be correctly recognized, appreciated, and responded to in this holy act of worship.

8. Improper partaking of the Lord's Supper leads to providential chastening by God (11:30-32). Failure to observe the inherent obligations is displeasing to God.

Clearly, these regulations require prayerful, reflective partaking in faith, understanding, and obedience. Therefore, the Lord's Supper must be withheld from the covenant child until he can partake responsibly and with understanding.

ADDENDUM:
THE QUESTION OF COVENANTAL CONTINUITY

Before closing my presentation (which focuses on the Pauline evidence), it may be helpful to provide a brief response to a common objection offered by paedocommunionists to presentations such as this. They often decry any refutation of their position if it focuses solely on the New Testament evidence, charging that Reformed theologians who do not deal directly with the Old Testament feasts are thinking like Baptists. [164]

Their argument in this regard may be summarized as follows:

1. The New Testament includes children in the covenant; hence, we practice infant baptism.

2. The New Testament tendency is to *expand* covenantal privilege, not to *restrict* it. For example, we see that females are given the new covenant sign of covenantal inclusion (baptism) even though the old cove-

---

[164] Leithart, "Response,"301; see also Rayburn, "Minority Report," M13GA, 342.

nant sign (circumcision) was restricted to males.

3. The Old Testament feasts included covenantal children.

4. Reformed theology emphasizes covenantal continuity between the testaments.

5. Therefore, the new covenant should provide the new covenant meal to baptized children as an expression of covenantal continuity.

A REFORMED RESPONSE

A Reformed response to this line of reasoning includes the following observations:

1. Reformed theology certainly recognizes continuity between the testaments. Nevertheless, there is *both* continuity *and* discontinuity. Clearly, discontinuity is part of the distinctive nature of Christianity. After all, we no longer practice ritual circumcision or blood sacrifice. We no longer engage in Jerusalem-centered, worship in the one temple. We allow females to receive the sign of the covenant (rather than only the male, as in the OT). The "continuity" argument is a canard when it is not balanced by real discontinuity.

2. The principle of expansion of covenant privilege is constrained within Biblical limits. For instance, women are not allowed to hold ordained office (1 Tim. 3:1-2) or to exercise instructional authority over men (1 Tim. 2:12), nor may children (our officers are called "elders," Titus 1:5; 1 Tim. 3:4-5). These restrictions apply despite Galatians 3:28 ("there is neither male nor female") that is often quoted by paedocommunionists and applied even to children (even though the text does not mention them and the context speaks to the contrary regarding children, see Gal. 4:1-2 mentioned above).

3. All Christian theology—including the Reformed tradition—emphasizes discontinuity in the differences between the meals of the old covenant and the new covenant. For instance, we reduce the number of worship meals from many to only one (the Lord's Supper). We no longer celebrate meals associated with sacrifices (e.g., Passover). The one new covenant meal focuses spiritual concern and concentrates responsibility.

4. We really do not know the age and circumstances of the old cove-

nant children who attended the feasts — although this is crucial to the argument for paedocommunion. We do not have enough information to be certain that all the family feasts included very small, uninstructed children. Rather, Nehemiah suggests that those who could hear the law "with understanding" (8:3, 8) were the ones who participated in the Feast of Booths (8:10-18).

5. Though the evidence is sketchy, it appears that the infants, very young, and pre-instructed children did not partake the Passover (the meal most closely associated with the Lord's Supper, Matt. 26:17-27; Mark 14:14-25; Luke 22:15-20; 1 Cor. 5:7).

> • In Exodus 12:8 the Passover meal includes roast lamb and bitter herbs, which might either choke or be spit out by the younger child. Unlike circumcision which can be applied to infants (and is so commanded, Gen. 17:12), the Passover meal does not accommodate the very young.[165]

> • In Exodus 12:26 the child speaks as an *observer*, not a participant in the Passover: "what do *you* mean by this service?"

> • During the numbering of participants when preparing the Passover (Exo. 12:4), children were not counted (Ex. 12:37).

> • In Exodus 12:48 the stranger who wants to partake of the Passover must be circumcised with his male children. But only *he* partakes ("then let *him* come near to celebrate it").

> • Deuteronomy 16:16 requires only adult males to come to the three great annual feasts (including Passover).

> • Deuteronomy 16 mentions (the possibility of) children (but at what age?) at the Feast of Weeks (Deut. 16:9-12) and the Feast of Booths (Deut. 16:13-17), but it omits any reference to children at Passover (Deut. 16:1-8).

> • Luke 2:41-42 states that Mary and Joseph attended the Passover annually, but that when Jesus "became" (*egeneto*) twelve they took him along with them "as was the custom of the feast."

6. The new covenant establishes a principle of heightened obligation

---

[165] See earlier footnote (number 26) on weaning in antiquity.

that effectively counters the argument from Old Testament feasts. As a general principle, the Lord informs us: "To whom much is given, much is required" (Luke 12:48). But the new covenant situation is not simply a matter of general principle. In the very context of comparing the Old Testament saints and the New Testament saints in their meals (1 Cor. 10:1-4, 16-17), Paul provides evidence of the heightened obligation in this age that began with the incarnation: "Now these things happened to them as an example, and they were written for our instruction, upon whom the ends of the ages have come" (1 Cor. 10:11; see also Acts 2:16-17, 24; Heb. 1:1-2; 9:26; 1 Pet 1:20; 1 John 2:18).

In the same way, in Hebrews the writer compares the old covenant administration with the new (e.g., Heb. 8:6-13), emphasizing our elevated responsibility in the new:

> • "Therefore we ought to *give the more earnest heed* to the things which we have heard, lest at any time we should let them slip. For if the word spoken by angels was stedfast, and every transgression and disobedience received a just recompence of reward; *how shall we escape*, if we neglect so great salvation; which at the first began to be spoken by the Lord, and was confirmed unto us by them that heard him" (Heb. 2:1-3).

> • "He that despised Moses' law died without mercy under two or three witnesses: Of *how much sorer punishment*, suppose ye, shall he be thought worthy, who hath trodden under foot the Son of God, and hath counted the blood of the covenant, wherewith he was sanctified, an unholy thing, and hath done despite unto the Spirit of grace?" (Heb. 10:28-29)

> • "See to it that you do not refuse Him who is speaking. For if those did not escape when they refused him who warned them on earth, *much less shall we escape* who turn away from Him who warns from heaven" (Heb. 12:25).

7. In the church that allows paedocommunion, it is possible that members may never be required to take vows (as they do in the Reformed tradition before they are admitted to the Lord's Supper). It also is theoretically possible that several generations of family offspring could pass through the church without ever having to take personal vows, e.g., when they meet with the elders to profess their faith.[166]

---

[166] I pastor Fairview Presbyterian Church, which was founded in 1787 by members of the Scots-Irish Peden family. We still today have many faithful Pedens here after 200

8. When all is said and done, the hard fact remains: the Apostle Paul establishes sacramental regulations that exclude young, non-professing, untrained children from partaking of the Lord's Supper.

---

years. Using the paedocommunionist approach, these could all have avoided personal vows before the elders because they were born into the church. For a history of the church see Mary Lou Stewart Garrett, *History of Fairview Presbyterian Church of Greenville County, South Carolina* (Fountain Inn, S.C.: Fairview Presbyterian Church, 1986).

EPILOGUE

It is our opinion that we have never published a more important book. Since 1999 we have addressed a number of serious issues that are before reformed churches. As we dealt with these issues, we recognized they would affect the sanctification of the believer, the well-being of the Church, and the glory of God. The issues, however, in this volume deal fundamentally with the nature of salvation.

We never thought we would have lived to see the doctrine of justification under attack by ministers from within reformed communions and those ministers advocating a doctrine that baptism converts by effecting union with Christ. These things, however, are being taught and many are confused.

Although the advocates of the Federal Vision, the New Perspective on Paul, and Norman Shepherd's doctrine of justification, may not be uniformly agreed on every nuance of the aberrant theology of justification and baptism, there is a great deal of uniformity among the adherents of these positions. Their doctrines attack some of the basic doctrines of salvation such as the nature and role of faith in justification, the imputation of Christ's righteousness, and the nature of Baptism and the Lord's Supper. With respect to what they teach, we may safely say that, at best, their doctrines are inconsistent with the position of the Reformed standards and, at worst, some are soul damning.

Those interested in studying more than we were able to present in the present volume, may consult *The Auburn Avenue Theology, Pros and Cons: Debating the Federal Vision* and three books published by adherents of the various aberrant views: *Reformed is Not Enough*; *The Federal Vision*; and *The Backbone of the Bible*. An honest reading of these books will manifest that we have not caricatured nor exaggerated the positions of these teachers. An excellent critique of the New Perspective is *Justification and the New Perspectives on Paul* by Guy Prentiss Waters. Dr. Waters studied under a seminal sponsor and leading adherent of the New Perspective on Paul, E. P. Sanders, and has an excellent grasp of the teachings that are troubling the Church. He also is an able proponent of the classic, and we believe Biblical, view of Paul and justification. We would also recommend that our readers look for two forthcoming volumes from the pen of Dr. Waters: one on Federal Vision theology and one on Norman Shepherd. For a penetrating critique of Shepherd see the review article by Cornelis P. Venema in the *Mid America Journal of Theology* 13 (2002). We would also refer the reader to Dr. Venema's incisive articles in the March, April, June, July, September, and October 2003 issues of *Christian Renewal* magazine. Finally, we suggest that our readers look for a forthcoming volume edited by R. S. Clark, *Covenant and Justification.*

With respect to the debate on paedo-communion, we did some serious soul searching about whether we should have a debate on the topic. Some thought we should not have given a platform for the presentation of this aberrant position. Paedo- or young children communion is a serious error, which attacks the vitals of biblical Christianity. When we oppose paedo-communion, we are not opposing the Church's allowance of children who are 7 or 8 years of age, for example, to be examined and upon creditable profession of faith and the ability to take vows to be admitted to the Lord's Table. Rather, we are opposing admittance of young children to the Lord's Table simply because they are children of the covenant. We are opposed to admitting children who have not given a creditable profession and who are not required to take vows. The position of paedo-communion in fact changes the nature of the sacrament. Our reformed standards rightly interpret the Scripture that one must exercise faith if the sacraments are to be a blessing. The advocates of Paedo-communion teach that the sacrament of the Lord's Supper is a blessing apart from faith. This is an incipient sacramentalism, not greatly different from the Roman Catholic view that the sacrament works in and of itself. We believe that this view of the Lord's Supper has affected the baptismal view of men committed to the Federal Vision. They are advocating a new sacramentalism.

Scripture teaches that children of Christians are members of the Church and for this reason are baptized. But it also repudiates the notion that they are united to Christ *savingly* by baptism and have a right to the Table of the Lord. In addition to the exegesis of Dr. Gentry, we would remind our readers that in Exodus 12 there is a difference between the act of the Passover, which embraced all of the covenant people in Goshen covered by the blood, and the institution of the feast to commemorate that act (12:14ff.). Only men were required to celebrate the Feast of

Passover. We also repudiate the notion that because other sacrificial meals included children, the Passover must have as well. This assertion is never proven. Moreover, the purpose of the Passover was greatly different from that of the Lord's Supper. In the Passover, the celebrant remembered God's great saving work and meditated on prophecy of the Savior to come. In the Lord's Supper, the participant communes with Christ by faith. Part of this communion involves observing the sacramental actions (WCF 29:7; L.C.170, 174). A little child cannot do these things. Moreover, even in the Old Covenant one who was born into the covenant people had to enter personally into the covenant by taking vows: "'Gather My godly ones to Me, Those who have made a covenant with Me by sacrifice'" (Psalm 50:5). Such covenanting would and does involve taking vows. According to Exodus 20:7 and Ecclesiastes 5:1-5, it is an awful and solemn duty to take vows to God and covenant with Him. We should be sure our children are ready for such a commitment.

We offer this book with the fervent prayer that God will deliver His Church from the errors that we address.

Soli Deo Gloria!

Joseph A. Pipa, Jr.
C. N. Willborn

LIST OF CONTRIBUTORS:

John Carrick is Associate Professor of Applied Theology in Greenville Presbyterian Theological Seminary and author of *The Imperative of Preaching: A Theology of Sacred Rhetoric.*

Kenneth L. Gentry is the pastor of Fairview Presbyterian Church, Fountain Inn, South Carolina and author of numerous articles and books, including *The Charismatic Gift of Prophecy.*

Andrew T. B. McGowan is principal of the Highland Theological College, Dingwall Scotland and a minister in the Church of Scotland. Dr. McGowan is the author of numerous articles as well as *The Federal Theology of Thomas Boston.*

Joseph A. Pipa, Jr. is president of Greenville Presbyterian Theological Seminary and also serves as Professor of Systematic and Historical Theology. Dr. Pipa has authored articles and books, including *The Lord's Day.*

Richard D. Phillips is pastor of First Presbyterian Church Coral Springs, Margate, Florida, chairman of the Philadelphia Conference on Reformed Theology, and author of several articles and books including *Chosen in Christ.*

Robert S. Rayburn is pastor of Faith Presbyterian Church, Tacoma, Washington. Dr. Rayburn has authored a commentary on Hebrews in the *Evangelical Commentary of the Bible* series.

Dr. Morton Smith has served as a dean and Professor of Systematic and Biblical Theology at Greenville Presbyterian Theological Seminary since its founding in 1987. Dr. Smith was founding professor at Reformed Theological Seminary, Jackson, Mississippi, served the Presbyterian Church in America for several years as Stated Clerk, and has authored a number of articles and books, including *Studies in Southern Presbyterian Theology.*

www.ingramcontent.com/pod-product-compliance
Lightning Source LLC
Chambersburg PA
CBHW021226090426
42740CB00006B/395